NatWest Business Handbooks

Small Business Survival

Roger Bennett

Pitman

Pitman Publishing
128 Long Acre, London WC2E 9AN

A Division of Longman Group UK Limited

First published in Great Britain in association with the National Westminster Bank, 1989
Reissued in the NatWest Business Handbooks series, 1991

© Longman Group UK Ltd 1989

British Library Cataloguing in Publication Data
Available on application to the British Library

ISBN 0 273 036246

The information in this book is intended as a general guide based upon the legislation at the time of going to press. Neither the Bank, its staff or the author can accept liability for any loss arising as a result of reliance upon any information contained herein and readers are strongly advised to obtain professional advice on an individual basis.

Typeset, printed and bound in Great Britain

Contents

Preface	vii	
Where is your business headed?	1	1
Troubleshooting	15	2
Sensible expansion	31	3
Cutting costs	47	4
How to collect a debt	75	5
Labour matters	93	6
Computerise or perish?	121	7
Selling your output	137	8
Advertising and sales promotions	165	9
Keeping within the law	187	10
Restructuring for survival	199	11
The wolf at the door	219	12
Thinking about the unthinkable	241	13
Index	255	

Preface

Many small firms that go under do so not because they are worthless businesses, but simply because their owners do not bother to rethink their basic aims and policies when profits begin to fall. Often, these businesses are fundamentally sound, and can be saved if only the people in charge devise and implement a handful of straightforward strategies for turning around their firms.

It was the sight of so many hard-working small business owners failing to achieve the results their efforts objectively deserve that prompted me to write this book. As a management consultant to small businesses I often find that small firms' real problems actually lie more in bad attitudes towards detailed day-to-day procedures than in particular inadequacies of marketing, personnel, organisation or control.

The concepts discussed in the following chapters are not difficult to understand, but they do require fresh approaches to how you *think* about your business. Frequently, low profit firms are not inefficient or prone to extravagant spending, nor do they offer inferior or unwanted goods; it is just that they are not capable of accommodating change. They fail to take account of changing markets, new patterns of competition and/or methods of doing business, and they do not gather the *information* (about market opportunities, costs, customer preferences, behaviour of competitors, new production systems, etc.) needed for survival in the fiercely competitive environment of today.

In preparing the text I have drawn on many years of personal experience of assisting small businesses to improve their fortunes. The book tells you how to revitalise your organisation, present and promote your output effectively, tighten your systems for credit and other forms of control, and generally how to plan and prepare for change. Specifically, you will learn techniques for:

- collecting your debts quickly and efficiently, and how to take people to court if they stubbornly refuse to pay
- cutting costs
- rationalising your workforce and dealing with unproductive workers
- locating and penetrating new markets.

Additionally, the book contains useful advice on dealing with troublesome creditors and, for the reader who is totally ignorant as far as computers are concerned, on how a cheap desktop computer can be used to improve the efficiency of your firm. For the business in very serious financial difficulty I explain the extent of the personal liability of a small business owner in the event, alas, of his or her business collapsing.

This is a practical book, intended to make you want to do things for yourself rather than simply sit back and rely on expensive outside advice – which you can't really afford and which might not be appropriate to the needs of your firm. In business, you have to *make things happen* rather than just hang around waiting for events. Accordingly, positive strategies for diversifying, advertising, repositioning products and segmenting markets are suggested, based on your willingness to do these things yourself without forever seeking external assistance. There are, I believe, ideas within the following chapters capable of improving the profitability of every small business.

I assume you own the firm, have been established for just a short time, and only employ a small number of workers. You are solvent but feel that the business is generating a lower return than is possible, and that the profits you achieve do not reflect the objective worth of the enterprise. For convenience I commonly refer to businesses that supply 'goods', but this in no way implies that most of the ideas suggested do not apply equally to service firms, including professional and consultancy businesses.

My thanks are due to Christopher Wright for valuable comments on the legal aspects of the text, to Pitman Publishing for quickly expediting its production, and to Rosalind Bailey who typed the entire manuscript. The section on UK health and safety legislation in Chapter 10 is based on a corresponding section in my book *Personal Effectiveness*, published by Kogan Page in January 1989. I am grateful to them for their kind permission to adapt this material.

Roger Bennett
Spring 1989

1 Where is your business headed?

Myths and realities about small business management □
Analysing problems □ The customer's view □ What are your
business's strengths? □ Your personal strengths and
weaknesses □ Problems beyond your control □ Where do
you need to be? □ Could you diversify? □ New products
□The way ahead □ Summary □ Checklist

Too many small firms collapse within a few years, sometimes just a
few months, of starting up. Yet many of these businesses could have
been saved if only their owners had spotted the first signs of serious
trouble at an early stage and acted to eliminate them. Do not be
intimidated by the reality of high rates of small business failure
(about 85 per cent of all new businesses go under within five years of
their inception), but do recognise that *all* businesses have to overcome real problems in order to avoid failure in the early stages. Only
then can long term success be achieved.

My purpose in writing this book is to encourage you to think
creatively and, above all, adventurously about the structure and
operations of your business: how you run it, the scope and variety of
its activities, its organisation, administration, and how you present
the business and its products to outsiders. There are numerous ways
in which the efficiency and profitability of a small firm may be
increased, and even if your business is presently experiencing severe
problems there is still an enormous amount you can do to improve its
fortunes.

Myths and realities about small business management

People who have never done it themselves cannot fully appreciate the
problems attached to running one's own firm. Friends and relatives
naively assume that because you own a business you are:

(a) loaded with money,
(b) spend most of your time on holiday, and
(c) that when you do occasionally visit the premises you do little

more than give orders to employees who, in fact, do most of the work!

Outsiders are often blissfully unaware of how much effort you actually put into building up the firm. They forget how you worked in the evenings, at weekends and on bank holidays and how you still thought constantly about the business on your 'days off'!

But no matter how industrious, thrifty and self-disciplined you are, you might still have a firm that is underperforming. And the realisation that the enterprise isn't earning you a proper living can be profoundly worrying.

Where is your business headed?

Do not be too disappointed if these comments sound disagreeably familiar: low productivity is not unusual in small firms and if your last quarter's returns were poor you are not alone. Yet no matter how bleak your current prospects appear there are still numerous measures you can initiate to increase your profitability. Many people have been down this road before you. They have confronted the sources of underperformance in their businesses, and have ended up with highly successful enterprises at their journey's end. The fact that you are reading this book *proves* you are serious about improving the business and ensuring its long-term survival.

Be realistic about your prospects

When you launched your firm you probably read one of the innumerable books currently available on how to set up and run a small business. Some of these texts are excessively – even childishly – optimistic and either omit all reference to the stark and sometimes unpleasant realities of potential business collapse, or fail to discuss them adequately. They do not tell you about the *real* problems of small business management: unpaid debts, angry creditors, threats of legal action, lazy and incompetent workers, the loss of important customers, insurance policies that turn out to be useless, inadequate premises, rent reviews that cripple your operations, etc.

Possibly you initiated the enterprise at a time which with the benefit of hindsight guaranteed it could not be wholly successful (especially if, like so many new businesses, you started up following widespread local redundancies and hence local economic recession). Now, you have to rethink fundamentally the entire situation and analyse, honestly and comprehensively, your firm's weaknesses and your personal contributions to its inadequacies.

Analysing problems

There is, in fact, a small handful of key variables that consistently cause businesses to falter. Your business might:

- be in the wrong place
- offer the wrong product to the market
- collect and base decisions on the wrong information
- employ the wrong people
- be too lax in controlling the credit allowed to customers
- cost too much, unnecessarily, to operate.

Associated with these central difficulties is a whole series of other troublesome issues resulting, perhaps, in shortages of cash, over-investment in land, buildings, machinery, furniture, etc. (fixed assets), excessively high levels of working capital (money needed to operate the business from day to day), poor organisation; and inefficient utilisation of staff. Later chapters will help you identify these problems within your firm and suggest practical measures for dealing with them. Much of what follows is based on the idea of *management auditing*, namely, the application of systematic and analytical procedures to help you establish:

(a) where your business is now;
(b) where it needs to be in the future;
(c) what you have to do to get it there.

Important questions

Think of your business as a *system*, with inputs (such as labour, cash, use of the premises, and so on) and outputs in the form of the products or services it offers. Ask yourself the following questions.

Why did I start the business, and am I actually doing now what I originally planned?

If you are in fact undertaking the lines of work you first intended, but are still not earning a living then you probably need to *reposition* the business *vis-à-vis* its actual and potential markets. Perhaps you didn't appreciate how hard it would be to market your product, and thus altered its design and presentation to make it easier to sell. But in doing this you may have lost your direction and wandered into areas in which the firm is inexperienced. Chapter 8 tells you how to 'segment' your markets so that you can then target your selling efforts more effectively.

Can I calculate quickly and accurately the following information?

- How long, on average, does it take to collect an outstanding debt?
- The average periods that (i) stocks of the things I buy from outside stand idle before they are used, and (ii) stocks of finished goods stay on the premises awaiting despatch?
- Average stockholding costs?
- How long elapses, on average, before I pay my bills?
- What rates of return am I obtaining on each of the activities I undertake?
- How long, on average, does it take me to issue invoices?
- What is the likely effect on sales and revenues of my offering a small discount for prompt settlement of accounts?
- Which of my products are the slowest moving?
- Which products contribute most to aggregate profits and why?
- Is the product with the highest profit mark-up on cost the best selling of the firm's products, and if not why not?
- When did each of my main competitors last change their prices?
- How many methods of distribution other than those I use at present are available to me?

If you cannot answer these questions fairly easily there is probably something wrong with your *management information system*. How this can be improved is explained later in the chapter.

Is work duplicated within the business, and how can costs be reduced?

Few people fully appreciate the extent of the hidden costs of running a small business. You must be totally ruthless when curbing unnecessary expenditure. Chapter 4 offers suggestions for how day-to-day efficiency may be improved. Heed these carefully, since no private sector business can possibly survive in the long term if its day-to-day methods of operation are inefficient.

The customer's view

- Now take a pen and paper and describe how you think your last three customers see the firm. Do they regard your business as being at the top end of the market or the bottom end? How many new customers are recommended to your service or product by existing customers? How frequently do you receive customer complaints? What images of the quality of your product or service do your premises, stationery and letterheads project?

What are your business's strengths?

Next, analyse the strengths and weaknesses of the enterprise, focusing on what the business is *really* good at, and where its performance might be improved. Answer the following questions.

- What are the major selling points of each product or service, and why should anyone buy from you and not another firm?
- How are your personal relationships with suppliers, employees and with your bank?
- Is your equipment up to date, or does much of it need replacing?
- Which three improvements in your administrative organisation would you most like to see?
- How long into the future can you reasonably expect your existing products to sell without having to alter their design or contents?

Your personal strengths and weaknesses

You should by now be starting to formulate a critical and objective overview of the business's current situation. Analyse your competence. Did you establish the business without possessing sufficient resources or business or technical expertise? Do you lack communications skills, evidenced perhaps by your reluctance to enter into business correspondence, use the phone, or by an inability to 'connect' with others on personal terms? You will find advice on interpersonal communication skills in various situations in Chapters 5, 6 and 8.

Problems beyond your control

Of course, certain problems such as:

- undercutting by competitors
- unforeseeable changes in public taste
- tax, rates and interest-rate increases;
- economic depressions
- technological innovations

originate externally and are thus beyond your control. But you should still be able to monitor and quickly identify these events – if you cannot there is probably something wrong. Later chapters explore how you might identify and develop new market opportunities and technical innovations, how you can spot inefficiencies and reduce expenditure, revise your scale of operations, and rationalise your product range. In short, you will see how to make things happen rather than merely sitting back and waiting for external events to sink your business.

Where do you need to be?

Total reliance on a single product, or selling several products but only to one market, invites difficulties for your firm. So many things can go wrong:

- a change in fashion
- sharp seasonal variations in demand
- reduced consumer incomes in the single market serviced
- competitors' actions
- unexpected rises in raw materials and other input prices
- VAT increases, etc.

Not only does a single product policy leave you vulnerable to changes in market conditions, it also creates rigidities in your production, organisation and distribution systems. Your plant and equipment becomes increasingly specialised, so that it cannot be used for other purposes when business is slack. Also, its resale value will be negligible if there is widespread depression in the industry to which the assets relate. Your staff, moreover, become completely attuned to the processes and skill requirements of a single product

and supply system, and become unable or unwilling to undertake other, unfamiliar, activities and routines. And even if your single product/single market policy is brilliantly successful, the time will come when your existing market is so saturated that no further sales increases can occur.

The need for diversification

Ideally, you should have a variety of customers across many different industries (so that a depression in a single industry does not hit you too hard), and will offer differing credit terms to various categories of customer according to their importance, reliability and how quickly they settle their bills. Diversification across markets is also useful for a small firm that has already captured a large part – perhaps the dominant part – of a small market segment which rivals have overlooked. To increase market share from 85 per cent to 90 per cent of an existing market segment is considerably more difficult than increasing from a 3 per cent share to a 15 per cent share of an entirely new one. Good credit control is essential if you are to diversify your credit arrangements, and advice on this is offered in Chapter 5.

Could you diversify?

Even if you are extremely good at what you are currently doing and operate within a seemingly stable industry you still need to look out for profitable diversification opportunities. Indeed, your only hope of survival in the long term may depend on your ability to introduce profitable new lines. Products and services can be defined as much by the manner in which they are sold and presented as by their physical characteristics. Thus, a change in selling methods, e.g., through:

- introducing direct mail ordering
- offering cash and carry facilities
- creating a new package design
- making easy payment terms available, etc.

can itself be a form of product diversification; as indeed are changes in:

- quality
- colour

- the 'theme' of a product range
- layout of operating instructions
- the literature that accompanies your product

since all of these can redefine and/or reposition your output in your customers' minds.

Markets change continuously, and you need to be able to identify and seize opportunities as they arise. This means you have to be able to spot chances quickly through an efficient management information system.

Management information systems

An effective management information system (MIS) enables you to monitor costs and revenues, and forecast certain events likely to affect the business; identify possibilities for improving efficiency, for introducing profitable new products and for entering new markets; and to search the wider business environment for developments of interest to your firm. It provides the information necessary for day to day control (ratios of stock to output, profit to working capital, etc.) and, importantly, generates data on changes in the long-term efficiency of your various operations and hence whether you need to abandon current activities in favour of alternative opportunities.

You must monitor rates of return on capital employed (see Chapter 3), cash flows, the firm's liquidity position and the performances of specific investment projects. Accurate marketing information is crucial to the success of your firm, and should include data on:

- the effectiveness of advertising
- responsiveness of sales to price changes
- behaviour of competitors
- the efficiency of distributors
- lengths of trading cycles (i.e., the periods that elapse between making a product and its sale to the final consumer)
- trends in various market segments
- frequency and causes of stockouts, the identification of slow moving items, and stockholding costs.

Another essential MIS function is to highlight potential problems with debtors and suppliers. Your system should be capable of answering the following questions.

- What is the average delay between delivery of goods or performance of service and the issue of invoices?
- How quickly do customers settle their accounts?
- What are the effects of offering discounts for prompt payment?
- What is the ratio of creditors to purchasers?
- How long on average do suppliers take to deliver goods?
- To what extent can payments to suppliers be delayed?

New products or services

If the information generated suggests you are in the wrong business you need to look around for new products and services. Either you must think up completely different products, or copy (taking care not to breach other firms' patents and trademarks) someone else's products while altering a few of their features. (Actually, attempts at imitating other products may themselves create the inspiration necessary to invent something entirely new.)

Write out lists of all the types of work your firm is competent to undertake and of all the alternatives to your product that exist or are feasible. Can you change the product's shape, size, contents, colour or structure? How do foreign versions of the product differ to yours? If you don't know how foreigners make or present this type of good ask your local Chamber of Commerce to suggest some foreign magazines that might illustrate overseas firms' approaches to the design and supply of this kind of product.

The small firm's advantage

Small firms frequently enjoy an advantage over larger rivals in the introduction of new products. Typically they are:

- more flexible
- do not have large amounts of capital locked into particular technologies or distribution networks and may thus be better equipped to respond quickly to fresh market opportunities.

Can you diversify into products related to those you already supply? Do your own suppliers or end customers do things which you might be able to do better? Ask your major suppliers and customers whether they have product needs which they experience difficulty in fulfilling. Even customer complaints can generate new ideas for products!

Introducing products

Having listed some possible new products you next have to examine critically their technical, marketing, and production-cost feasibilities. Analyse the supply costs of the various options, and assess the profitability of each alternative. In particular:

- how many customers are likely to buy the intended new product
- where are potential consumers located and precisely why should they want to buy the item
- to what extent will the intended product enhance your business's image – will it cause you to appear conventional and old-fashioned, or will supplying the product make you seem innovative and up-to-date
- how do you expect market demand for the new product to develop, and what are the cash flow implications of the forecast pattern of sales?

Once you are happy about these matters you check to ensure that the product embodies selling points that will appeal to customers, that it will perform satisfactorily under normal conditions, and that it is safe in storage and in use. Now you draft a timetable for introducing the product, bearing in mind the fact that if the launch is successful, competition will quickly and inevitably emerge.

When to withdraw a product

Many businesses fail because they do not phase out old products as new ones are introduced. This results in:

- complicated and expensive production and organisation systems
- several independent production processes
- many varieties of raw materials drawn from several different sources
- non-interchangeable components and spare parts
- differing customer types (and hence the need for different advertising messages and media), etc.

Rationalisation and standardisation of the product range may offer substantial economies, so existing products should be withdrawn as soon as their production and sale ceases to be financially worthwhile.

   Products can be likened to people: they are conceived, born, they mature and die. The impending demise of a product might be evidenced by declining sales and unit profitability, and by an increase in the amount of effort needed to achieve the lower level of sales. It may be worthwhile cutting the product price – perhaps in combination with a special promotion (a coupon offer, for example) – just to see what happens. If the response is poor the product should be phased out. Otherwise, increasing amounts of time, effort, money and other resources will be devoted to maintaining a product whose natural life is over.

1

The way ahead

So overwhelming might the problems outlined in previous sections appear that you are beginning to wonder whether you really want to continue the business. What are the alternatives? Can you get a steady job if the business collapses? There is no point ruining your health or peace of mind merely to struggle on with a no-hope enterprise. If you decide there is absolutely no chance of the firm succeeding (especially if you cannot even cover the fixed costs – rent, rates, heating and lighting, etc. – of the establishment) then you should immediately cancel any orders on the books that will not generate profit and which do not carry a prohibitive cancellation penalty (though payment of a small penalty may be in fact financially worthwhile), and start to wind up your operation. If, conversely, you do decide to carry on – and I hope for your sake that this option exists – then you must recognise and accept that drastic, possibly ruthless, turnaround measures may be necessary. You might have to make loyal and hard-working employees redundant, and you will almost certainly need to redirect the fundamental orientation of the firm and radically alter its working methods. The steps involved are as follows:

- Conduct a searching analysis of your individual and of your firm's strengths and weaknesses.
- Establish a skeleton staff of totally flexible workers to implement crisis measures.
- Define new cost centres, put an immediate embargo on all new capital expenditures, and introduce a programme for significantly reducing the costs of operations. Link all expenditures to immediately identifiable short-run benefits.
- Tighten credit control procedures and seek emergency sources of finance to inject into the firm.

- Prepare emergency cash flow forecasts to pinpoint critical dangers and activities.
- Reorganise the firm's administrative structure and, simultaneously, redefine its target market segments, advertising strategy and sales promotions methods.
- Smarten your business's image, revise its price structure and carefully examine the adequacy of your present selling and distribution systems.

You also need to ask whether you really need your existing premises. These issues are explored in subsequent chapters.

Summary

Many firms experience low rates of return, but there is much that can be done quickly and easily to improve a small business's fortunes. You must not be discouraged by the fact that your firm is not as profitable as you first expected. And it is essential that you adopt an innovative and creative approach to the business's future.

In fact, a handful of key problems consistently cause underperformance in small enterprises, so provided you (i) know what these are, (ii) can swiftly identify them within your business, and (iii) stand ready to implement decisive policies for overcoming immediate crises, there is no reason why your profits should not improve.

Think of your firm as a system, with inputs of labour and materials and so on, and outputs of finished goods and/or services. The business exists to convert these inputs into outputs and then to distribute the resulting products. This involves deciding what lines of work the firm should undertake; and doing the work as efficiently as possible. In determining these matters you must consider:

- your product's present and potential positions *vis-à-vis* various market segments
- the strengths and weaknesses of the firm, its opportunities for development and the external threats it faces.

Relying on a single product or market invites trouble. You should actively seek to diversify your output and market coverage. Markets change continuously and you have to be able to grasp opportunities immediately they become available. This means searching for new products, carefully analysing the profitabilities of existing output, and withdrawing existing products *before* they become a financial liability. Sound information systems are thus vitally important for the long-term survival of the business.

To revitalise the firm you will probably have to reorganise its administrative structure, redefine its markets and marketing objectives, tighten its procedures for credit control, and introduce new and better advertising, sales promotions and other marketing policies.

1

Checklist

1. How do your firm's current operations compare with those you originally intended when you started the business? How do you explain differences?
2. What is your actual rate of profit compared to the rate of profit you predicted when you began operations?
3. Did you start the business when local economic conditions were not conducive to its survival, and if so, how have the effects of local economic recession affected the business's performance?
4. What outstanding difficulties have you experienced since starting up? Are these difficulties the ones you most expected when you began the business?
5. How quickly and accurately can you identify trading and other business problems when they arise?
6. Which inputs (of labour, raw materials, components, etc.) have caused you most difficulties and why?
7. Which aspects of your firm's operations have been most successful and why?
8. Do you feel technically competent to deal with the new products you have introduced and/or new markets you have recently entered? How might you obtain training to help you cope with these matters?
9. How long would it take you to find out:
    (a) the weekly cost of holding one unit of stock;
    (b) how long on average it takes to collect outstanding debts;
    (c) the average period that elapses between your receiving suppliers' invoices and settling the amounts owed?
10. Have you truthfully answered the questions asked on page 5 above?
11. How many new products might it be feasible for your business to introduce over the next three years?
12. What are the essential features that differentiate your product from that of competing firms?
13. What is the average length of your trading cycle?
14. How recently did you examine the efficiency of your distribution system? If the answer to this question is 'A long time ago', why have you neglected this vital aspect of your operations?

2 Troubleshooting

Do-it-yourself management consultancy □ What you need to study □ The competition □ The business environment □ Cash flow problems □ Breaking even □ Causes and consequences of bad management □ Summary □ Checklist

When you are ill and go to the doctor you expect the doctor to diagnose the cause of your ailment. He or she will ask a series of questions and from the answers conclude why you are feeling unwell. Doctors normally apply one of two approaches to diagnosis – inductive or deductive – depending on the available information and the seriousness of the complaint.

The deductive approach involves asking general questions first and then narrowing down the range of possible origins of the problem as the consultation proceeds. Questions become increasingly specific until the reason for your illness is discovered. There are two difficulties with deductive questioning, (i) the vast range of questions that might be asked, and (ii) the fact that asking a particular question can put an idea into the patient's mind – people asked whether they have been having headaches may suddenly decide that they have, even if this is not actually the case.

Inductive diagnosis means the doctor takes one look at you and, from his or her many years of experience of treating similar illnesses, provisionally assumes a certain cause. Then you are asked questions to confirm or reject this opinion. The problem here is that the initial assessment may be incorrect so that the doctor then pursues several wild goose chases before reaching the correct diagnosis.

Do-it-yourself management consultancy

Discovering what has gone wrong with a business is much the same. You may inwardly feel that you know the source of poor performance, yet be unable to establish conclusively the cause of the complaint. Typically you need to begin the investigation with a general assessment of all aspects of the operations of the business and then narrow down the list of things that might have gone wrong. A good management consultant would guide you in these respects, but you may not be able to afford outside advice, and so must do this work independently (and anyhow the work is itself interesting).

Imagine you are an outsider brought in to analyse the efficiency of your firm. You must be objective, rational, realistic and above all brutally honest about the situation.

Cause and effect

The aim is to establish connections between causes and effects, and then to impose new management structures and patterns of interpersonal relationships (you might, for example, have previously been too soft with your debtors or employees) in order to remedy the business's faults. Then you will be able to predict how your business responds (or should respond) to changes in the things that cause difficulties. Suppose, for instance, that you know by how much your sales will probably increase if you reduce your selling price by a certain percentage, and that you have also identified the relationship between the volume of production and unit cost. You can now work out the likely consequences for production costs and schedules of an aggressive price-cutting marketing strategy, and incorporate these directly into your business plan. Ignorance costs money in the commercial world, and the resources devoted to collecting relevant information on the causes and effects of various activities are usually justified.

How to begin

One useful mode of analysis is to specify exactly what you initially wanted (and still hope to achieve) from the business and then work back through your entire organisation highlighting the inefficiencies which have prevented you achieving your objectives. This requires you to think of your business as a system with inputs and outputs under your control. You set up a theoretical, perfectly functioning model of how your business *ought* to perform and then compare the idealised model with what actually happens.

Suppose, for example, that you run a wine bar and that when you started you anticipated a certain average number of customers per week, each spending a particular average amount, thus generating an income of a predicted level well in excess of your anticipated costs. What precisely needs to happen for this to occur? Presumably, the answer to this question will involve:

- a certain proportion of potential customers in the wine bar's catchment area becoming aware of the establishment's existence, using the establishment, and repeating their custom

- each customer unit (person or group) spending some minimum amount per standard period of time (half an hour perhaps) while in the bar
- a certain average hourly turnover of custom and/or seat/table occupancy
- wage and other expenses not exceeding predetermined limits
- a constant supply of inputs (wines, foodstuffs, etc.) at reasonable prices.

The actual list will of course be much more exhaustive than this, and will relate to the specific circumstances of the business. In general, however, you would need to ask *how* each of your objectives could be achieved and *why* targets have *not* been met. You want to know:

- what resources, activities and other inputs are needed
- what processes are required
- how you and your employees must behave towards customers and towards each other
- what information you have to gather
- how materials are to be stored and manipulated.

Now compare the ideal configuration of events and activities with the reality of your business and determine the changes necessary to improve its performance. Some fundamental changes – in premises, marketing methods, staffing levels, ways of controlling costs – are dealt with in other chapters. Here we are concerned with identifying causes of difficulties.

What you need to study

The symptoms of poor performance (declining profitability, low sales, soaring expenditures) are obvious, but their causes may be hidden. Experiments may thus be necessary to determine the sources of problems.

Experiments and research

You can experiment with:

- the price of your product (special price reductions, special offers and so on)

- how you package output
- where you place advertisements
- the allocation of tasks to various employees
- staff incentive schemes, etc.

Normally, you would not wish constantly to change your activities. But the circumstances of a low profit business are not normal, and your firm could fail unless drastic measures are implemented. Also, experiments create a spirit of adventure among those who initiate them. They encourage innovative and analytical approaches to problems.

Where you cannot experiment you need to conduct business research. This can be internal or external, done at your desk or 'in the field'. Let's begin by looking at the state and behaviour of the competition.

The competition

There is much wishful thinking when newly established firms evaluate the calibre of their competitors. Proprietors convince themselves of the superiority of their own businesses, to the point where they perceive competitors in a totally unrealistic manner. If your business succeeds you must expect other firms to respond aggressively – if they do not you have a clear indication that you have failed to make a significant impact on chosen market segments. Three reactions from competitors are likely: an increase in their advertising and other promotional activities, price cuts and their copying your products and initiatives. Look ahead. Anticipate competitors' behaviour and prepare contingency plans for dealing with various responses to your actions. And be prepared for dirty tricks from competitors, including:

- attempts to persuade your suppliers (via financial inducements) not to accept your orders, or at least to insist on cash payment
- circulating unfounded rumours to your largest customers that you are on the verge of bankruptcy
- pretending to be recruiting staff, inviting your own employees to apply for (non-existent) vacancies, and then interviewing them simply to gather information about your current operations
- persuading retailers and/or distributors not to handle your products.

Monitor continuously your competitors' activities, and never underestimate their worth. If you have employees, a good way of following competitors' actions is to make each employee personally responsible for keeping tabs on one particular competitor – by perusing their advertisements, cataloguing the selling points of their current products, watching their staffing levels, price policies, etc.

Beware the predatory competitor

Paradoxically, the greater your success the greater the danger competitors can become to your long-run survival! Suppose that you are so technically efficient and that your advertising is so effective that you now dominate the local market. At this point (supposing, for example, that you have a three-quarters share of the market) the only way you can increase your sales further is by expanding the *total size* of the market (which task is both difficult and expensive). Yet a less successful rival can increase its market share – and hence its sales – at your expense by cutting its prices and taking some of your existing custom. You have little alternative but to respond by cutting your prices. But your own sales are unlikely to increase in consequence because you already dominate the market. Thus, you lower your prices and accept the resulting decline in profits.

Unfortunately, however, this enforced cut in revenue occurs just at the moment that funds are most needed, since in order to dominate the market in the first instance, you had to:

- invest in new equipment
- undertake expensive advertising
- enter high value bulk purchasing contracts with suppliers
- employ more workers
- hire a warehouse to store extra goods, etc.

To finance these activities you borrowed heavily, and the loan plus interest is now due for repayment. The reduction in profits forced on you by a competitor's actions means you can't find the money. Your very success in outpacing competitors is actually causing the failure of your business!

The business environment

The worst time to start a new small business is during an economic depression when consumer incomes, and hence the general demand for products, are falling. Yet these are precisely the conditions that typically prevail when governments most vigorously encourage the establishment of new firms. Perhaps you started your enterprise during a tax regime that suddenly altered, or depended on government or local authority support that unexpectedly collapsed, or arrived at work one morning to find double yellow lines on the streets where previously your customers parked their vehicles. As a small business you are unlikely to experience strikes within your own organisation, but you could be affected by strikes (or other mishaps) among your suppliers, distributors or large industrial customers.

Plan ahead

Such difficulties arise from factors beyond your control and you are not responsible for their consequences. But you should plan ahead and make provision for various environmental eventualities. Planning enables you to decide today, unhurriedly, how you will react to diverse future situations. It means you do not have to take crucial decisions, which could make or break the business, in a crisis atmosphere when you do not have time to consider all relevant facts objectively. The business that plans is ready to adapt its activities to suit altered environments and it can take action now to help it cope with possible future occurrences. Planning forces you to think hard about your organisation, its strengths and weaknesses, and its future prospects. Many pitfalls might then be foreseen and thus avoided.

Cash flow problems

Cash flow problems certainly make themselves known to the poorly planned small business, if only through there not being enough money in the bank to settle outstanding invoices. Yet the business might otherwise be financially viable and have excellent prospects. You must analyse how cash flow difficulties arise; it is not sufficient merely to observe that cash inflows fail to arrive in appropriate periods. Prepare lists of all your receipts and expenditures for the last six months and highlight major weekly differences. Almost certainly, you will find that inflow problems relate either to unexpected reductions in sales or to credit customers taking unacceptably long periods to settle their balances. Outflow problems are usually caused by natural (or man-made) catastrophes that could and should have been insured against, or by excessive and/or unanticipated expenditures.

Predicting and monitoring cash inflows and outflows and analysing the differences between them are crucially important for the small firm, since failure to do this is one of the commonest causes of the collapse of small businesses.

Planning the cash flow

One way of planning the cash flow is to anchor *all* spending against sales revenues. Hence, expenditures on anything other than current wages and production supplies are deferred until after pre-specified sales revenues (not sales volume or credit) have been achieved. This is a cheap and simple control device that avoids many cash flow problems. But it has the severe disadvantage of automatically reducing certain expenditures when perhaps they ought to increase, since sales might themselves depend on various activities whose funding is arbitrarily withdrawn just because sales are reducing. And you do not wish to give the appearance of being in trouble. External signs of financial problems such as:

- failing to re-paint the reception area
- not cleaning offices or the fascia of the premises
- continuing to run ageing and obviously unreliable vehicles, etc.

can be most damaging to the image of the business. Good quality stationery, bold letterheads, printed (rather than typed and photo-copied) sales literature and so on, can be crucial for marketing the firm. However, linking costs to sales revenue can be extremely useful to an enterprise facing immediate cash flow difficulties and, sensibly applied, it might save the business.

Breaking even

A frequent cause of cash flow problems is failure to realise the revenue implications of various pricing policies. Sometimes, price cuts lead to such big increases in sales that the effects of a lower price per unit are easily outweighed by the additional revenues generated by an increased volume of business.

For instance, a firm selling 5,000 units per quarter at £5.00 per unit realises £25,000 from sales. Suppose the firm has £10,000 per quarter in overheads (rent, rates, lighting and heating, etc.) and that each unit costs £2.00 to supply. The firm is making £5,000 profit per quarter. Now suppose the selling price is reduced to £4.00 per unit. This business must now sell 5,000 units just to break even, let alone make any profit, and must sell 7,500 units if its existing profit level of £5,000 per quarter is to continue.

To see this, remember that the breakeven point occurs where total revenue equals total cost. Revenue is price times number of units sold, i.e., (£4.00 × X) where X is the number of units. Total cost consists of overheads of £10,000 plus cost per unit times the number of units produced, i.e., (£2.00 × X). Thus, to break even we need:

> total revenue = total cost
> i.e. $4X = 10,000 + 2X$
> so that, $X = 5,000$ units

To make £5,000 profit, total revenue must exceed total cost by this amount, viz:

> $4X = (10,000 + 2X) + 5,000$
> so that $X = 7,500$ units

is the number of units required. Accordingly, you must always work out how many extra units have to be sold to make a price cut financially viable. In the example given it might in fact be impossible to increase sales from 5,000 to at least 7,500 units. And if competitors cut their prices in response, with the result that sales do not increase at all, then all the existing profit is wiped out (£4 × 5,000 gives £20,000), leaving just enough to break even.

Before even considering a price cut (or increase) you need to calculate an array of possible prices with their break-even points and cost/revenue implications clearly indicated. Note that a low price associated with a high break even might be appropriate for a market that is buoyant and expanding and where production costs are not likely to increase without warning; but may be totally unsuitable for other situations. A big wage increase for staff, raw materials price rises, or an increase in the rent of your premises will disrupt your intended point of break even and hence all your planned production schedules.

Causes and consequences of bad management

Some problems might be due to your own incompetence. Face up to this: accept your past failings, but resolve never to repeat your mistakes. Common managerial indiscretions include the following.

Not enough customers

Relying on just a couple of really big customers for most of your orders and not seeking to diversify your market can spell disaster for your firm. One of these large customers might:

- decide to withdraw its business
- go into liquidation
- itself experience financial problems and not be able to settle the outstanding balance it has accumulated.

Too few suppliers

Not seeking alternative sources of supply is equally dangerous. You may perhaps have negotiated an attractive discount for bulk purchases of raw materials from a particular supplier. But in doing this you failed to realise the longer term implications of relying on a single source of supply. The following difficulties might be especially severe.

- The discount might be withdrawn, by which time your production line may have been adapted to suit the specific characteristics of the output of the supplying firm.
- Deliveries from the single supplier might be regularly late and cause numerous hold-ups in your manufacturing system.
- The proportion of defective items in each delivery may become unacceptably high.

Reliance on just a couple of suppliers means, moreover, that if they unexpectedly increase their prices and if you cannot easily pass on such increases (via a higher selling price) to your own customers then your profit margin is reduced – at least in the short to medium term. And a declining margin could mean the end of the business.

Finding alternative suppliers capable of delivering the possibly substantial amounts of raw materials you require – on time, at an acceptable level of quality and at a reasonable price – can be difficult, time consuming and expensive. So take an interest in the technical aspects of your inputs: their origin, manufacturing processes, quality options, etc. This will not only help you improve your product but could also enable you to identify new and better sources of supply.

Staff problems

Employing staff who are lazy, inept or dishonest (or all three) is another obvious source of trouble. If this has occurred it is largely your fault; you ought not to have hired such workers in the first instance, or they should have been taken to task as soon as they began to under-perform. Why did you not recognise the signs of staff dishonesty or incompetence? After all, lack of enthusiasm, refusal to co-operate or exercise initiative, conflicts and bad interpersonal relationships among employees are easily observed! An inefficient employee can be the most expensive (and damaging) resource your business ever acquires. Conversely, competent staff make enormous contributions to the well-being of the organisation. Employee relations are therefore important in even the smallest of firms. These matters are considered further in Chapter 6.

Capital and current spending

Failing to distinguish between capital spending and current spending creates enormous difficulties for the hard-up firm. Too many small business proprietors regard all incomes and expenditures as part of their normal monthly cash flow, regardless of the purpose to which the money is applied. Thus, for example, a firm's single delivery vehicle might be its most important, and expensive, asset, yet the business's owner may make little effort to create a reserve out of current income to replace the vehicle when it wears out. Sometimes proprietors wrongly assume that the rate of depreciation applied to an asset on the advice of an accountant – who will select the method of depreciation that saves the maximum amount of tax – is the actual rate at which money should be put aside for the asset's replacement. For instance, at the time of writing the Inland Revenue will only allow you to depreciate a motor car by at most 25 per cent of its initial cost in any given year. But how long that vehicle actually lasts depends principally on how much you use it and whether it is well maintained. Hence, you should put aside a reasonable amount each month to cover all foreseeable asset replacement costs, and then add a contingency allowance (say ten per cent) for good measure. And remember that maintenance costs increase sharply as assets age.

Many small businesses have gone under when confronted with large maintenance bills or when a major capital asset unexpectedly needs replacement. Remember too that tangible assets are necessary to provide security for bank loans. You may be able to rent a replacement capital asset temporarily if you happen to be short of funds when your existing one fails. But you cannot offer rented equipment as security when borrowing money.

Market trends

Suppose you have an excellent product – technically superb, well packaged and presented, and priced reasonably. Your firm is doing what it is good at and you love the work. What, you ask, could possibly be wrong with that?

Unfortunately, you may be offering for sale a product that is mechanically and functionally first rate but which consumers increasingly do not wish to buy! Markets alter in terms of the ages, sex, income levels, geographical location, etc., of potential customers and also in relation to consumer tastes and preferences. There is little point in producing technically excellent goods which consumers are not willing to purchase. Thus, instead of simply trying to sell the goods you have already decided to make (and becoming increasingly frustrated by consumers' poor reactions), you should monitor current trends among consumers, look for new market opportunities and be prepared to diversify and/or modify your offerings to satisfy current consumer preferences. Of course, large and prosperous organisations can to some extent create consumer demand through skilful advertising, but this consideration does not normally apply to small businesses. And even the most vigorous and expensive advertising and other promotional campaigns will fail if products are not wanted by consumers. This question is explored further in Chapter 8.

Change in the environment

Never assume that environmental conditions will not alter. We live in a rapidly changing world and you should assume as a matter of course that:

- new products and materials *will* be introduced
- consumers *will* change their buying behaviour
- a friendly, grant awarding local authority *will* be replaced by one that is parsimonious and hostile
- new production methods are bound to emerge, etc.

Clinging on to existing products and methods when better alternatives are available to competitors guarantees long-term disaster.

How long is it since you compared your own products to those of competitors, especially those relatively new to the market? List all the changes in the wider environment – laws, taxation, consumer tastes, local authority regulations, input prices, operating costs, employee relations – that you can think of that might affect the business and alongside each item briefly outline its probable consequences. Then consider each of your firm's activities (selling, manufacture, raising finance, and so on) and ask yourself what changes are likely to occur in each area. Change is inevitable. Accept change. Look ahead and plan the implementation of its consequences.

Spare capacity

Carrying too much spare capacity is not uncommon among small firms, whose owners typically dislike being under too much pressure with production deadlines, machine time and labour utilisation constraints, lack of storage space, etc. Matching current workloads with available capacity requires careful scheduling and a great deal of effort. How much easier it is to maintain a comfortable margin of spare capacity, so that any order can be met without additional administrative work. But consider the real cost of surplus capacity. A machine (or person, or warehouse) idle for one hour a day is costing the business 14.3 per cent of its potential contribution (assuming seven hours a day normal working). Avoid spare capacity, even if tight schedules are inconvenient. As soon as spare capacity appears, consider subletting the surplus and/or cutting your prices; do not breathe a sigh of relief, spare capacity (including office space and storage facilities) is costing you money despite its convenience. Spare capacity is a frequent symptom of unprofitable expansion, which is dealt with in Chapter 3.

Wasteful advertising

Failing businesses sometimes naively assume that they can turn around their fortunes by increasing expenditure on advertising. They insist that their products are excellent, and genuinely believe customers will clamour to buy these products when informed of their existence. Advertisements must be carefully targeted if their costs are to be recovered. And only in exceptional circumstances should advertising be undertaken where its effectiveness cannot be measured. Advertising can be enormously expensive and wasteful of resources. Chapter 9 tells you how to avoid unproductive advertising.

Discretion is sometimes better than valour

Do not take on more than you can chew. In particular, never initiate a fight with competitors when realistically you stand little chance of succeeding. Large firms frequently possess substantial reserves which they can and do use to 'see off' smaller rivals that initiate price or advertising wars against them. Avoid attacking larger competitors unless you are sure you can win or those firms attacked you first. Discretion is infinitely preferable to valour in most circumstances.

What about the workers?

Lack of sympathy for workers who experience personal family problems which interfere with their jobs (causing them to take time off to look after children, for example) or who have difficulty coping with the level of their work, can alienate and render unprofitable workers who are fundamentally sound and who possess great potential. Minor concessions such as:

- allowing flexible working hours
- paying certain small expenses
- consultation in decision making

can transform the situation, and cause disaffected individuals to become highly satisfied employees. Chapter 6 examines these issues.

Further problems

Other examples of poor management include:

- naively trusting people who ought not to be trusted (whether they be members of the public, suppliers or employees)
- not realising the extent of your tax liability for the current financial year
- not planning the maintenance of machines and other vital equipment
- not expanding the business in a sensible and conservative way (see Chapter 3 below).

Control problems often figure prominently in the case histories of businesses that experience low profitability. Thus, you might start out as a one person operation with direct, personal and intimate knowledge of every aspect of your firm, taking all decisions yourself, knowing all your major customers and suppliers by name, and enjoying low overheads. Then you employ staff to liaise with outsiders. You haven't the time to supervise them closely (you are too busy building up the firm) and anyway it would not be proper to deny them the authority to take decisions independently. But the staff become slipshod in their work. They upset customers, do not properly inspect suppliers' deliveries, and allow overdue accounts to accumulate. The telephone isn't answered; letters leave the office badly typed, etc. All this has happened behind your back – you have lost effective control of your business!

You must *plan* the development of the business. Allow for steadily increasing expenditure on overheads (extra warehousing, premises, administration) in line with the growth in sales. And as your business grows increase the frequency with which you inspect vital management information: the order book, outstanding credit, delivery periods, market share, etc. These matters are discussed in the next chapter.

Summary

To be good at small business management you have to be able to diagnose accurately the basic causes of business problems, and relate such causes to their operational effects. You should set up an ideal model of how the business would function in the best possible situation and then compare this with your firm's actual performance, analysing differences as you go along.

You may need to experiment and undertake considerable amounts of research prior to deciding on the measures necessary to improve profitability, but once you have chosen your actions you must stick to your plan, implementing tough new policies to overcome your difficulties. Beware of dirty tricks by competitors and continuously monitor their activities. List and describe current operational problems under headings for

(a) those created by outside influences, and
(b) those subject to your personal and immediate control.
And be totally honest in your analysis.

Planning is essential for successful small business management, particularly regarding the timing of receipts and payments. You need a system for relating current levels of spending to some measure of the business's overall performance. And you must carefully examine the break even and cash flow implications of various selling prices.

Prosperous firms are usually those which in the longer term avoid overreliance on just a handful of customers or suppliers. They regularly seek out fresh markets and new supply sources. The chapter concluded with a brief description of some of the many things that can go wrong in a small business, citing particular instances of bad management and their effects. Later chapters suggest solutions for many of these difficulties.

2

Checklist

1. Can you pinpoint at least four *specific* reasons why your profits have not been as good as expected?
2. By how much do you think your total profits would increase if you cut all selling prices by (a) five per cent, (b) ten per cent, and (c) fifteen per cent?
3. What are the revenue implications to the answers to the last question?
4. Make out a list – similar to that on page 17 above – of the sorts of things that are necessary for your business to prosper.
5. What are the three marketing policies your leading competitor could most easily introduce in attempts to disrupt your own marketing efforts?
6. How well-equipped is your business to adapt quickly to the following:
   * an increase in the rate of VAT on your output
   * a big price cut by a major competitor
   * a strike among the employees of the firms that deliver your most important supplies?
7. When did you last prepare a cash flow forecast?
8. Suppose your three major suppliers increased their sale prices by ten per cent, how would this affect the profitability of your business?
9. How much do you know about the technical aspects of the firm's raw material inputs?
10. Do you really understand the difference between capital spending and current spending? If not, reread page 24 in the text.
11. What is the probability that you will not experience an equipment breakdown within the next three months, and how would a serious equipment failure affect your cash flow?
12. Do you carry spare capacity, and if so how much is it costing you?

3　Sensible expansion

Why expansion doesn't always increase profitability □
Distribution matters □ Consequences of expanding too
rapidly □ Business ratios □ What to look for □ Measuring
productive efficiency □ How to avoid unprofitable expansion
□ Summary □ Checklist

Some seemingly successful small firms expand so rapidly that they
run into all sorts of administrative and financial difficulties which,
paradoxically, cause their average unit profitability – the average
return achieved on each pound invested in a business – to be lower
than before the expansion occurred. Whereas prior to the expansion
the enterprise might have obtained an average return of, say, fifteen
per cent on capital employed (measured perhaps by fixed assets plus
working capital – see below); after the expansion the percentage
average rate achieved may be only ten! Disorganised and unprofitable expansion frequently causes serious financial difficulty in small
businesses, and disorderly and unplanned growth should be avoided
at all times; indeed, it has led to the collapse of many firms.

　To prevent haphazard expansion and the problems it creates you
need first to understand how unprofitable growth arises, and second
to be able to identify possible sources of 'overtrading' within your
firm. Then, if you are in fact growing too rapidly for your own good
you must seek ways sensibly to reduce your scale of operations.

Why expansion doesn't always increase profitability

You start a new business, and it flourishes. Order books are full;
sales expand. Everyone agrees you have a reasonably priced first-
class product that supplies a consumer need. Your staff are hard-
working and enthusiastic; customers are delighted with the goods
you produce. Accordingly, you start to expand the scale of your
decidedly successful operations. But this, alas, could be the worst
thing you can possibly do because rapid growth typically means
disturbing a highly efficient existing administrative system (it must
be efficient otherwise the firm would not have achieved the success
that caused it to expand). Also, you incur numerous unforeseen
expenses, and encounter many unanticipated organisational difficulties

during the expansion. To produce the extra goods needed to satisfy the increasing volume of sales you have to spend extra money *now*, on such things as:

• additional supplies
• more wages
• higher electricity bills to run even more machines
• extra stationery

but you do not receive any income from additional production until some considerable time in the future after the goods have been sold.

Credit problems

Usually, a growth in sales is accompanied by an increase in the amount of credit you give to existing (and possibly new) customers so that the period between incurring expenses and collecting the money from the sale of your goods becomes very long. Moreover, the number of bad debts you incur (i.e., debts for which the likelihood of the debtor paying up is so remote that all hope of retrieving the money has to be abandoned) begins to increase.

You will probably have to borrow at high interest to finance the gap between the additional spending on extra labour and supplies and the receipt of income from extra sales. Also, you may have overinvested in fixed assets to cope with the expansion.

Wasted space

Perhaps you increased the size of your premises in order to house the additional staff you hired and to provide more warehousing space and access to new machinery. Whereas previously you fully utilised every spare inch of your premises – with people almost on top of each other and boxes of goods in every available corner awaiting despatch – you now have plenty of space. But this necessarily means you are now paying money for space on which there is *zero return*. If you pay £10 per square foot annual rental, then every square foot of space not used represents an extra £10 per annum invested in the business without that money generating any profits at all, which means that the *average* return on each square foot of premises rented quickly begins to fall.

Parkinson's law begins to apply

Similar considerations apply to machines and labour. Suppose, for example, that previously you had three employees – all of whom worked extremely hard and were fully utilised throughout all seven hours of their working day – but that in order to satisfy increased consumer demand you have now increased your labour force to six. This solves the production/clerical work problems caused by expansion, but could mean that through easing the pressure on labour you now have six workers, each of whom is only fully employed on average for five hours of each working day. 'Parkinson's law' begins to operate – work quickly expands to fill up the time made available for its completion and, in consequence, the *average* return on the wages you pay to each employee (assuming you pay a flat rate weekly or monthly wage) goes down. Likewise with machines. Before, you had three machines constantly in operation. Now you have five, but each is only used for part of the day. Again the average rate of return on each pound invested in machinery will decline.

Supply problems

While the average returns on your investments in inputs are falling, your average costs of operating the business are going up. Suppliers might not be prepared to grant credit on really big orders because the risk to them of your default is too great. Accordingly, whereas previously perhaps three-quarters of your supplies were purchased on credit (meaning in effect that suppliers are lending you interest-free funds), you find that after the expansion possibly less than half of your much bigger total purchases are on credit terms. Most supplies now have to be paid for in cash, which you draw from the large overdraft you operate at enormous interest cost. Moreover, your existing suppliers might not have been able to satisfy your increasing demands, so that you went to new and different suppliers whose deliveries in fact turned out to be extremely slow, and a lot of the goods were defective and had to be returned.

More clerical work

Extra staff not only mean a higher wage bill but also more employer's National Insurance contributions and additional clerical work for you in working out their PAYE. Controlling the staff becomes more difficult, especially if recently recruited staff are not familiar with the firm's line of work. You might not be skilled or experienced in staff management and thus find that employee relations problems come to dominate your working life. Administrative overheads can increase alarmingly after hiring additional staff. More space and desks are needed, more stationery is required, and the expansion in the firm's general operations creates the need for more letters to customers and suppliers, extra photocopying, more printing, typing, internal memoranda, co-ordination meetings, etc. And of course, opportunities for staff malingering, indeed for employee fraud, theft and petty dishonesty, expand as the workforce increases.

Distribution matters

Higher sales may require that you augment or change your existing distribution system. Yet in so doing you might lose effective control over how your goods are sold. Increased production means that someone, somewhere, has to carry extra stock. Stockholding is expensive, as goods must be:

- warehoused
- recorded
- packaged to avoid natural wastage and pilfering
- monitored and moved in and out of stores.

Also, stock is an idle asset – money tied up in stock could be used to earn interest or, even better, generate further profits for the firm.

Using a wholesaler

You can, of course, pass on the cost of stockholding to a wholesaler who will also bear the risk of collapse in sales. Unfortunately, wholesalers demand big discounts on bulk purchases – discounts so big that use of a wholesaler might not be financially worthwhile – and they typically stock competing brands: there is no reason they should promote your product rather than the output of competing firms. Conversely you might decide to retail your own products, acquiring retail premises for this purpose. In this case, however, you have to incur even more fixed costs and will probably need to borrow very heavily, at high interest, to finance the deal. And you must assume all retailing risks.

Many businesses fail through taking on these sorts of retail distribution obligations without properly considering the extra work involved or the additional expertise and business experience required. Even mail order and other direct marketing methods (see Chapter 9) can involve heavy initial costs.

Small versus large orders

Distribution costs are affected by the sizes of order that customers place (an increased volume of low unit sales can greatly increase distribution costs through increased expenditure on packaging, order processing, invoicing, debt collection and so on) and by the costs of selling:

- salespeople's wages and expenses
- increasing travel costs as more sales staff cover bigger territories, etc.

These costs may, of course, be avoided by concentrating on selling to just a handful of really big customers. You might, for example, produce an 'own label' version of your product for a large multiple retailer, or place the bulk of your output with a couple of wholesalers. But what happens if one of these customers (who might take as much as fifty per cent of your production) decides to take its custom elsewhere, or squeezes you for extra discounts, or goes into liquidation owing a huge bill? You are likely to go bust since much of your productive capacity will be geared to the needs of that customer and you will probably not be able to sell this output elsewhere.

Consequences of expanding too rapidly

Increase in competition

Apart from disturbing existing production systems and possibly upsetting well-established personal relationships within the firm, a conspicuous expansion will itself signal to competitors your business's success and the fact that you are engaged in a highly profitable field. This can lead to disaster, because:

(a) your existing competitors might decide to expand their operations;
(b) other firms not presently engaged in your line of work may decide – following your profitable example – to enter your area or industry and begin to compete!

And the increased competition can occur precisely when you are at your most vulnerable; when you have borrowed heavily, have just paid out large amounts of cash for additional labour and raw materials and possibly are experiencing acute cash flow problems for the first time.

Problems with administration and finance

Common difficulties include the following:

- Deliveries to customers are frequently late on account of the administrative problems caused by the firm's fast growth and the production bottlenecks and distribution breakdowns that are increasingly encountered.
- Debtors are slow in paying bills, excusing themselves by pointing out deficiencies in your own clerical system – your invoices miss customers' end-of-month cheque issues; invoices, delivery and advice notes sometimes conflict and are regularly inaccurate.
- It takes so long to settle these problems that you are constantly short of cash. Liabilities increase, current income falls, you have exhausted your financial reserves on the purchase of new equipment, while much of the firm's working capital is tied up in stock and in unpaid debtors' bills. You find it difficult to put together enough money to pay your own creditors, payments to creditors are delayed for several weeks, resulting in creditors threatening to withdraw credit facilities (hence creating even more cash flow problems for the firm).

Owners of firms in this situation are sometimes incredulous about what is happening to them. They cannot believe that cash flow problems are occurring given that the business to date has been a huge success. After all, increasing sales and hence the prospects for higher profits were the original impetus to expand.

The mistake made here is the confusion of *absolute* cash inflows with *profit per unit of resource employed* within the firm. True, the *total* amount of profit generated by higher sales continues to increase, but if you divide this by the value of the resources used to create the higher profit, you find that the average profitability of each pound invested in the business is actually lower than it was before.

Identify the problem

You need to compare a few key statistics before and after expansion.

A good starting point is to measure your 'rate of return on capital employed'. This is defined as profit earned during a period, say three months, divided by the value of tangible fixed assets (plant and equipment, premises if you own them, vehicles, furniture, etc., but not including goodwill) plus current assets (stock, debtors, and cash), minus current liabilities (short-term debts that have to be settled in the next six months). If you are expanding sensibly, this ratio should not decline in value over time. Measure your profits as net profits before drawings, tax, loan repayments and the payment of interest on loans (since obviously some interest costs have to be incurred in order to finance the expansion, and such loans should not therefore be classed as part of your normal operations). Stock should be valued at cost or market value, whichever is lower. And always deduct probable bad debts from the figure for debtors in current assets.

Valuation of fixed assets presents a problem because of the need to deduct depreciation for wear and tear. Note that you do not have to use the same depreciation method for this purpose as you employ to save the maximum amount of tax, so choose a sensible figure that reasonably reflects the loss in asset values over the period considered.

Business ratios

If the rate of return on capital employed begins to decline you must investigate the cause. Look at movements in ratios:

- for profit to sales (showing whether extra sales are really contributing to unit profitability)
- for sales to capital employed (which tells you how much you have to invest to generate extra sales)
- any other ratio that might be relevant for measuring your firm's efficiency, e.g., profit/working capital (where working capital equals current assets less current liabilities); sales to fixed assets; sales to working capital; debtors to working capital; sales to overheads; and so on.

The current ratio

Crucially important for effective financial control is the ratio of the firm's current assets to current liabilities. This is called the 'current ratio' (or sometimes the 'working capital ratio') of the enterprise. It shows the degree of liquidity of the business, i.e., how easily the firm can (theoretically) settle its debts if all outstanding balances must be simultaneously cleared ('theoretically' because working capital includes debtors and of course some customers might not actually pay their bills!). Current assets of cash, debtors and stock are or should be immediately and easily converted into purchasing power, while current liabilities (trade creditors and accrued expenses) are debts which might have to be settled at short notice and hence drain the business of short-term funds. Also, even if you measure stock at the lower of cost or market value there is still no guarantee that in a real emergency all your stock on hand could be sold. Leaving this aside, a value for this ratio of more than one means the firm is, in principle, fully solvent and can settle all its short-term debts from its own resources. Note that a current ratio of less than one is not necessarily bad – it could simply indicate that the business is economising on stocks, debtors and cash while maximising the period over which it settles its own debts. This might be suitable for a firm in a stable commercial environment where volatile change is unlikely; fixed assets could perhaps be liquidated in an emergency.

In general, however, a decreasing current ratio between one period and the next often indicates 'overtrading'. Expansion has been so fast that the growth of short-term liabilities has exceeded the accumulation of current assets.

The liquidity ratio

The fact that some current assets take longer to liquidate than others gives rise to the need for a ratio which measures a firm's capacity for immediate settlement of its current liabilities. The 'acid test ratio' (also called the 'liquidity ratio', or the 'quick' ratio) achieves this objective since it incorporates only those current assets which can be instantly converted into cash. Thus, stocks of raw materials and work in progress (which take some time to liquidate) are ignored. The ratio is:

$$\frac{\text{Cash} + \text{Debtors} + \text{Realisable Investments}}{\text{Current Liabilities}}$$

A more severe version would exclude debtors on the grounds that few debtors would actually meet their obligations instantly on demand. The liquidity ratio should normally have a value near to one, meaning that current liabilities are fully covered. However, values in excess of one are undesirable because superfluous liquid funds should always be quickly reinvested in order to generate additional profits for the firm; they should not be held in the form of cash or low yield financial investments.

Finally, you should break down the current ratio into its component parts, and look carefully at alterations in such ratios as stock/current assets, debtors/current assets, etc., as the business increases its sales.

What to look for

You need to establish whether you are getting the same value for money from a bigger firm as you obtained previously when output and sales were less. Through continuously monitoring the quick ratio (in conjunction with detailed cash flow forecasting) you ensure that you will always be able to repay loan interest and capital sum repayments to your bank and honour your other financial obligations. Thus you will not be forced to wind up your successful business through short-term lack of funds.

Before spending an extra penny on expanding your operations look ahead to check that every additional pound put into the business will yield the same rate of return, proportionately, as that which you have *already* achieved and will not reduce average profits per pound put into the business.

Seek out possible inefficiencies in the use of working capital. Excessive stockholding, for example, is revealed through reductions in the 'stock turnover ratio', measured as cost of sales/average stock where 'cost of sales' is the value of opening stock plus stock purchases during the period less stock at close. The ratio shows the speed of inventory turnover. If, for instance, the accounting period is one year and the ratio has a value of two, then a unit of stock is held on average for six months. Values lower than two mean that stock is held longer than six months, and vice versa. (High values are appropriate only for firms which face irregular and unanticipated market demands where sudden changes in taste can lead to heavy, unexpected sales.)

Generally, fast stock turnover is desirable because rapid transformation of stock into sales means an increase in the intensity of the trading cycle (i.e., how many times goods are produced and converted into cash within any given period) and hence higher returns on capital employed. Usually, perishable goods have the highest turnover rates, while consumer durables and luxury goods take longer to sell. Often, there are direct relationships between profit margins and stock turnover rates. Lower selling prices, while associated with lower unit prices, might cause stock to turn over so rapidly that higher total profits eventually ensue.

The average amount of raw materials stock you carry can be reduced by buying in smaller quantities which, nevertheless, are delivered more frequently. This only works, however, if suppliers' delivery arrangements are reliable and you have alternative sources of supply available if particular orders do not turn up on time. Also, you need to balance the savings in your stockholding costs against the loss of bulk-purchasing discounts possibly available on larger orders.

Other useful ratios

Other useful ratios are:

- profits to sales
- administrative expenses to sales (the various categories of administrative expense – selling, secretarial, documentation, etc. – might also be usefully expressed as a proportion of sales)
- credit sales to total sales.

Movements in the credit/sales ratio indicate changes in the firm's dependence on credit selling and, by implication, its sensitivity to a lengthening of the average period before debtors settle their outstanding accounts. The ratio of bad debts to sales shows the risk of selling on credit. Another ratio worth computing is that of net current assets (i.e., current assets minus current liabilities) to fixed assets. This indicates the extent to which physically realisable plant and equipment, premises, vehicles, etc., are available to settle outstanding debts. A high value means there are few assets that can be sold off in the event of liquidation.

You must also study several crucially important *operating* ratios as expansion proceeds. The most important of these for a small business that makes things are the various manufacturing and machine capacity ratios, whereas an assortment of labour and other resource utilisation ratios might be more relevant to a service firm.

Measuring productive efficiency

First, work out how much value is added to your raw materials inputs during the course of manufacture. This can be done by deducting:

(i)   the costs of raw materials;
(ii) other direct manufacturing costs (labour, machine running costs, etc.)
(iii) manufacturing overheads (e.g., the costs of renting those parts of the firm's premises used exclusively for manufacturing, lighting and heating costs for these areas, and so on);

from the value of sales. Then you divide this 'value added in manufacturing' figure by the current value of the assets – machines, premises, tools, etc. (but not consumable items such as oil or other supplies which go into 'direct manufacturing cost') – that are used in manufacture. If this ratio falls as your business grows then the *average* return from your investments in the machines, tools, premises, etc., devoted to manufacture has deteriorated. Your total sales (and profits) may have increased, but the expansion of sales has led to a decline in the efficiency with which you are using your manufacturing resources: profitability per pound spent on manufacturing has gone down.

A simpler ratio is that of sales to assets used in manufacturing, which ratio can be sub-divided into ratios for sales divided by the various categories of manufacturing assets: value of machinery, premises, and so on. Similarly, the value added in manufacture can be divided in turn by each of the manufacturing costs. The ratio of manufacturing costs to sales shows the proportion of each pound's worth of sales that is spent on manufacturing the item. An efficient business expansion would cause this to fall as the firm obtained economies of scale, that is:

- reductions in unit production cost through discounts on larger purchases of raw materials
- full use of equipment on a greater volume of production
- integration of processes
- longer production runs to spread overheads over more units, etc. as the business grows.

Machine efficiency

Machine efficiency before and after an expansion of scale and output can be measured by:

(a) the proportion of the working day that each machine is fully utilised;
(b) ratios of actual output to maximum possible output and of machine operating costs to the value of output;

(c) relationships between fixed and variable machine costs as the firm expands.

Ratios of wage payments to output, overtime to output, maintenance costs to output, machine set-up costs to output and the average costs of stoppages to output are also worthy of examination.

Labour efficiency

Work out the costs of supervising your employees (measured perhaps in terms of the amount of your own time that has to be devoted to this task) and divide this by the value of output before and after expansion. For what proportions of the working day are each of your employees fully occupied? What is the ratio of actual hours worked to 'productive' hours during which employees are directly contributing to the growth of the business? The ratio of total output to total hours worked is a telling figure, as is the simple ratio of labour cost to hours that employees are working. Labour cost can be divided by productive hours worked and then by actual hours worked. Then you might look at the ratios of hours spent on maintenance, machine set-up, idle time, etc., to total hours.

How to avoid unprofitable expansion

There are two golden rules for business expansion:

1. Expand conservatively and circumspectly.
2. Never link management objectives to sales, but rather to *unit profitability*.

Conspicuous expansion might be avoided through increasing operations via a wholly owned subsidiary, through discrete use of sub-contractors (who are firmly instructed not to display the fact they are doing your work), or through a joint venture with another firm. The latter course helps you spread the risk and financing requirements of an increased scale of operations, and it could enable you to acquire the experience and expertise of other people at very low cost. Or you might perhaps buy out another business – possibly a failing one that can be had for a negligible outlay – to carry your increased output under its own name, thus avoiding advertising the fact you are doing well and expanding operations. Current or potential competitors must not be alerted to your success or they might be encouraged to:

- extend their own operations
- cut their prices
- increase their advertising and sales promotions, etc.

thus sabotaging your capacity to grow. Driving around in an ostentatious motor car or otherwise openly pursuing an opulent lifestyle might, therefore, be damaging to your long-term future.

Look before you leap

Never accept a really large order without carefully considering all its implications for the welfare and development of the firm.

- Can you really cope with the extra work?
- Will you need to withdraw resources from other work or intended projects in order to complete the job, and if so what are the likely consequences of this?
- What happens if the order is suddenly cancelled or if, having done the work, the customer is unable (or refuses) to pay?
- Are special designs, set-up costs or alterations in existing production methods necessary?
- How will you finance the acquisition of extra supplies and materials needed to produce the additional output?
- When will you be paid and what are the cash flow implications of various sets of credit terms?

If you do take the order do not assume that it will be repeated or that it will lead to bigger and better things. Thus always seek to expand output first by using *existing* resources more intensively – run your machines for longer, stay open in the evenings and at weekends, have your current employees work overtime, sub-contract and incorporate the extra costs incurred into a higher unit price; but do not expand the scale of your capital base until you are compelled to do so. And make absolutely sure that the sale of the higher output is assured. Note that rented machines, premises and equipment can be quickly and costlessly discarded, whereas assets purchased outright cannot be disposed of so easily.

Continuous monitoring of the consequences of changes in scale of operations is essential. Predict the returns on every new asset you acquire and frequently compare actual and target returns. The targets quoted should relate to percentage rates of profit on each pound's worth of capital employed, not simply to the volume of sales. Expanding your operations may be the gateway to a fortune, but can so easily cause the failure of your firm.

If the problems outlined in this chapter sound familiar (and a few quick calculations should be sufficient to determine whether you are tending to overtrade), then you need to slim down your operations, to rationalise and to disinvest. These matters are considered further in later chapters.

Summary

Rapid growth creates numerous difficulties, even for the highly profitable small business. Haphazard, disorganised and unplanned growth can even cause an expanding firm to collapse as its immediate financing needs outstretch its cash inflows in the short period.

It is essential that you understand how overtrading can occur, and are able to recognise its presence in your own enterprise. This requires you to calculate a few key statistics in order to compare rates of return achieved before and after the firm's expansion. These statistics relate to your return on capital employed, the business's working capital and liquidity ratios, stock turnover rates and manufacturing indexes.

When you expand, do so circumspectly. Never advertise the fact you are doing well or you could attract new competition. Inconspicuous growth may be achieved through the acquisition of another business, by sub-contracting, or simply through the more intensive use of existing labour and other resources.

Never accept huge orders without first considering all the implications of your firm becoming overdependent on particular customers.

Checklist

1. Has the second of your employees worked as hard as the first? Did your third employee work as hard as the second?
2. What is the relationship between the volume of your sales and the amount of credit you give to customers?
3. Has the incidence of bad debts increased significantly within the last year?
4. Do you fully utilise every room in your premises?
5. Are all your employees and equipment fully utilised throughout the working day?
6. How much time do you spend working out employees' tax and National Insurance?
7. Did you buy yourself a big car and otherwise visibly spend a lot of money on yourself when your firm began to grow?
8. How did competitors react to your expansion?
9. What is the average value of orders placed by customers?
10. What proportion of your trade is conducted with customers who place low value orders? Is this trade financially worthwhile?
11. Has the average period taken to deliver goods to customers increased since you started to grow?
12. Have you computed values for the ratios mentioned in the text? If so, were you surprised by the results of the calculations?
13. How sensitive is your firm's working capital to changes in its individual components?
14. How can you improve your stock turnover ratio?
15. How much value do you add to your inputs in the course of their processing and manufacture?

3

4   Cutting costs

Cost centres □ Administrative costs □ Do-it-yourself organisation and methods □ Premises □ Production costs □ Marketing costs □ Insurance □ Fraud, theft and cheating □ Managing your time □ Summary □ Checklist

Two critical and obvious measures are necessary in any attempts to revive a business's fortunes: increasing the firm's revenues and reducing its costs. The former can occur through:

- higher prices (made possible perhaps by repacking the product, improving the image of the enterprise, or entering the top end of a new market segment)
- increased turnover created by aggressive selling, advertising and other sales promotions, possibly in conjunction with price cuts.

Policies for raising revenues need time to plan, research and implement. Cost reductions, conversely, are available *now*, and their cash flow benefits are immediately felt.

Low profit businesses must be totally determined in cutting costs, concentrating on short-term expediency rather than the long-term consequences of reduced expenditure for efficiency and market share. Grasp the nettle. Aim to *halve* your administrative and secondary production costs. You may not achieve this, but the very process of trying will itself be worthwhile.

Two things are needed for effective cost cutting: accurate information, and an innovative and adventurous frame of mind. First you must identify precisely the true cost structure of the firm. To do this you have to specify 'cost centres' to which various expenditures may be ascribed.

Cost centres

Cost centres can be activities (packaging, advertising, assembly, etc.), particular machines, products, offices or pieces of equipment, or individual members of your staff. If you choose a machine as a cost centre then you work out all the costs of running that machine; if costs are assigned to a function, 'running the office', for instance, then you compute all the costs associated with the relevant function. Equally, you could ask the question 'How much does it cost to service all the work of a certain employee?'.

Which to choose depends on the nature of your firm. Select cost centres according to how easily you can measure the expenditures involved. Prepare two lists: one for 'direct' expenditures immediately absorbed by a cost centre (e.g., the raw materials and/or machinist's wages used in making a product); the other for indirect costs such as lighting, heating, secretarial support and other overheads. Then establish rules for apportioning overheads, say, in proportion to the direct expenditures incurred by each cost centre.

Overheads

Overhead apportionment systems are necessarily subjective. Thus you could just as easily relate overheads to the relative sales values of products (so that a product selling for £50 per unit is assumed to absorb twice as much overhead as a product with a sales price of £25, regardless of direct cost) as to the *volumes* of output of various products. In the latter case, a product with a weekly production run of 100 units is assumed to use up twice as much lighting, heating, rent, etc., as one with a production run of 50 units – even if no extra floor space is required. However, provided you are consistent you should be able to analyse cost movements and compare various costs.

Zero-base budgeting

If you control your business through budgets, put all of these onto a 'zero-base' footing. This means beginning each new accounting period (quarters, for example) with the supposition that no money will be allocated to existing budgets whatsoever, so that you and your staff are compelled to justify the funds assigned to various activities every single budget period. This forces you to re-specify plans and to re-examine cost structures and working methods continuously as the business develops. Normally, zero-base budgeting is not a good idea because of the enormous amount of time used up in periodically assessing all the firm's costs and resource requirements. Yet zero-base approaches are an essential stop-gap measure for the firm in immediate difficulties; they identify high cost activities and impose rigid and necessary financial discipline in the short term.

Need for a proper attitude

Effective cost reduction depends critically on your adopting appropriate mental attitudes towards running the business. It is useless, for example, to cancel your copy of the *Financial Times* while ignoring escalating costs of entertaining customers or servicing company vehicles. Be nihilistic: question every expediture that arises – probe, analyse operations, and personally verify all invoices sent to the firm.

If you have employees, tell them about your deteriorating fortunes (they will find out anyway) and of the pressing need to reduce costs. It is essential that staff participate enthusiastically in reducing expenditures without your having to tell them what to do. They must *want* to switch off lights, save energy, economise on travel expenses and so on.

Target cuts should relate to specific cost centres rather than apply overall: a general but vague commitment to reduce total costs is unlikely to succeed. Thus, the campaign needs careful planning, and detailed records of its subsequent success must be maintained. If a particular target reduction is not achieved, write out a detailed explanation of the reasons for failure. Look for cuts in each of the areas outlined below.

Administrative costs

Photocopying costs can be frightening, and excessive use of a photocopier must not be allowed. Unnecessary costs arise from taking too many copies – 20 when only 17 are needed, a round 100 instead of 83! Multiply these extras by the cost per copy and the frequency with which the practice of taking too many copies occurs and you have a substantial opportunity for reducing costs. To avoid this needless expense you could:

- display a prominent notice on the photocopying machine reminding you and your staff only to take the actual number of copies needed
- have all copying done by a person who is aware of the problem
- place a restriction on the number of copies of a single document that anyone can take without permission.

Remember too that every photocopy taken and not thrown away creates the need:

    (a) for extra space where it can be filed;
    (b) for someone to create and manage the file;
    (c) physically to file the photocopied document.

Any spare copies accidentally taken should be used as note paper.

Letters are expensive. Typing is the major cost, so wherever possible write notes on compliment slips to accompany enclosed documents rather than typing separate letters. And be sure you can justify every letter you despatch.

Avoid status differentials

It may not be a good idea for you to have better quality furniture than your employees because this creates status hierarchies attached to the possession of certain physical possessions – hatstands, filing aids, special chairs, desk accessories, etc. – which cause petty resentments among the staff and cost money. If you have two employees, one of whom is paid more than the other, and if you personally have superior office furniture to the higher paid employee, then you create a working environment in which he or she will want better accessories than the lower paid member of staff. And the more employees you have the more you will then need to pander to their demands for status differentials.

It is better, I suggest, for you all to share the same office, have similar furniture (preferably second hand, which is cheaper) and use the same equipment. By sharing an office, moreover, you are able to observe at first hand how hard your employees are working.

A common problem is for staff jealously to guard any item of furniture or equipment allocated to them, even after it ceases to be of practical use. Nothing is ever thrown away. Drawers, shelves and cupboards which should be used for stationery, component stocks and working equipment are used instead for storing personal belongings, or become stuffed up with out-of-date files. Turf out the lot. Start afresh with the absolute minimum of furniture, cabinets, filing units and similar equipment.

Offices

Offices have three functions: they are places of work, social environments, and they help represent the firm's 'corporate image' to the outside world. But do you *really* need an office? Perhaps you can do your routine administration, filing, duplicating, etc., at home. And you should certainly question whether the business needs its own photocopier. Why not negotiate a deal with the business next door whereby you use their photocopier (and perhaps other secretarial facilities) at just above marginal cost? A good typist/secretary/ administrator is a wonderful asset – but a bad one can cause havoc throughout your organisation. Secretaries need time off for holidays (perhaps at inconvenient times), occasionally fall ill, sometimes arrive late and leave early. You have to compute their tax and National Insurance and provide them with desks, typing chairs, potted plants, etc. Is it all really worthwhile? Couldn't you simply hire someone to come in one day a week (or even half a day) to do the accumulated typing? Again, why not pay for this from a neighbouring business? Another possibility is for you to dictate letters into a hand-held machine which you pass over once a week to a secretarial agency. There are few instances in which business letters have to be typed and despatched in less than a week, and you can always use the phone or a handwritten note in these circumstances.

Note too that you can have stickers printed with your business address that you can attach to ordinary letter paper. This is much cheaper than using printed stationery. If you possess a word processor you will already know how easily you can create letter-heads for standard letters.

Do-it-yourself organisation and methods

Here's a short and simple programme for improving your administrative efficiency using the management consultant's technique of 'organisation and methods'. O & M is work study applied to clerical and administrative procedures, especially in relation to document creation, storage and retrieval. It aims to simplify work and avoid duplication of effort. Much clerical work involves paper, and the more unnecessary paperwork can be abolished the better. Thus you should seek to eliminate redundant procedures, combine documents to reduce the number of documents transmitted, and shorten the transit time for documents in circulation. Write out a list of all the clerical activities your business undertakes (issuing invoices, credit control, placing orders with suppliers, etc.) and then ask the following questions in respect of each operation.

1. What is being done and how?
2. What is the purpose of the activity; is it connected with any other operation, and if so, how?
3. Who performs the operation, and what special skills, training

and experience are needed for its execution? Must a certain person (e.g., yourself) perform the operation or will anyone do?

4. Where does the activity take place? Does it have to take place there, and if so why?

5. When are operations performed? Is starting one activity dependent on completing another? What will happen if the operation is not completed on schedule?

6. How are operations completed. What equipment and other resources are necessary? Might alternative methods be used?

7. What are the costs, including overheads, of individual operations?

Answers to these questions often reveal cost cutting possibilities. And the investigations needed to collect the required information should enable you to draft a 'flowchart' showing the movements of documents between various stages of processing. The best way to do this is for you to follow key documents (an invoice, for example) through your system. List everything that happens to the document. Each time you or an employee perform an operation on the document (e.g., filling in a form, calculating a figure, putting a letter into an envelope) draw a circle on the left-hand side of your description of the happening. Whenever you move a document between locations draw an arrow on the left of that item on the list of events. Indicate a delay in processing the document (e.g., in an in-tray or out-tray) by a capital D. If you have to store the document in a filing cabinet, or in a card index or similar device show this with a triangle; if you inspect it (proofreading, checking for accuracy, reading the information it contains, etc.) mark the item with a square. To illustrate, consider the progress of a supplier's invoice through your system. This might be recorded as follows:

		Invoice received in post from supplier
1	O	Open letter
1	[ ]	Read contents
1	>	Refer for checking against receipt of supplies
1	D	Hold in pending tray
2	[ ]	Check that goods have been received as per invoice
2	O	Sign a 'goods received' slip
2	>	Send invoice to the accounts clerk
2	D	Hold in pending tray
3	[ ]	Check amount owing against purchase order
3	O	Authorise payment
3	D	Clerk asks you for cheque
4	O	Record details from invoice in firm's ledger
1	△	File invoice

4	D	Cheque request held in pending tray
5	O	Write cheque
3	>	Return to accounts clerk
5	D	Hold in pending tray
6	O	Prepare accompanying letter/compliments slip for cheque
4	[ ]	Check amount of cheque against invoice
7	O	Place cheque in envelope
6	D	Put envelope with today's mail
		etc.

This is a simple example, but the approach can obviously be used for analysing more complicated events. Its advantage is that it forces you to investigate in detail every aspect of your clerical procedures, and such analyses frequently reveal many unnecessary delays and duplicated activities. The number alongside each symbol shows how often it has occurred at that point in the list. Look for high numbers, since they indicate excessively frequent operations, delays, document transits or inspections.

You can use the results of these investigations to:

- reorganise your procedures more efficiently
- redeploy staff
- replace manual operations with operations using office machines (including perhaps a desktop computer – see Chapter 7)
- smooth out work flows.

You may find that you can combine operations, complete two or three inspections in one go, or avoid delays by re-routing documents.

The exercise should result in better co-ordination of activities, faster and simpler procedures, fewer clerical errors and tighter management control. Seek always to minimise the time spent shifting documents. Thus workstations should be near to each other, and work should not be allowed to accumulate in one out-tray while the next in-tray in the system is empty.

Filing systems

You probably don't use more than a quarter of the information your internal administration generates. And the widespread introduction of desktop computers to small businesses has increased enormously the volume of data that a small business can produce. All this information has to be stored (albeit electronically), and the extent of your filing operations can quickly assume terrifying dimensions.

Retain only the documents that are essential and discard the rest. Overextensive filing systems waste space and create rigidities in organisations. The more you file the longer it takes to locate essential documents, and the greater the probability of losing key facts.

File alphabetically under each of the firm's major activities. This is the cheapest of all filing methods because:

- no index is required
- files can be referred to directly
- the system is understandable, flexible and easy to use (although some cross-referencing might be necessary through your being unsure of which heading to apply to a particular document).

Never file documents relating to different functions in the date order they are received (with the possible exception of invoices), or dreadful chaos may ensue.

Cutting administrative costs is important, but do recognise the constraints involved. In most private companies administration accounts for less than ten per cent of total costs, so saving just a few photocopies (as opposed to continuous excessive use of photocopying facilities) or making the secretaries use their typewriter ribbons for a little longer will not contribute all that much to total profitability in the long run. It is perhaps better to identify the really big sources of expenditure (premises, raw materials, labour, processing, distribution) and seek economies there.

Premises

Bad choice of premises creates tremendous long-term problems for the newly established business. If your premises are clearly unsuitable for the purpose for which they were originally intended you need to do something about it – and fast. Perhaps you weren't sufficiently careful in your initial choice of building and/or location, and possibly you didn't look far enough ahead: premises suitable for the launch of a business might be totally inadequate for its subsequent operations. Have any of the following difficulties emerged?

- Inadequate parking space for customers or suppliers.
- Lack of custom due to insufficient numbers of your target consumer groups living around or commuting to the local area, and/or inadequate public transport facilities to support potential transient trade.
- Poor heating, gas, electricity and water supplies.
- Frequent break-ins.

- Too many competitors nearby.
- Difficulties in recruiting local staff possessing the skills needed by the firm.
- Remoteness of raw materials suppliers, support services (waste disposal for instance), etc.
- Intolerable noise outside.
- Exorbitant maintenance costs.
- Large areas of unused space in overly wide corridors, staircases, etc.

If any of the above significantly reduce the efficiency of your business you need to consider a move. But first, ask yourself the simple – though incisive – question 'Do I *really* need premises at all?'.

Working from home

No time is spent travelling to work if you work from home. If you need to meet customers or suppliers only occasionally and your home is not a suitable venue then perhaps you can hire a room in somebody else's premises for the odd half day. You cannot usually manufacture from home, but you can certainly run an office (see Note 1), while garages, attics and spare bedrooms can often be commandeered to provide storage space. Telephones, filing cabinets, photocopiers and office equipment do not work any less efficiently when located in a bedroom rather than on business premises. Also, you can hopefully use members of your family to do odd jobs for you for free (answering the telephone, filing or a little typing).

Your house contents insurance will not normally cover business equipment or stock, so check your policy and take out extra cover where necessary. Take care not to upset the neighbours. Delivery vans parked outside, callers who have the wrong address and go next door by mistake, etc. will not help! If for tax purposes you claim that your home is a business, e.g., by setting off domestic gas, electricity, and telephone bills against your profits, then your home ceases to be exempt from capital gains tax – which fact might make this course highly expensive in the long run.

Low cost premises

If it is impossible to work from home, but you cannot afford to continue in your existing premises, then consider using a GPO box number for your business mail and a professional answering service for incoming telephone calls. The latter costs only a few pounds a week, and the personnel involved are adept at concealing the fact that callers are speaking to an agency and not the receptionist of a business. You collect your calls daily and reply from home.

How much space do you *really* need? Space costs money, not only for rent but also for heating, lighting and business rates; the less space you have the lower the expense. You might consider running the business from a single tiny office in a low-rent part of town, although two major problems arise when this is done:

- ringing telephones and people conducting conversations while others are trying to work;
- clattering typewriters or noisy word-processing printing machines.

The former problem might be solved through judicious use of a telephone answering machine, the latter by a strict rule that no typing shall occur before (say) 3.30 pm. Have a polite message on your answering machine, which you should clear twice a day – perhaps at 1.00 pm and 4.30 pm – in order to return important calls. Small offices are cheap to heat, light, ventilate and service. You don't need central heating (an electric fan heater will normally suffice) and rates are low.

Sale and leaseback

If you own your premises consider subletting part of them or, if you are really short of cash, investigate the feasibility of a 'sale and leaseback' agreement. Sale and leaseback means that you sell your land and building for just less than their current market value to a purchaser who in return contracts to lease the premises back to you for a certain period (five or ten years perhaps) at a moderate rent. You will have to pay the legal fees involved in drafting the special contract, and you will probably be liable for capital gains tax on the disposal, but at least your firm survives.

Work space premises

'Work space' premises offer interesting opportunities to businesses that are hard up. These usually result from property developers or local authorities renovating old buildings and letting out floorspace 'units' within them to small businesses. You occupy part of the floor of a building (your 'share' of the floor may be delineated only by painted lines on the floor itself) and thus share heating, lighting and telephone switchboard facilities. In some schemes you can also share the owner's secretarial, mailing and photocopying services (using your own headed notepaper and business documents, of course). There is a common cleaning service, and communal rooms for meetings and the reception of visitors. Business expansion can be accommodated by taking over adjacent workspaces.

There are problems involved in work space premises:

- there is noise from neighbouring units
- you lose privacy
- your stocks, materials and equipment need special protection.

Also, units are typically let on a very short-term basis, subject perhaps to a single month's notice. Nevertheless, their low cost might be just what is needed for your business to survive.

Work space premises are not really suitable for firms which need impressive building fascias and interior decorations designed to project favourable images to outsiders. In this situation you might select instead cheap alternative premises but spend a lot of money on decorating the outside entrance and immediate reception area, with comfortable chairs, expensive low-level coffee tables, attractive lighting and colour schemes, etc. The rest of the building need not be so luxurious, save perhaps for a single small room used for interviewing visitors.

Keep the shabbiest parts of the premises well hidden from outsiders; people often connect dilapidated buildings with low quality service from the firm, even though in principle this need not be the case.

Production costs

Reductions in the range of customer support services offered (acceptance of non-defective returns, repair and maintenance services, free advice on how to use goods after purchase, and so on) can cut costs dramatically, especially on slow moving and relatively unprofitable lines. Otherwise, look carefully at the *functions* of your products. A product 'function' in this context is a characteristic that makes it operate properly (e.g., by lifting a weight, heating a room, carrying goods, cutting a substance, or whatever). You ask the question 'What is this product intended to do?' and then ask 'Is there a cheaper way of achieving this purpose?'. In consequence, you may decide to abandon certain (costly to produce) designs, replace certain input materials with cheaper materials, or change the process of manufacture. Products consisting of many component parts are more suitable for this approach than single unit items since multi-component products usually contain much scope for cost reduction through removal of unnecessary functions. Every single aspect of an item should possess an identifiable purpose, fulfilled at minimum cost and effort.

Production staff

Staff utilisation is obviously important, as are indirect labour costs such as training, record keeping, doing employees' PAYE and National Insurance, etc. If you employ skilled labour, consider deskilling jobs to enable the work to be done by cheaper unskilled workers.

Do skilled employees spend part of their time doing unskilled work? Can work be cheaply sub-contracted to outsiders? Might overtime working be reduced, or extra work be undertaken by part time staff paid the standard rate?

Machines

Identify the sources of machine breakdown, and implement measures to avoid these interruptions (through planned maintenance for example). Look for ways to reuse scrap and waste materials (e.g., as packaging). Is the existing quality level of your input and output really necessary, and how much could you save (bearing in mind the implications for marketing) by reducing quality?

Examine your purchasing policies critically. Would bulk purchasing at a discount outweigh the costs of storage and materials deterioration? Do you possess a proper search procedure for ascertaining the lowest cost sources of supply?

Purchasing

It is too easy to continue using the same old suppliers and ignore cheaper and possibly better alternatives. Any potential supplier will be only too pleased either to send you literature or pay you a call. Have a policy of contacting at least one new supplying firm each month. You lose nothing other than a second class stamp for the letter asking for information, and perhaps half an hour of your time. Always ask suppliers to present estimates for exactly the same quantities and specifications, since then you are able to compare like with like when assessing quotations. And ask suppliers to include in their proposals a brief summary of:

- the measures they will implement to ensure continuity of supply and prompt regular delivery (thus enabling you to economise on stockholdings);
- the extent of guarantees and after sales service offered. You also need at least one reference from a business the firm has recently supplied.

An important consequence of the Consumer Protection Act 1987 (see Chapter 10) is that purchasing firms increasingly need to assure themselves that suppliers are properly insured against claims for damages resulting from defects in their products. If a supplier is not so insured and a large defective product claim registered against both the supplier and purchaser jointly then causes the supplier's insolvency, the purchasing firm can find itself responsible for the entire amount. Read suppliers' terms of business carefully, looking particularly for any clauses that seek to limit or exclude the suppliers' product (or other) liability. If you find these, either take legal advice and then renegotiate the terms before placing an order, or get yourself another supplier.

Stockholding

Lower stockholding through reliable delivery is important for several reasons other than the wasteful tying up of working capital (which represents an idle asset) that excessive stockholding involves. In particular:

- the more stock is held the more is broken, naturally deteriorates or is pilfered
- large stocks engender feelings of complacency among production staff, leading to sloppy work scheduling
- storage, protection and security costs increase
- the accumulation of stock necessitates installation of an expensive and complicated system for stock control.

Stores procedures

Keep your stores procedures as simple as possible, arranging stock as straighforwardly as you can on shelves instantly visible to you and the staff (never pile different items on top of each other). Consider the feasibility of maintaining stock according to a straighforward 'two bin' system. Here, you fill two bins (or boxes, or shelves, or whatever) with a certain component or material. Each bin is of such a size that when one is empty an order for new supplies is placed for a delivery which arrives before the other one is exhausted. This is appropriate where stock usage is reasonably constant over time. If it is not – if exceptional demands occasionally occur – then you need three bins. Instruct your staff to tell you the instant they begin using unusually large amounts of stock.

Make or buy?

As there is no profit margin on components produced within the firm, and as you have complete control over their quality, design and time of delivery, you might conclude that it is always better to manufacture your own components than to buy them from outside. But this is not always the case. An external supplier will usually have produced many more units than those delivered to your firm, and will have obtained substantial economies from mass production (long manufacturing runs, use of specialist skilled labour and so on) and thus might offer highly competitive prices as a result.

Consider also the fact that you might be able to delay payment for purchased component inputs, which means, in effect, that outside suppliers are lending you interest free money. Moreover, you do not have to employ as much labour, or use as much fixed plant, or buy as much equipment (some of it having to be paid for now, in cash) as when you buy from outside.

Marketing costs

Special problems apply here because certain aspects of marketing (especially advertising) generate income. A reduction in advertising is likely to reduce sales. Nevertheless, the effectiveness of current advertising should be regularly assessed (see Chapter 9), and distribution and transport costs cut to the bone. Look for possible cost reductions in the following areas:

- packaging materials and equipment
- costs of discounts and special offers
- salespeoples' expenses.

Salespeople

Sales staff paid hourly rather than on a commission basis can be extremely expensive to employ, since a salesperson who does not sell contributes little to the firm. Monitor the efficiency of your salespeople and carefully analyse the number of calls they make, costs per call, costs per order, the order/call ratio and the average monthly profit contributed by each salesperson. People sometimes forget the high costs of obtaining orders, so commission systems based on unit *profitability* per order (rather than on sales revenue or sales volume achieved) are usually more cost-effective. Other marketing cost savings might be possible through:

- increasing a salesperson's territory (and rewarding that person for their extra work)
- better route planning
- analysing the returns on visits to various customer types.

Note the high cost of processing small orders. Costs of invoicing, credit control, packaging and despatch frequently make small orders unprofitable. Equally, the cost of providing after-sales service to small consumer units is alarming. Discounts given on small orders, transport costs, credit control expenses and the risk of bad debts may result in certain customers not being worth the effort involved.

Another costly activity is to spend too much time selling to 'safe' established customers who are easy to do business with rather than seeking out completely new trade.

Mail-order costs

Businesses that sell much of their output through mail order sometimes experience difficulty through actual or alleged non-delivery. Two costs are involved:

- the costs of the goods 'lost' in transit
- the clerical and stationery costs associated with issuing payments reminders, checking delivery details with the Post Office, etc.

Firms can insure against non-delivery with the GPO, but the cost of cover may be substantial and there will be a delay before reimbursement. For small value items, these hidden clerical costs can exceed the value of the goods and it might be better not even to bother trying to follow up small unpaid invoices relating to mail-order delivery.

Normally, small value mail orders should not be accepted unless they are clearly profitable or unless they are confidently expected eventually to lead to much bigger orders. Alternatively, you could impose a minimum price for small orders, regardless of their size. This fixed charge must be big enough to cover postage, packing, order processing, release from stores, invoicing and other clerical duties, and so on. Profit margins are thus maintained and unremunerative small orders actively discouraged.

Packaging and distribution costs

If you package your output in expensive containers, examine the feasibility of offering a sizable refund on packaging materials returned to the firm. Possibly you can use the availability of the refund as a means of attracting repeat business, say, by inviting the customer to place a further order at a small discount available only at that time.

Weigh up the cost and benefits of distributing your products through a wholesaler rather than supplying retail outlets direct. In using a wholesaler you lose control over its final resale price, and your markup per unit of output is reduced (wholesalers buy in bulk and thus demand substantial discounts). But several cost savings may accrue, since by selling to a handful of wholesalers you save:

- the expense of employing a salesperson
- travelling costs to procure small orders, and other marketing expenses
- warehousing and other stockholding costs (you are effectively using the wholesaler's warehouse to carry your stock)
- transport costs
- the clerical work attached to issuing invoices to many retail outlets
- credit control and debt recovery expenses, and the risk and costs of the inevitable bad debts.

On the other hand, using a wholesaler means you lose the ability to determine how your output is sold, and at what price. There is no reason why a wholesaler should promote your goods rather than those of a competitor, and the wholesaler will recover all its stockholding and administrative costs by substantially raising your product's resale price, perhaps to a level you feel detrimentally affects its sales prospects.

If you decide to supply retailers direct and if many outlets are involved, then note how much cheaper it is to deliver using your own vehicles rather than the vehicles of outside carriers or by rail, provided you have sufficient business to justify using a vehicle full time.

Transport

Vehicles are a major expense for most businesses. Compute the likely running and maintenance costs of any vehicle you wish to buy as well as its capital cost, and remember that its *usefulness* is more important than its comfort or prestige. Estate cars are worth having because they can be employed as delivery vehicles as well as for transporting personnel. Make sure you absorb all the costs of transport into your product price; do not assume that the firm's car exists really for your own personal use.

You need a *transport budget*, plus detailed records of when, by whom, and for what purpose each vehicle is used. Take care to ensure that:

- vehicles can be repaired at short notice
- deliveries and visits to customers always follow the most economical route (not necessarily the shortest, depending on traffic flows)
- underutilisation of a vehicle is quickly identified
- vehicles are depreciated at the maximum allowable rate (details are contained in a leaflet available from your local tax office).

Insurance

There are so many potential hazards associated with running a business that to insure against all of them may appear neither justified nor financially worthwhile. And the high cost of insurance is indeed one of the many unanticipated supplementary costs that new firms frequently ignore when drafting their first business plans. Insurance bills often come as a shock, and they tempt some businesses to do without. But to ignore insurance completely is to court disaster, so you need to think carefully about the risks, costs and benefits involved.

Compulsory insurance

Employer's liability insurance is legally compulsory if you employ anyone full or part-time on or off your premises. It covers your employees for any injuries that may take place during the course of their work.

Not legally compulsory but *virtually a must for most businesses* are:

- property (obviously), plant and equipment, stock and work in progress. Any motor vehicles must of course be insured. Commercial vehicles require separate insurance, while private vehicles used for business purposes need extra 'commercial use' policies
- consequential loss, i.e., compensation for loss of business and disruption following a disaster (quite apart from the loss of capital assets). 'Keyman' policies which pay a lump sum upon the death of the insured 'key' person, come under this heading
- public liability insurance to protect against liability to third parties killed or injured through defects in the firm's premises or through the negligence of employees

You should also seriously consider insuring against:

- personal accidents
- theft including pilfering by staff, customers, break-in thieves, etc.
- goods-in-transit
- 'professional liability', i.e., liability arising from wrongful and/or negligent professional advice given to clients
- credit insurance against defaulting customers
- legal expenses insurance to cover the legal costs of disputes in which the business innocently becomes involved
- product liability cover against defects in products causing injury to customers. This type of insurance is increasingly important in view of the great amount of legislation (under EC as well as domestic law) in this area and the escalating costs of out-of-court settlements of product liability cases. Note the need (following the Consumer Protection Act 1987 – see Chapter 10) to ensure that suppliers and/or co-producers are similarly covered.

Together, these insurances add up to a considerable amount of money, and can affect substantially the business's cash flow.

Choosing which insurances to carry requires your having to *manage risk*. You must balance the substantial cost of cover against the possibly remote chance of loss. Do you really need all your insurances? And are you fully aware of the disclaimers and let-out clauses invariably hidden in the small print of your policies?

Managing risk

Risk is attached to most business operations. You can never be certain how much things will cost in the future, whether business conditions will change, or what unexpected losses might occur (fires that destroy stock, for example). This does not mean you should insure everything – only that you must be fully aware of the extent of business risks. For instance, a market gardener knows there is a chance of night frosts in late spring that can wipe out crops. Yet by planting later in the year this risk (and the costs of insuring against it) can be avoided. The market gardener must therefore weigh up the benefits of planting early against the extra costs of insuring against abnormal weather.

Types of risk

You cannot insure against normal business risk. If, for example, the demand for your products suddenly falls, you alone must bear the consequences. Conversely, the risks of physical destruction of property and of natural disasters may be fully covered, as may 'social hazards' such as damage due to theft, forgery or civil riot.

Natural disasters cannot be prevented; social hazards, however, can sometimes be avoided. Thus, by carefully selecting your staff, checking references and not putting temptations for dishonesty before employees you can minimise the risk of staff pilfering, possibly to the extent where insurance against this is not worthwhile. The more secure your premises, the fewer valuable goods you leave 'lying around', the more anti-shoplifting and other theft control devices you install, then the more you can economise on security insurance.

Other preventative measures

Other tips for reducing your business risk are:

- the fire proofing of buildings and materials
- installation of sprinkler and alarm systems
- making your employees safety and fire conscious
- using a credit information service to avoid selling on credit to unsuitable customers
- using security firms for high value deliveries.

Never run water pipes (which can burst during cold weather) over valuable stores or equipment, and do not store goods in the basement if there is any chance of flooding. Use your common sense. If you live near a football ground or between two public houses in a rough area then either have small windows instead of large plate glass windows or invest in metal shutters. If your premises are in a high burglary risk district then install a good alarm system and make sure everything valuable is locked up or bolted down separately – make burglars work for their money! You should also ask for a visit from your local Crime Prevention Officer who can be contacted at the nearest Police Station.

Check your policies

If you choose not to insure against certain risks (e.g. window break-age, motor accidents other than third party) but instead create a reserve into which you pay a predetermined sum each quarter, then not only will you earn interest on your contingency deposits but also you will know with certainty that you will be able to replace lost or damaged items. With insurance, on the other hand, you face yet another risk: that the insurance company – to which you have been contributing premiums for years – might not pay up (or may be extremely slow in paying) following a loss. Be particularly careful if you are running a business from home that your household policy is extended to cover your commercial activities. Are you sure, for example, that:

- your property insurance covers *rebuilding* costs and not just the market value of the premises, as these could be much higher than market value?
- your furniture and fittings are covered up to their current *replace-ment* costs rather than (the insurance company's) estimate of their second-hand value?

Insurance principles and jargon explained

Insurers will only insure risks that are assessable, and even then they build into insurance contracts a number of devices to minimise the extent of their loss. You must have a personal interest in the thing insured so that, for instance, you cannot insure against other peoples' losses. And the principle of 'indemnity' always applies.

Indemnity

This means that you should only be placed in the same position after the loss as you were in before the loss occurred. On the face of it this seems fair enough – you ought not to be able to make a profit from insurance or otherwise you have an incentive to cause losses, by deliberately starting a fire, being careless, arranging for other people to steal your goods, and so on. However, nasty shocks for insured people sometimes arise when the indemnity principle is applied. Suppose, for instance, that your van is written off in a motor accident. The van is well maintained, regularly serviced and in excellent condition. In fact it is almost like new and would cost several thousand pounds to replace. But, according to the insurance company, it only has a low 'book' value, and the insurer will only pay a few hundred pounds compensation for a vehicle of that year.

Similarly, you might insure your equipment for £20,000, lose a quarter of it in a natural disaster, and claim £5,000 compensation. 'Oh no!', says the insurance company after its loss inspection. This equipment, according to the insurance company, was initially worth £30,000 so that in its opinion you were 'underinsured' in the first place. Hence they will only pay two-thirds of the £5,000 (i.e., £3,333) on the basis that you had only insured two-thirds of the original total value of all your equipment. Numerous problems arise, moreover, over determining the true value of specific replaceable items.

Proximate cause

This piece of jargon means that insurance companies only accept liability if they believe a loss was caused 'proximately' (i.e., immediately) by the occurrence of a risk *specified* in the insurance contract. Suppose, for instance, that all your windows are smashed in by a gang of drunks. You claim for the loss you have incurred, but the claim is rejected because the insurer insists the damage was caused during a 'riot' or civil commotion and such events are not covered by the particular policy you hold! Or suppose your stock is destroyed in a fire. An insurance company will want to know what caused the fire in the first place. If the ultimate cause was an event excluded from the contract (e.g. your negligence) you might not succeed in your claim.

Material facts

When taking out a policy you must (i) not make a false statement, and (ii) must disclose all 'material facts' about your circumstances. A material fact is any information that might influence the insurance company in deciding whether to accept the insurance and if so, at what rate of premium. If the information you provide is inaccurate, or you simply forget about some matter that the insurer subsequently insists you should have disclosed, then the policy becomes void and the insurance company does not have to honour your claims.

Having decided which insurances you really need (cancel the others), go through each policy carefully, making quite sure you fully understand all the detail they contain. How much you are entitled to in the event of loss, and in what circumstances might proper compensation not be paid? Usually, insurance companies offer special policies that guarantee indemnity at replacement cost rather than second-hand market value. These policies – while more expensive – are certainly worth investigating.

Fraud, theft and cheating

Possibilities for fraud and theft exist within any business, especially those with many employees: there might be pilfering, shoplifting, goods sent to non-existent customers, cheques issued to non-existent supplying firms, and so on. When employees undertake financial transactions on your behalf it is normally better to have different people performing different tasks (sales records and cheque issue for example) and, wherever possible, to minimise the practicability of collusion. Change the personnel undertaking these tasks regularly and without notice.

Cash and cheques

If your incoming mail regularly contains cash, postal orders or stamps it is prudent to open the daily post yourself, though do this discreetly (say by always being the first to arrive at work) so as not to appear distrustful of your workers. Bank your takings as often as possible – having lots of cash around invites theft. An advantage of trading under a business name rather than your own is that it becomes rather more difficult (though not impossible) for an employee to purloin cheques issued by your customers. If I trade as 'R Bennett' then a dishonest employee might open a bank account falsely using my name and pay into that account some cheques addressed to me. The employee might then forge and/or falsify internal documents to avoid discovery of the theft, at least in the short term. If, conversely, I trade as 'RHA Management Consultancy' and ensure that customers write cheques in favour of that name then the dishonest employee must convince a bank that a legitimate business exists under that name prior to opening the account. This is not impossible, but the trouble involved may discourage an opportunist thief.

What theft is

Problems arise over the definition of theft, especially where employees have free access to materials and equipment and are encouraged to take work home in evenings. Theft means dishonest appropriation of someone else's property with the intention of permanently depriving the other person of that property. But it is not dishonest to take property if the person genuinely believes that it belongs to the appropriator, or believes sincerely that its owner has consented or would consent to the property's removal. Be absolutely clear, therefore, about which equipment may or may not be removed from the building by your staff.

Shoplifting

Retail outlets inevitably experience shoplifting. Shop layout is obviously important here, as is the need to alert sales staff to shoplifting techniques. Offer your staff cash incentives for every shoplifter they catch. A security camera prominently displayed overlooking the shop can discourage shoplifting, even if the camera doesn't actually work and is there just for show. Place lots of mirrors around the shop.

Managing your time

The biggest of your administrative expenses could in fact be the cost of your own time. Think of time as a resource, just like a raw material, and seek to allocate your time in the most productive ways. Time spent writing an unimportant letter, for example, might be better used visiting a customer or inspecting the quality of supplies, so rank your activities in order of importance and consciously adjust the time you spend on each job.

Avoid interruptions

The efficient use of time requires your maximising the creative output of each working day. This is not as easy as it may first appear: the sorts of activity a small business owner undertakes (meeting people, talking on the phone, writing letters, dealing with customers and suppliers, inspection, day-to-day decision taking, forward planning and control, etc.) are varied, scattered, and prone to frequent interruption.

Sources of interruptions

Many interruptions arise from routine communications that disrupt more creative work. Set aside some predetermined part of your day (between two and three in the afternoon, for example, by which time all the day's mail will have been delivered) and handle communications during that period. Stick to this rigidly – if outgoing letters cannot be completed within the time allotted to communication duties then leave them until the following day when they will be given priority. Also:

- wherever possible deal with each item of correspondence only once; it is surprising how often the attention paid to certain letters is duplicated
- group together similar tasks: write all your letters in one go, make your phone calls one after another and when you use the phone have before you all necessary information and a list of the points you wish to make.
- write notes on the outcome of a call immediately after it finishes. If you see outside people, try to see them by appointment and during a prearranged period.

Plan your working day

Great anxiety, over-exertion and stress can result from trying to keep abreast of current communications duties while simultaneously pursuing more creative goals. Hence, you should:

- forecast your future workload, assign priorities and plan your time;
- predict how much time you need for particular jobs, record the times actually taken, and analyse any differences.

To avoid the accumulation of a large backlog of petty administration, reserve some limited period each week purely for routine work. The best time for this is when you are tired, since doing mundane, non-critical duties gives relief and relaxation from the exhausting effects of more demanding activities. Undertake critical tasks when you are fresh and most creative. If your normally feel energetic in the early morning, do your difficult work during that period. If conversely you 'warm up' during the day then do mundane work in the mornings and leave creative activities until later in the day. People commonly err in using their intellectually productive hours for work that is interesting but which does not require the exercise of discretion or intense mental effort. Suppose, for example, you are most alert in the mornings. You open your mail at 9.00 am and immediately become interested in petty administrative matters, which occupy you for three or four hours. When eventually you come to consider more substantial issues you are too tired to attend to them properly, so they are put aside and never fully resolved!

Dealing with interruptions

You must learn to deal with interruptions, to switch your attention from one thing to another without loss of momentum or upsetting the balance of your working day. If you find this hard to do, initiate a 'time awareness diary' recording every task you undertake. After a few weeks extract from the diary a comprehensive list of all the activities you have completed. Alongside each item put a grade (A, B, C, etc.) indicative of its importance and state whether it was urgent or routine. Then rearrange the list in order of task priority and ask whether you devoted sufficient time to major priorities. The answers may surprise you, so next specify some proportion of your total time you feel you ought to devote to each category of task and thereafter try to structure your time in these proportions.

Note

1. However, you do need planning permission from your local authority. This is normally given without question, provided your business will not cause a nuisance to neighbours. If your property is leasehold and/or carries a mortgage you must check these to ensure that the lease or mortgage agreement does not prohibit the use of the property for business purposes. Note that there exists a 'grey area' between domestic and commercial activities. And you do need to exercise discretion. Building societies are usually prepared to adjust the terms of a mortgage to allow business use of domestic property in appropriate circumstances.

Summary

Effective cost cutting requires that you assume an appropriate attitude of mind as well as investigating the costs of particular business activities. Profligate firms rarely survive in the longer term, so the adoption of a proper perspective on costs and revenues is essential for the future well-being of the enterprise.

Crucial to the success of any cost-cutting exercise are (i) the definition of relevant cost centres, and (ii) the accurate measurement of costs, although for firms which produce many products there is no easy way of apportioning overheads to cost centres – all systems for allocating indirect costs are necessarily subjective to some extent.

Question the need for every significant item of expenditure and, in the short term, use zero-base budgeting. Seek economies in production, the utilisation of premises, distribution and in general administration (perhaps using concepts derived from 'Organisation and Methods'). Recognise, however, that administration typically accounts for only a small part of total expenditure and hence that to achieve really big savings you will probably have to look elsewhere.

Simplify your ordering and stockkeeping system, and reduce to the absolute minimum the average amount of stock you hold. Be fully aware of the risk of your stores being pilfered (and of other forms of theft and cheating) and implement appropriate measures to pre-empt such difficulties.

Efficient management of time is critically important for the owner of a small business. Time is a resource, to be allocated rationally just like raw materials or any other input to the firm. Plan your time; avoid interruptions at inconvenient moments, and try to complete your work in blocks consisting of tasks of a similar nature.

Checklist

1. What is the proportion of administrative cost to the total cost of running your business?
2. How recently did you undertake a thorough analysis of the costs attached to a particular aspect of the firm?
3. Have you prepared budgets for next month, next quarter and the next half year? If not, why not?
4. What are the marginal and average costs of each photocopy that you take?
5. How much have you spent on the furniture and equipment used by (a) yourself (b) each of your employees?
6. List six reasons why you need an office for your business.
7. Do an O and M analysis of your credit control system.
8. Go through the filing cabinet nearest to your desk and calculate the proportions of essential and non-essential information that it contains.
9. Are your premises fulfilling the purposes for which they were originally intended? If not, why not?
10. Find three alternative locations for your business and establish the rent and rates payable on suitable premises in those areas.
11. Have you investigated whether the functions your output serves might be equally well served by a product that costs less to produce?
12. What could you have done to avoid your last three equipment breakdowns?
13. Find the names and addresses of three alternative suppliers of your primary raw material.
14. How much would it cost to arrange for the input components you presently buy from outside to be manufactured or assembled within your own business?
15. Is a large proportion of your total sales accounted for by a small number of customers?
16. How much do you (or could you) save by using your own vehicles for delivering your output instead of relying on outside carriers?
17. Does your premises' contents insurance cover the full value of goods you might have to replace (assuming you need to purchase brand new equipment) or does it just cover the second-hand values of lost or destroyed items?
18. What measures have you introduced to avoid your stores being pilfered?

19. How much time did you spend making unproductive telephone calls last week?

_____

5 How to collect a debt

The cost of credit □ Improve your credit control □ Debt collecting □ How to take somebody to court □ Enforcement □ Summary □ Checklist

Not all firms find it necessary to give credit – wine bars, restaurants, small shops and certain other retail outlets are examples of businesses that typically trade in cash. Yet the majority of businesses cannot survive unless they offer their customers reasonable periods in which to settle bills. Two questions immediately arise: how long is a 'reasonable' period, and what do you do when a customer is obviously not willing to settle an outstanding account.

The cost of credit

Credit is outrageously expensive: you lose money every time a customer delays payment of a bill. If a £1,000 invoice falls due on 1 January and is not paid until 31 March, you lose the use of £1,000 for a *quarter of a year*. At worst, you could have put this £1,000 in the Post Office (for example) and earned three months' good interest. More profitably, you could have employed the money collected on 1 January to buy further inputs (labour, raw materials, stock, etc.), have processed them and sold the resulting output in order to achieve even greater returns. By letting customers extend payments in this way the intensity of your 'trading cycle' is severely reduced – you 'turn over' your sales revenue less often than you should. Looking at the problem from another perspective, just suppose your customers take an average of six weeks to settle their bills and that you sell an average of £2,000 worth of goods each week. You have already paid for the labour, raw materials and overheads used in each week's £2,000 worth of sales, so that at any moment in time you need 6 weeks times £2,000, i.e. £12,000 of finance – straight from your own pocket – simply to run the firm! Reduce the credit period to three weeks and you instantly release *six thousand pounds' worth* of working capital. If a debt becomes 'bad' (i.e. the customer never pays), this can cost your business a great deal of money, particularly if you are trading on low profit margins. Chasing debts can also cost you dear in terms of time. Obviously, you need to be as diligent as possible in chasing debts!

Credit checks

Although the need to offer credit must be accepted as an inevitable fact of business life in most circumstances, always recognise the adverse affects that slow settlement of debtors' accounts will exert on your firm's operations, and that the decision whether or not to give credit is yours alone. Certain customers may go bankrupt owing you large amounts of money, and there exists the possibility of deliberate credit fraud by some clients. This latter risk can be minimised by carefully checking out the credit-worthiness of customers who demand credit facilities. Ask the customer for a banker's reference and that the customer complete a form requesting a credit account. The form should ask for the following information.

(a) Name and address of the customer's bank and when an account with that bank was first opened. You need to be suspicious if the business claims to be well established yet the account was only opened within the last couple of years, bearing in mind how easy it is to open a new account using a false name and address. If the account is, say, less than two years old then ask for details of the customer's previous bank and for permission to approach the previous banker for a reference.

(b) The customer's home address if this differs from his or her business premises.

(c) If the customer is a limited company, its registration number and date of incorporation.

(d) Names and addresses of any partners in the customer's business.

(e) The name and address of at least one other firm presently supplying that customer on credit, plus permission to approach that firm for a credit reference.

Credit control agencies

A credit control agency will prepare and issue such a form on your behalf on payment of a small fee and will, moreover, inspect centralised County court records to check whether the customer is in the process of being declared bankrupt or, if it is a company, wound up, or has any County court judgements awaiting settlement, or whether any court enforcement orders or attachment of earnings orders (see below) are outstanding. If the customer is a limited company the agency will inspect its documents at Companies House (though you can do this yourself either by post or by visiting Companies House) to see the extent of its mortgages and charges (see Chapter 12) and will report back to you accordingly.

Credit limits

Acting on the information you have gathered you can now set credit limits (a good figure would be the expected value of three months' sales to each company in question).

Credit refusal

You may prefer to refuse credit altogether. This means either not trading with the company at all or insisting on cash before or on delivery. Cash before delivery can be achieved by proforma invoicing the customer and perhaps arranging for an agreed percentage of the value of the proforma invoice to be paid up-front.

Need for Security

For very large credit transactions you will want a binding assurance that you will eventually get your money, regardless of the state of the customer's trade. Effectively, you are lending to the customer during the credit period and it is only reasonable that the loan be secured, as if it were a loan from a bank. Security might be offered to you through a fixed charge on the firm's assets or through your retaining title to the goods until payment occurs. If the customer is a limited company you will need at least one of its directors to offer a personal guarantee – enforceable on his or her personal estate – that the debt will be honoured. These options require legal advice, the cost of which should be incorporated into the price of the output.

Reservation of title

When you sell on credit you accept that the purchaser can sell the goods to a third party prior to your being paid. If your credit customer then reneges on the debt you must try to collect the money from that person or firm; you cannot normally approach the third party and reclaim the goods which in law now belong to the third party. The exception is where the firm builds into its terms of sale a 'reservation of title' clause whereby you retain legal ownership of the goods until you have been paid. This is not a straightforward matter; the circumstances in which courts will accept the legitimacy of such contracts are complex and you must consult a solicitor before attempting such a sale. However, the possibility is perhaps worth investigating if your output is high-value and such that its reclamation from customers in a resaleable condition is practicable.

How title to goods may be 'reserved'

A reservation of title (RT) clause makes the transmission of ownership of property conditional on receipt of payment. There are two types of RT clause: 'simple' and 'extended'. The former occurs in the circumstances already outlined, i.e., where the seller retains ownership until cash payment is received or a cheque is cleared. This is legal under both the UK Sale of Goods Act 1979 and European Community law. More difficult, however, are 'extended' RT clauses, which come in two forms.

1. The buyer is regarded as an *agent* of the supplier and, if the goods are sold to a third party, the money received is viewed as being *'held in trust'* on the supplier's behalf. Thus, should the first buyer become insolvent before paying the supplier, the latter has a charge (see below) on that firm's assets even to the point of being able to reclaim the goods in question from the third (or subsequent) parties to whom they were resold.

2. The clause may state that if the goods supplied are used as inputs (i.e., as raw materials) to other goods then the original supplier retains a financial interest in the final goods that result, unless the final goods possess a different 'commercial identity' from the original goods input. For example, a case in 1983 (see Note 1 at end of this chapter) established that a supplier of leather to a handbag manufacturer did not have title to handbags sold to the public by the manufacturer, despite the existence of an extended RT clause.

Improve your credit control

First you must calculate how long, on average, it takes to collect a debt. An indication of this period can be obtained from the following formula:

$$\frac{\text{Amount owed to you at the end of the year}}{\text{Total value of sales during the year}} \times 52$$

Thus, if your business sold £100,000 of goods last year but was still owed £25,000 at the year's end the average credit period suggested by the formula is:

$$\frac{25,000}{100,000} \times 52 = 13 \text{ weeks}$$

Of course, an exceptionally big order already delivered but not yet paid for immediately prior to the end of the financial year could distort this figure by misleadingly increasing the value of debtors on the top of the formula. So take a random sample of, say, 50 invoices issued during the last year (and I assume here that invoices are properly issued the moment goods are despatched) just to check that the average debt collection period revealed by the formula does actually represent the true situation.

5

Identify overdue accounts

Next, devise a system (a simple system will suffice, and there are several commercial systems on the market) for identifying overdue accounts the instant they are in arrears. The system must enable you to gather together all invoices that are, for example, one week overdue, two weeks overdue, one month overdue, two months and so on. Dated cardboard folders might be all that is required to generate this information in the required form, but whichever way you do it you will probably find that a handful of customers predominate in the records for long overdue accounts, and you need to consider seriously whether continuing to service these customers is financially worthwhile (the profit mark-up on transactions with such customers might be effectively wiped out by the implicit costs of delays in payment).

Know your customer

On the other hand, late payers may be big and valued customers who can be relied upon to pay eventually. In this case you should time your invoices to coincide with customers' accounting systems, details of which you can obtain by phone. There is no reason why customers should not be willing to tell you the day of the month they settle invoices and, importantly, the names and telephone extensions of the staff involved. Once you have established a personal relationship with the accounts clerk (sometimes called ledger clerk) who deals with your bills you can telephone him or her to ensure that high-value invoices are internally processed (checking for numerical accuracy, inspecting the goods, etc.) on time. The purchasing and accounts departments of large organisations can be extremely helpful in these respects.

Debt collecting

Much time, effort and money is taken up in writing letters, making telephone calls, issuing copy invoices, and so on, in order to collect overdue accounts. It might be worthwhile, therefore, considering offering customers an inducement to settle early through a discount for prompt payment. Unfortunately, however, such discounts are extremely expensive – a two and a half per cent discount offered for payment within 30 days actually works out at a staggering 30.4 per cent on an annual basis (remember you are giving the discount 365/30 times per year which, multiplied by 2.5, gives an annual percentage rate of 30.4).

You could consider instead giving discounts for very large cash orders. Money lost on discounting is recovered through increased sales volume. The threshold for discount can be tailored to appeal to new customers in new market segments.

Better, perhaps, and more important, is a rigorous system for politely pursuing debtors the moment their accounts are overdue.

● Prepare two standard letters asking for settlement of unpaid bills. One should be sent two weeks after the account is due, the other two weeks later. If you are not very good at writing letters, go to your local library and borrow a book of standard business letters any one of which will contain examples of letters for credit control.

Don't be afraid to use the telephone

If the account is still unsettled – use the telephone. Take care in how you make this call, since much hinges on the customer's response, especially if your business is desperately short of funds. A direct and poignant appeal for prompt settlement (even if the bill is not all that much overdue) can evoke a sympathetic and potentially life-saving response. When making the call:

- jot down the major details of the invoice and the points you wish to make, and be sure you speak to someone in a position to expedite payment, preferably the relevant accounts clerk
- explain the position briefly and check that the listener understands what you have said
- be brief, and always polite – nothing guarantees that a slow paying but honest customer will impose further delays more than offending a sensitive accounts clerk.

Ring in the morning so that if details have to be checked at the other end your contact can telephone you back later in the day. If your contact does not return the call you then have an excuse to ring again. Do not fear being nervous when making such a call; indeed, obvious nervousness in your voice might actually help your case in that it emphasises to the listener the urgency of the matter in relation to your cash flow.

5

The next step

If the call does not result in payment, wait another week or so and call again. Thereafter there is little point making further telephone calls: more formal and severe measures are now required. But before initiating tough debt collecting action first ask yourself *why* the customer refuses to pay the bill. He or she might simply be hard up, and if so there is little point in your spending much time chasing the debt. If the customer is also in business, try to think of a way the bill might be settled in kind, say by the firm doing some work for you free; or extract an agreement (which needs to be in writing) that the customer will supply you with some of its output at cost price (so that you can sell the goods at a profit) as soon as its trading position strengthens. A debt collection agency (see below) will not purchase a debt from you if the possibility of settling the bill is remote, and there is no point in going to court if the debtor obviously hasn't the means to pay a substantial part of the amount owing. Your best strategy here is to minimise your loss. If, instead of cash, the creditor offers physical goods that have a resale value you should take them – you have nothing to lose.

If, conversely, the debtor is clearly solvent yet still refuses to pay you have three options:

(a) trying to collect the debt yourself through a personal visit;
(b) selling the debt to an agency;
(c) recovering the debt through the courts.

The first option – personal attempts to recover the debt – is perhaps the least attractive. Debt collecting in Britain is covered by section 40 of the Administration of Justice Act 1970, plus the precedents established by a number of test cases brought under this Act and others (see Note 2). Of course, it is illegal to use or threaten violence, or even to harass unduly those who owe you money. Courts have ruled that, for example, calling on someone's home late at night is unlawful (as is sending several men or a man with a large dog!). Other unlawful practices include:

- approaching a member of a debtor's family and making abusive or threatening suggestions
- pretending to be a policeman or court official, or threatening criminal (rather than civil) proceedings
- discussing a person's debts with his or her neighbours or posting notices about the debt in shop windows near to where the customer lives.

You have to play strictly by the book, though by all means visit the debtor to establish the cause of non-payment. Perhaps he or she has been ill, faces temporary cash flow problems or has simply behaved irresponsibly in some way.

Using an agency

The second alternative is to use an agency for collecting the debt (agencies can be found in *Yellow Pages*). Either you can pay an agency a hefty commission on the value of the final settlement, or you can sell the debt outright in exchange for cash. This enables you to convert the debt into *some* cash (provided the agency believes it will be able to recover the amount owing), but it is very expensive – you only get a percentage of the amount due, perhaps as little as 25 or 30 per cent.

An interesting and potentially useful variation on the collection agency theme is the use of an agency letterhead, even though you do not feel that extensive further action to recover the debt (including court action) is financially worthwhile, especially if the amount is too low to interest a collection agency *per se*. In return for a small fee some agencies will send an impressive letter to the recalcitrant debtor saying the agency has been instructed by you to initiate legal proceedings to recover the amount owed. This might shock the debtor into payment, since slow payers are often more impressed by correspondence from a seemingly bona fide debt collector, which the debtor assumes *will* take legal action, than from a small firm which the debtor assumes does not possess the knowledge or resources necessary to pursue the debt. In fact, you have no intention of taking the customer to court, and are using this device merely as a ruse to engender settlement. Some businesses even invent non-existent agencies with nothing more than a mailing address behind them just for this purpose.

Tell your bank

Slow payment of outstanding balances can cause acute embarrassment regarding your own consequent inability to settle debts, and honouring them in the absence of a cash inflow may result in your accumulating a substantial overdraft. Do not conceal from the bank the fact that you are experiencing problems in collecting debts. Banks after all are themselves intimately involved in the debt business, and bank managers typically possess great experience in this field. Your bank may be able to put you in touch with a respectable debt collector, or 'credit factor' who will purchase (at a big discount) for cash the invoices you issue to customers and will then collect for themselves the amounts owed.

How to take somebody to court

Ultimately you will have to take an unrepentant debtor to court. You should realise that this is not cheap and is likely to be time consuming, however. If the debt is below £500 then unless the case involves complex matters of law or if fraud is alleged, you must use the County court 'small claims' procedure. This, in comparison with standard County court proceedings, reduces the formality and inconvenience involved, though all court appearances are harrowing to some degree. County courts themselves can currently handle cases involving sums of up to £5,000 for each alleged breach of contract. There is no jury; cases are adjudicated by either a judge or, if the amount claimed is relatively low, by a 'registrar' sitting alone. Proceedings in small claims cases are intended to be conducted in a straightforward manner, and you are not obliged to use a solicitor. If you do choose to be represented when using the small claims procedure you cannot claim your representative's costs from the other side if you win the case. (Although minor administrative costs are recoverable, see below.)

Starting an action

You begin the action by obtaining from your local County court (the address and telephone number will be in your telephone directory) form N202 'Particulars of Claim', which you complete (only brief details of the case are required) and return. Alternatively you can type out your own 'Particulars of Claim' on a separate sheet of paper under this heading. You state the facts of your claim and the sum of money you are owed. If you wish you can visit the County court office in person and do this 'over the counter' on the spot. The forms used in County court proceedings have been considerably simplified in recent years. Examples of them and how they should be filled in (with specimen claims) are explained in a free booklet, *Small Claims in the County Court*, which you obtain from the County court office and which tells you precisely what to do. (Also useful is the *Which?* guide, *Taking Your Own Case to Court or Tribunal*, published by the Consumers' Association.)

The summons

The cost of initiating an action is very low (currently between £7 and £43 depending on the type of action and how much is involved). You must now complete a 'Request' form from which the court prepares a 'summons' which is served on the debtor. The Request is a simple document, and the court staff will help you complete it 'over the counter' if you so desire. The court now sends the 'defendant' (i.e., the person or firm that owes you money) the summons containing details of the allegation and gives the defendant 14 days in which to reply. If the summons is returned undelivered the court will tell you about this and you will then normally ask the court bailiff to serve the summons on the defendant in person. An additional (recoverable) fee is payable for this work. You receive a thing called a 'Plaint Note' which formally registers the case, allocates a number to the case, and is accompanied by a notice allocating a date for the hearing. Four possibilities now arise:

1. The debtor pays up, in which case you are entitled to claim from the defendant the fee you had to pay for initiating the case.
2. No payment is received and the defendant does not reply to the summons that has been served on that person, either by post or by the court bailiff. The court now sends you a form (N14) called a 'Request for Entry in Default' which is a statement of when you want the money (including the cost of issuing the summons) to be

paid. The form is easily completed and no technical legal jargon is involved.

3. The debtor admits the claim and asks for time in which to pay the amount owed. In this case the debtor must complete a form listing his or her means and assets and set out any offer he or she wishes to make. If you refuse an offer of partial lump sum settlement the court will fix a date for the court registrar to decide how the debt is to be paid (perhaps by instalments).

4. The case is contested (i.e., the defendant replies to your summons and appears in court). If the amount is less than £500 the case is heard in private, otherwise in open court (unless both parties agree to arbitration – see below). Should the debtor reply to the summons and state that he or she will contest the case but then fails to turn up for the hearing you will normally win the case automatically, and be able to claim from the defendant your travelling expenses to attend the hearing and small expenses for witnesses. Otherwise the case is heard in the usual way (see Note 3).

Arbitration

Cases involving more than £500 can be settled via arbitration in a manner analogous to the small claims procedure, provided both parties agree. The advantages of arbitration compared to a formal trial are that:

- the hearing is held in private, not in open court
- procedures are relatively informal (the strict rules of evidence do not apply)
- the arbitrator (normally the court registrar, though any suitable person may be appointed if both parties so desire) can adopt any procedures which he or she considers fair, convenient, and appropriate for expediting the case.

However, solicitors' costs *will* be allowed in disputes concerning more than £500 unless both parties agree to their exclusion.

The side which loses an arbitrated case does not have the same rights of appeal as the loser of a dispute tried in the conventional manner. Appeals from arbitrated judgements are complex, costly, and need to rely on some proven incompetence or inconsistency on the part of the arbitrator.

If you win any kind of County court case and the defendant does not pay up it is *your* responsibility to 'enforce' the judgement.

Enforcement

Unfortunately, winning a case is not the end of the story. You may now have to enforce settlement of the debt, since responsibility for making the debtor pay up after a court order has been issued lies with you and not the court. Enforcement can be tedious and expensive, so think carefully before embarking along this road – there is absolutely no point in proceeding if the debtor has no money or assets to sell (bankruptcy of the debtor might be a better option in this case, since when bankruptcy proceedings are threatened previously undisclosed assets sometimes suddenly appear). However, enforcement costs are recoverable from the debtor if you do eventually succeed.

Enforcement proceedings

The judgement order issued by the court following your successful action will require the debtor to pay the money owed either at once or by instalments. You begin enforcement proceedings immediately an outstanding amount becomes overdue. If you know the debtor has assets, move straight away to one of the enforcement methods outlined below. Otherwise, a further court hearing to establish the extent of the debtor's assets may be required. To arrange this you write (see Note 4) to the County court covering the area in which the debtor resides, asking for an 'oral examination' of that person (or of the company secretary or named director of a limited company, though in this case you are only allowed to ask about the company's assets and not the private means of its directors). The court sends you a form N316 which you complete and return with the appropriate fee. This fee is increased periodically but does not amount to more than a few pounds. Then the court arranges a date and venue for the examination and issues an order to the debtor to attend. Failure to obey this order can result in a prison sentence for contempt of court. At the hearing you ask (or get the registrar in charge of the hearing to ask) for particulars of the debtor's income from employment (if any) and from other sources, the income of the debtor's spouse, details of bank and building society accounts, ownership of stocks and shares, property, etc.; and whether that person is owed any money and if so by whom. (For further details see the reference quoted in Note 3.) There are five ways of enforcing settlement as outlined below. Which to choose depends on the specific circumstances surrounding the case.

1. Attachment of earnings

If the debtor is working for someone the best solution may be to ask the court to order the debtor's employer to pay part of the debtor's weekly or monthly earnings direct to you. The amount payable is decided by the court, taking into account the debtor's need to support his or her family. You apply for this type of order on form N337, upon which you specify the debtor's employer and place of work. A small fee is payable when you return the form. The court then serves the application on the debtor by post. If there is no reply you will have to pay the court bailiff to serve the application personally. No further action is possible until the application is served, so if the debtor has moved you need to discover his or her new address before proceeding further.

2. Attachment of debts

5

The debtor might be owed money by someone else (referred to as a 'garnishee') who can be ordered by the court to pay the amount owed (or some part of it) to you instead of the debtor. This is useful where the debtor is unemployed but known to have money in a bank or building society account since money in such an account is technically 'owed' to the customer. The problem, of course, is that as soon as debtors get wind of the fact that 'garnishee orders' are being sought against them they immediately withdraw all the money from their bank and other accounts. Moreover, a garnishee order applies only to the money held in an account on the day the order is served on the bank, not to money paid in thereafter.

To obtain a garnishee order you must go in person to your local County court, complete form N49, swear on oath before a court official that the information given is true and pay the relevant (subsequently recoverable) fee. The order is served on the bank or other debtor of the debtor who owes you money. On receipt of a garnishee order the third party pays the amount due into court (assuming enough money is available in the account) after deducting a small fee for its clerical expenses.

3. Warrant of execution

This is the commonest of the methods; it means that the court directs a bailiff to seize and sell sufficient of the debtor's assets to settle the outstanding balance. The warrant instructs the bailiff to visit the debtor's house, business premises or anywhere else the debtor's goods might be found, and physically remove and sell whichever goods the bailiff thinks will raise enough money to cover the debt plus the cost of removing them and putting them up for auction. Clothing and bedding up to a certain value (currently £250) cannot be taken, nor can the debtor's 'tools of trade'.

Although warrants of execution are frequently used, problems do occur, specifically:

(a) the bailiff cannot force entry to the debtor's home (though business premises can be so entered, and refusing to allow the bailiff to enter domestic premises will eventually result in the debtor going to jail);

(b) costs of removing, storing and selling goods can exceed their auction value, and if the bailiff believes the amount raised will not cover these costs then the goods will not be taken;

(c) some if not all of a debtor's valuable household goods (refrigerators, television sets, etc.) may have been obtained on unexpired hire purchase and cannot be seized since they do not 'belong' to the debtor;

(d) only goods belonging to the debtor can be taken, not those which belong to the debtor's spouse or any other person.

To obtain a warrant you complete form N323 and pay a small fee which varies according to the value of the outstanding debt. You must find and give to the bailiff the debtor's current address. If you know the whereabouts of any of the debtor's property you should tell the bailiff.

4. Equitable execution

This is appropriate where the debtor receives rent or other regular, non-employment payments and/or proceeds from the sale of land. The court will appoint a receiver who collects these payments and turns over the money to you. Heavy administrative costs are involved, and you need proper legal advice before attempting this procedure.

5. Charging orders

A charging order is an order preventing the debtor selling his or her land or securities (stocks, shares and debentures) until the outstanding debt has been settled. The debtor must own the land or securities before the charge is imposed. This method is useful where the debtor's major asset is a house or a portfolio of shares, and he or she has little money income. Charging orders can be extended to force the debtor to sell the land or securities in order to settle the outstanding balance, but special court proceedings are necessary before this may occur, and the process is complex and expensive.

If none of these measures succeed in obtaining the money you can apply to have the debtor declared bankrupt, since non-compliance with a judgement or order is one of several acts that render the debtor liable to bankruptcy (or company liquidation) proceedings. The threat of bankruptcy, plus all that it involves (see Chaper 13) might prompt a debtor who – through various delaying tactics, changes of address, withdrawal of funds from bank accounts, putting goods in other peoples' names, etc. – has messed you around for months suddenly to settle the debt (and previously accumulated collection expenses).

Clearly there are many problems and pitfalls associated with legal action, and you should never rush into litigation if you have any doubts about the strength of your case. Note, moreover, that there is nothing to prevent the debtor using a solicitor in a small claims action, hence injecting formality and legal jargon into the proceedings and leading perhaps to your having to hire a solicitor yourself, bearing in mind the fact that solicitors' fees are not recoverable if the debt is under £500.

Delaying tactics by the defendant – making vague promises, changing address, opening and closing bank accounts, offering trivial defences to the claims you present, asking for adjournments, shuffling assets – can wear you down to the point where you simply haven't the energy to proceed. And you might feel fundamentally ill at ease in a court environment. Court registrars are themselves lawyers and tend to think in legal terms. They frequently use language unintelligible to the average lay person and, because they lack practical business experience, communication can be difficult.

Notes

1. *Re Peachdart Limited* [1983] 3 WLR 878.
2. Notably the 1974 Consumer Credit Act (see Chapter 10).
3. For details see section four of the pamphlet, *Small Claims in the County Court*, mentioned above.
4. Specimen letters for this and other enforcement purposes are contained in the HMSO pamphlet, *Enforcing Money Judge-*

ments in the County Court, (form Ex 50C), which can be obtained free of charge from your local County court (see your local telephone directory under 'Courts: County' for the telephone number).

Summary

The need to give credit is a fact of life for most small businesses, but credit is expensive, and a certain number of credit customers will not settle their bills. You shouldn't offer credit to just anyone who asks for it – check each applicant's credit-worthiness, using an agency if necessary.

Accurate information about the credit side of your business is crucially important for your long-term survival. You need to know how long, on average, it takes to collect a debt; who the slow payers are, and why they take so long to settle their accounts.

Debt collecting is tedious, costly and may be emotionally unpleasant. Certain small debts can cost more to collect than their face values, so great efficiency in debt collecting procedures is required. Draft standard debt collecting letters, and never be afraid to use the phone. You can sell debts to a collection agency, or even pass all your invoices to a credit factor. The latter will pay you a proportion of the face value of invoices in cash and then collect the full amounts owed. However, both these possibilities are expensive to implement.

If you possess unambiguous evidence of the existence of a debt, and there are no complicating factors such as alleged non-delivery of the goods, defective produce, etc., then legal action should be considered; especially if less than £500 is involved. The County court small claims procedure is very straightforward compared to normal litigation, although even here legal complications may arise. And there is no point in suing someone who does not have the means to settle an overdue account. Moreover, enforcement proceedings themselves can be laborious and expensive.

Checklist

1. What proportion of your output is sold on credit?
2. Suppose you were to insist on cash or cheques with all orders, what would happen to the level of your sales?
3. How much are the discounts you offer for prompt payment actually costing you each year?
4. Do you ask applicants for credit accounts to provide you with banker's and other credit references?
5. How long did it take you to collect the amounts owed under your last six credit invoices?
6. Do you know the names and telephone extensions of the people who deal with suppliers' invoices in the accounts departments of your three largest customers?
7. Have you ever telephoned a debt collecting company to ask how much they charge? (Agency telephone numbers can be found in the *Yellow Pages*.)
8. Have you mentioned your debt collecting problems to your bank and asked for advice?
9. How many long overdue debts for amounts less than £500 do you have on your books?
10. Have you read the HMSO pamphlets referred to in Notes 2 and 3 on page 89?

5

6 Labour matters

Full- or part-time workers □ Employees who don't work hard enough □ How to deal with a lazy employee □ Redundancy □ Dismissal □ Rights of employees □ Recruiting new staff □Motivating your workers □ Incentive schemes □ The law on health and safety at work □ Vicarious liability □ Summary □ Checklist

Karen Lanz's text, *Hiring and Firing* (already published in this series) contains a detailed and comprehensive review of personnel issues. Here I present a brief overview of these matters, emphasising the need for maximum efficiency in the management of a small firm's labour. A good employee is one of the most valuable assets your business will ever possess; bad workers, conversely, can cause disaster.

You must be extremely cautious when recruiting labour: interview carefully, monitor the new entrant's work, and regularly discuss problems that arise. It is not necessary to draft rigid job specifications for the employees of a small business, because precise job descriptions invite 'who-does-what' disputes when in fact total job flexibility is usually needed.

There are of course, important legal constraints on how you recruit staff, but you will not get into trouble with the law provided you:

(a) do not discriminate unfairly on the grounds of race or sex or because someone is married;

(b) issue written contracts of employment and pay agreed wages on time;

(c) deduct the correct amounts of PAYE and Class One National Insurance contributions from employees' pay and turn these amounts over to the Inland Revenue at the end of each month;

(d) issue P60's at the end of each tax year.

Full- or part-time workers

Before you hire anyone ask yourself first whether you *really* need to have 'employees' at all. The computation of PAYE and National Insurance is time consuming and administratively troublesome, and all sorts of interpersonal relations problems may arise among your workers. Perhaps you can sub-contract work to other firms or possibly make do with part time labour, which is much cheaper than hiring permanent full-time employees. Other advantages of using part-time and/or casually employed staff are that:

(a) they have fewer legal rights (maternity and redundancy pay, the right to claim unfair dismissal, etc., as outlined below) than full-time workers;

(b) since they can be laid off with minimal legal repercussions you can alter the size of the labour force quickly as market circumstances change;

(c) unsatisfactory employees may be easily dismissed;

(d) casual workers have no statutory rights to time off for union work or public duties;

(e) there are no annual pay rises, superannuation, promotion or sick pay for casual part-timers other than the statutory minimum.

On the other hand, casuals typically lack commitment, have usually less training and experience than full-timers, and may bitterly resent being employed on a casual rather than permanent basis, especially if they do the same work as better paid full-time staff.

There are few opportunities for job enrichment (i.e., deliberately making a person's work more varied, interesting, responsible and demanding) in relation to casual part-time work, which can result in low morale, frequent absenteeism and high staff turnover rates. And employee grievances persist indefinitely among casual workers – complaints are passed on from one generation to the next.

If you employ full-time workers then remember that they may not share your total loyalty to the business, which to them is probably (and understandably) little more than a means of earning a living. Employees may see you in a manner very different to how you see yourself: it is after all *their* hard work that will cause the business to succeed and they rightly feel entitled to a fair reward for their endeavours.

Small businesses cannot afford idlers

There is no room for free riders in a small firm experiencing financial difficulties (or in any other business for that matter). Everyone must pull their weight and be willing to undertake whatever duties and changes in working practices are necessary to improve the business, no matter how personally inconvenient they happen to be. Ultimately, jobs depend on the long-term survival of the firm!

Working for a small business

An advantage of working in a small business is that the employee has opportunities to experience a wide range of work activities. Jobs need not be as narrowly defined and specialised as is common in large organisations. This fact embodies strengths and a weakness. Strengths include:

- more job satisfaction
- higher morale and greater motivation
- the chance to acquire many skills and competencies through participation in a variety of working relationships
- possibly, management training.

The disadvantage is that simultaneous involvement in many (perhaps fragmented) assignments creates numerous opportunities for duplication of effort, inefficiency and, albeit unconscious, work avoidance.

6

Employees who don't work hard enough

Employees need not be overtly lazy before they start avoiding important duties; they might simply be trying, perhaps unintentionally, to exchange easier or more enjoyable duties for the tasks that really need to be done. Some jobs are necessarily less attractive than others and, not unnaturally, those who should perform unpleasant tasks may constantly seek alternative ways of filling their time.

A worker may be completely unaware of the extent of his or her task evasion. There is no question of deliberate malingering, yet nothing is achieved. Interesting duties are padded out to make them last longer; extra and unnecessary tasks are invented to run in parallel with jobs that are actually required. And the worker becomes so busy completing these contrived duties that he or she has no time or energy left to deal with really important matters! Thus, the employee will:

- double-check documents
- carefully peruse marginally relevant pieces of correspondence
- investigate closely problems with obvious solutions
- query insignificant mistakes
- ask for guidance on unimportant issues, and so on.

Sometimes employees behave like this because they wish to feel important, and do not associate the mundane lower level duties you want them to perform with the status they believe they ought to command. Often employees want to take decisions, and have their own ideas about the decisions they should be allowed to take; indeed, about the entire distribution of work and responsibility within the firm. These perceptions may differ from your own and it is thus essential that you try to divide work between you and your employees in a manner which seems *to them* to be just.

Allocating duties

Put yourself in your employees' place. Would you feel exploited or degraded if you were told to do the work you expect of your employees? Could the duties you delegate be considered beneath someone's dignity or not an integral part of their normal routine?

Ideally, the division of work you impose should be seen to be equitable by employees, so regularly ask workers for their views about the duties they believe they can and should perform. Work roles are sometimes unclear – people may think they ought to be doing one thing when actually they ought to be doing something else. In consequence everyone assumes someone else will complete a disagreeable or difficult task, with the result that it is never actually completed.

Need for total job flexibility

What, then, can be done to overcome such difficulties? I do not favour organisation charts and rigid job specifications for the employees of small businesses. Total job flexibility should be the ultimate objective, including employees' ability and willingness to undertake managerial work. You own the firm, so you have nothing to fear (e.g., being dismissed to make way for a brighter or younger subordinate) from 'training up' your workers. And the more precisely defined are the tasks which employees *ought* to do, the greater the opportunities for their not doing work not strictly covered by job descriptions!

Organisation charts and job specifications, moreover, quickly become out of date, and they can never comprehensively define all the potential duties of an employee of a small business. Rather, you should:

- delegate interesting as well as routine work to employees
- regularly rotate employees' workloads in order to observe how well one worker completes particular duties compared to the individual who previously undertook them
- share with employees various aspects of your managerial duties.

This stimulates workers' interest and motivation, and malingering is difficult when duties are undertaken jointly with the boss.

How to deal with a lazy employee

A malingerer will minimise the effort he or she puts into a job and will attempt to shorten the length of the working day. Here, work avoidance is deliberate; the employee:

- is persistently late
- takes unnecessary breaks
- does 'walkabouts' around the premises
- tries to appear absorbed in tasks while actually doing nothing.

Of course, such individuals do some work just to avoid argument; files are shifted from one place to another, there are regular telephone calls to suppliers and other outsiders, and no shortage of conversation. Eventually, however, you realise that you are being ripped off: the employee wants the job, but is not prepared to expend any effort when undertaking the activities it involves.

The situation is intolerable. The worker is costing you money by the hour: immediate and drastic measures are needed. Here's what you must do.

- Tell the worker you think his or her work is unsatisfactory and why this is so. Specify detailed instances of unsatisfactory work, with dates, times and supporting documents where appropriate. Plan the discussion well in advance and never begin such an interview when you are tired, angry, upset or depressed.
- State that the discussion is more than just a 'friendly chat'; that you are seriously disturbed by the problems the worker is creating and that you intend remedying the situation.
- Ask for comments and/or explanations. Were there mitigating circumstances (domestic problems causing frequent absences and latecoming, for example)?
- Examine and question the reasons given for poor performance. Find out why the worker has been malingering. If the employee denies

everything, point to your evidence (which you must collect prior to the discussion) of unsatisfactory work.

- Remind the employee of his or her responsibility to achieve a certain minimum standard, and ask what you can do to help overcome current difficulties.
- Tell the worker that he or she should consider the interview as constituting a 'warning' about inadequate performance. Follow this up with a letter detailing your allegations, specifying dates and occurrences, and stating that if performance does not improve then he or she will get the sack.

You must, by law, give an employee 'reasonable' time to remedy deficiencies, and you must make crystal clear (preferably in writing) the standards you expect. Standards must be realistic, and the consequences of failing to achieve them explained fully. If the employee's work does not improve and he or she cannot advance any reasonable explanation for continuing to underperform then you have to repeat the above mentioned procedure twice more. The second interview will be more pointed than the first; the third should issue a final and unambiguous warning of dismissal. All these discussions must be followed by letters confirming the warnings you issued during the interviews. These letters should:

- point out that previous warnings were ignored
- specify in detail further instances of incompetence or misbehaviour, and mention that no satisfactory explanations or mitigating circumstances have been brought to your attention (but that if any exist you must be informed immediately).

Such actions are administratively troublesome, unpleasant and you may be tempted not to bother – simply firing the worker when the situation gets out of hand. But you can end up losing a costly unfair dismissal case if you ignore the abovementioned procedures; the days when an employer could fire a worker, albeit an idle and incompetent worker, at will have long since departed. Today, you must follow carefully specified procedures, (outlined below) when sacking employees. The government-funded Arbitration, Conciliation and Advisory Service (ACAS) publishes a Code of Practice entitled *Disciplinary and Other Procedures in Employment* (HMSO 1986), which sets out in detail the procedures you need to apply. Obtain a copy of this, read it and adapt its recommendations to your particular needs. And similar considerations apply to redundancy situations where existing workers (industrious and competent though they might be) cannot be retained simply because you no longer have any work for them to do.

Redundancy

If you need to make someone redundant and he or she has worked for you for more than two years full time, or two years part time doing more than 16 hours a week, or five years part time doing more than eight hours a week, you have to offer a redundancy payment, although 35 per cent of this is recoverable from a central government fund if your firm employs less than ten workers.

The amount of payment depends on the age of the worker and how long he or she has worked for the firm, subject to an upper limit which varies from time to time. (Details of current rates are available from the office of your local job centre.)

Redundancy applies to the *job*, not a worker. It means that you have no further work available of the type previously undertaken by the employee affected, and must not be confused with dismissal for incompetence or a similar reason. You are obliged by law to seek alternative work for anyone threatened with redundancy, give adequate warning (plus paid time off to look for another job), and must consult with the employee's trade union.

Selecting people for redundancy

If you make one person redundant but not another you have to be able to demonstrate that in selecting that particular worker for redundancy you applied fair and objective criteria when making your choice. Hence you must consider the lengths of service, capabilities, ages, qualifications and experience of all staff previously employed on the type of work that has disappeared, and should take into account each person's suitability for alternative employment within the business. You cannot lawfully declare one worker redundant while simultaneously hiring someone else to perform that person's work.

Who to retain

If most of your workforce has to go, keep a skeleton staff best able to face up to the challenge. Only retain flexible and energetic workers, but recognise that they will not want to stay for very long unless your firm's performance (and hence their security of tenure)

improves rapidly. Note that there is no presumption that younger or
older employees will perform better in these circumstances – young
people are perhaps more adaptab'e to fast changing environments,
but may lack the experience and commitment of older colleagues
(especially those who will have difficulty in finding another job).
Each retained worker can act as a cost centre in his or her own right,
and be made accountable for specific business rescue activities.

Guarantee payments

Workers today are legally entitled to 'guarantee payments' for individual days when they are under contract to work but no work is
actually provided – you cannot simply lay someone off for the day
without wages just because the firm is short of work.

Dismissal

Under the Employment Protection (Consolidation) Act 1978 (which
also covers redundancy and guarantee payments), workers with:

(a) more than two years' continuous full-time service, or
(b) two years' continuous service if the employee works part time
more than 16 hours a week, or,
(c) five years continuous service if more than eight hours a week
are worked;

have the right not to be 'unfairly' dismissed. This means you cannot
fairly dismiss an employee covered by the Act unless that person is
genuinely redundant, or is guilty of 'gross' misconduct or demonstrably inadequate performance, or unless you have some other
'substantial' reason for the dismissal. Normally you must give a
worker notice (or payment in lieu), although dismissal without
notice – known as 'summary' dismissal – is permissible provided the
employee's behaviour makes impossible the fulfilment of his or her
contract, e.g., through persistent drunkenness, violence, abusiveness
to customers, wilful disobedience or incompetence that immediately
and directly damages the business. Any worker whom you dismiss
after he or she has completed six months' service with the firm (no
matter how many hours the employee works each week) is legally
entitled to a written statement of your reasons for the dismissal.

Gross misconduct

The term 'misconduct' has no legal definition – each case must be considered individually. Theft and violence are obvious instances of gross misconduct, though it is up to you to prove that

(a) the misconduct actually occurred,
(b) that it detrimentally affected the work of the firm, and
(c) that you acted reasonably at all times.

Inadequate performance

This means the worker cannot complete his or her work satisfactorily and/or does not have the necessary qualifications for the job. A sick worker may be fairly dismissed on these grounds, subject to the sick leave agreed in the employee's contract of employment. Always keep documentary evidence of the incompetence of any workers you intend to dismiss, and do not write glowing references for them prior to dismissal since such letters might subsequently be used in evidence against your allegations of inadequate performance.

Other substantial reasons

Other reasons for fair dismissal might include being rude to customers, 'organisational efficiency' (though the exact meaning of this must be established in each case), a temporary job coming to an end (provided the job holder was told from the outset that the job was temporary), or if the continuation of a person's employment would cause you to break the law, e.g., by employing a driver who has lost his or her licence.

You are entitled to co-operation and obedience from those you employ, although the orders you give must be reasonable, legal and not involve dangerous working practices. Orders given must be covered by the worker's contract of employment, and dismissal for disobedience is 'fair' only if the failure to obey is wilful and 'significant'.

In any of the above circumstances you cannot legally dismiss the worker until he or she has been warned both verbally and in writing (preferably several times) and given the chance to improve. And following dismissal the worker is legally entitled to a written statement of the reasons for his or her sacking.

Automatically unfair dismissals

Certain dismissals are 'automatically' unfair as far as the law is concerned. Thus, if you:

- sack a pregnant woman just because she is pregnant, or
- dismiss someone for joining or refusing to join a union, or
- sack workers when a business changes hands

then your actions will automatically be deemed unlawful. Note also that your behaviour short of sacking a worker can lead to an unfair dismissal claim, since if you act so unreasonably towards an employee (e.g., by cutting wages or by lengthening the working day) that he or she feels there is no option but to quit then the worker can allege that 'constructive' unfair dismissal has occurred.

What you stand to lose

Unfair dismissal cases are heard by three-person industrial tribunals, comprising a legally qualified chairperson plus two lay representatives. If you lose you must pay compensation. This will consist of some or all of the following, according to circumstances.

(a) A *basic* award depending on the employee's length of service. The maximum basic award for someone with many years' service is currently £4,920.

(b) A *compensatory* award (up to £8,500) to cover loss of earnings and/or accumulated pension rights.

(c) An *additional* award of up to £4,264 should you fail to comply with an order to reinstate the worker. These are extremely rare – only one per cent of claims result in this type of award.

(d) *Special* awards (which can be considerable – there is no upper limit in certain cases) if the dismissal is automatically unfair and you refuse to obey a tribunal order. Again, these are extremely rare in practice (much rarer than additional awards).

The fact is that the total compensation award by tribunals to workers who win their cases averages little more than £2,000, and most claims are actually settled out of court before the tribunal is required to rule on the question of compensation. Note that only persons with the requisite lengths of continuous service may claim they have been 'unfairly' dismissed. (Note also the important fact that a series of renewable short term contracts issued one after another builds up continuity of employment just like a single contract for a longer period.)

Wrongful dismissal

Actions for 'wrongful' dismissal are possible through an ordinary civil court, usually the County court. A worker with only a few days service may claim to have been *wrongfully* (as opposed to 'unfairly') dismissed. The sacked person initiates a breach of contract action and sues for damages equal to the monetary loss incurred through not receiving proper notice of dismissal,

Rights of employees

An important right conferred by the EPCA is the right of employees to receive a written contract of employment within 13 weeks of starting work. An 'employee' in this sense means someone who is to work more than 16 hours a week, or who has already worked eight hours a week for at least five years. The following information must be included in the written statement:

(a) Names and addresses of employer and employee.
(b) Job title.
(c) Date of commencement.
(d) Usual hours of work.
(e) The rate of pay and how and when payment will be made.
(f) Terms and conditions regarding (i) sick pay
(ii) holiday pay
(iii) pension schemes.
(g) Grievance and disciplinary procedures.
(h) Special conditions relating to membership of a particular trade union.
(i) Length of notice to be given by either side.
(j) Arrangements for working overtime.

Contracts of employment are important because they establish the existence of an obligation to pay wages in return for a predetermined amount of work. Breach of a contract of employment will on the one hand provide the firm with grounds for fair dismissal, and on the other enable the worker to sue for unpaid wages. The contract is the ultimate determinant of the work an employee must do.

In addition to the minimum information required by statute the written statement should, in your own interests, include as much supplementary detail as possible – especially on potentially contentious issues such as shift work obligations, compulsory overtime, etc.

Apart from the period of notice specified in a contract of employment, certain minimum periods are imposed by law. The Employment Protection Act demands that at least a week's notice be given to a worker with more than one month's but less than two years' service, and one extra week's notice for each year of employment thereafter (so that, for instance, a worker with eight years' service is entitled to eight weeks' notice) up to a maximum of twelve weeks.

Pregnancy and maternity

Employees' maternity rights are governed by the 1978 Employment Protection Act, the Employment Act 1980 and the Social Security Act 1986. It is unlawful to dismiss a protected worker simply for becoming pregnant. Additionally, the woman is entitled (i) to return to work up to 29 weeks after her confinement and (ii) to be reinstated in her old or an equivalent job. Also, the woman is entitled to maternity pay, which is the responsibility of the employer but which the firm then reclaims from the Department of Social Security.

There are two levels of payment, 'higher' and 'lower'. If the woman has worked with the same employer for more than 16 hours a week for at least two years (five years if she has worked between eight and 16 hours a week) she can claim 90 per cent of her normal weekly pay (minus the value of state benefit) from her employer for six weeks, plus the lower rate (set by statute, currently about £35 per week) for up to twelve further weeks. Women with between six months' and two years' service are entitled to the lower rate for up to 18 weeks.

The only circumstances in which you can fairly dismiss a woman for being pregnant are if you can *prove* that her pregnancy makes her physically incapable of performing her duties, or if continuing to employ her would cause your firm to break the law (there is legislation prohibiting the employment of pregnant women in certain dangerous occupations). In both cases, you must seek suitable alternative work for the woman, on the same pay, and be able to *prove* that you have done so. All pregnant women – regardless of length of service – are legally entitled to paid time off to attend 'reasonable' numbers of antenatal appointments. However, firms are entitled to ask to see letters confirming that female employees are actually pregnant and that appointments have in fact been made. Note that you cannot fairly dismiss a woman for reasons 'connected' with pregnancy. Thus, dismissals of women suffering from emotional tension brought on by pregnancy, or suffering from postnatal depression, or who miscarried and were consequently ill, have been declared unfair by industrial tribunals.

Certain formalities have to be followed by a pregnant employee who wishes to be re-employed after the birth of her child. She must give written notice of her intention to return to work at least 21 days before she goes on maternity leave, and must produce on request a doctor's certificate stating the expected date of confinement.

If you write to her within seven weeks of the confinement asking for confirmation of her intention to return to work she *must* reply within 14 days, or as soon as is 'reasonably practical' thereafter. Then she can return to work any time up to 29 weeks after the birth (with a possible four week extension on medical grounds), provided she gives at least 21 days advance notice of the date of her return. To qualify for this right, the woman must have been continuously employed for at least two years immediately prior to the eleventh week before the expected date of confinement.

These rules are stringent, and a woman who is ignorant of them or fails to meet deadlines loses her right of return. Dismissal of a temporary replacement worker (employed specifically to cover the woman's absence) after the woman returns is explicitly allowed under the EPCA. The woman who returns is legally entitled to her previous job, not a job of inferior pay or stature. If her old job has disappeared (through departmental reorganisation, for example) then the firm is obliged to seek a suitable alternative.

Further complications can arise through the Employment Act 1980, under which small firms (i.e., those employing not more than five workers) can claim that it is not reasonably practicable for them to reinstate women who have taken maternity leave and, provided they can offer concrete reasons why reinstatement is impracticable, can escape their obligation to reinstate. However, the law is extremely uncertain in this area and it is impossible to generalise about the extent of a small firm's liability.

Laws that prohibit discrimination

The Sex Discrimination Act 1975 aims to eliminate discrimination between men, women and married persons. Under the Act, it is generally unlawful for an employer to discriminate on sex or marriage grounds in recruitment, in the terms and conditions of employment offered, or in the provision of access to training or promotion opportunities. 'Direct' discrimination occurs through treating people less favourably on account of their sex or because they are married. 'Indirect' discrimination means imposing a condition such that the proportion of members of one sex who can meet the condition is considerably less than in the other, e.g., a statement in a job advertisement that all applicants must be over six feet tall. 'Victimisation' results from people being less favourably treated because they complain of not receiving their statutory rights, or because they help someone else complain of unfair treatment.

There are several exceptions to the Act. These include:

(a) employment mainly outside Great Britain;
(b) employment in religious organisations that operate a sex bar;
(c) certain occupations (coal mining for example) where Parliament has decided women should not be employed;
(d) employment in the armed services.

Also exempt are jobs where sex is a 'genuine occupational qualification'. Examples are actors who play male or female roles, jobs in single sex schools, hospitals or other institutions, and jobs where 'decency or privacy' require employees of a particular sex (lavatory attendants for instance).

The Race Relations Act 1976 offers similar rights to ethnic minorities. As with the Sex Discrimination Act there are several exemptions, notably where race is a genuine occupational qualification. Other exemptions are:

(a) employment in a private household (though note that this violates EC law and is unlikely to remain much longer; also, victimisation of an employee in a private household is still unlawful); and
(b) employment outside Great Britain.

Responsibility for seeking to eliminate racial discrimination in employment lies with the Commission for Racial Equality, which publishes Codes of Practice to guide firms in these respects. Similarly, the Equal Opportunities Commission issues Codes of Practice in relation to the avoidance of sex discrimination. Both Commissions conduct research, and initiate legal action against firms that unlawfully discriminate.

Industrial tribunals and discrimination

Workers who believe they have been subject to sexual or racial discrimination, or who wish to register complaints under a variety of other employment regulations and statutes (including health and safety and equal pay legislation) may initiate actions in industrial tribunals, the operation of which has been described in a previous section.

Recruiting new staff

Aim for low cost recruitment, avoiding expensive press advertisements or recruitment agencies (which charge a fee of up to ten per cent of the annual salary of the person eventually selected) wherever possible. Word of mouth recruitment is cheap and highly effective in certain circumstances, particularly in high unemployment areas. Put the word around that you are looking for workers, supplementing this with a few letters to existing contacts within your industry, the local job centre and perhaps to local colleges. A notice outside your premises or in a nearby shop window might be sufficient to attract the right person.

Interviewing

When interviewing, seek to identify in candidates the personal qualities your business most needs, and try not to be swayed by irrelevant subjective criteria. Consider only the skills, qualifications and experience required for successful completion of the job, and do not hire someone simply because he or she is more like yourself than the other applicants. (Owning and running a small business usually requires talents that differ significantly from those needed for working for someone else and following their instructions.) Prior to the interview ask yourself the two following questions:

1. What exactly do I want the appointed person to do?
2. What are the personal characteristics that will enable an individual to perform this work successfully?

Relevant personal qualities might include:

(a) the ability to mix easily and get on with others (including customers, suppliers and/or other workers);

(b) possession of a certain technical skill;

(c) alertness and the ability to interpret complicated issues;

(d) the ability to withstand stress, cope with irate customers, work independently, etc.;

plus whichever further attributes you deem appropriate for the job. Prepare a checklist of these points for use in interviews, and consider how they can be assessed in candidates. Thus, for example, you might require a person who need not be physically strong but who must possess good eyesight, has passed a certain technical examination, has a minimum amount of experience of a particular type of work and has already worked in a certain industry, who is emotionally stable, willing to work overtime, etc. You are unlikely to find anyone who matches this specification exactly, but at least you have some objective criteria against which to evaluate the people who apply.

Obtaining information

Use interviews to obtain *information* about candidates. Do not talk about yourself and your achievements; avoid pomposity, and do not ask aggressive questions which serve only to upset the candidate and interrupt the free flow of conversation. Act naturally when interviewing; remember that the person you hire must work with you as you are, not as you transitorily appear during a half-hour discussion. Ask open-ended questions rather than those requiring simple 'yes-no' answers, and do not make insensitive remarks after an answer has been presented.

Try always to put the interviewee at ease. Be polite, pleasant and sympathetic to his or her inevitable nervousness. Avoid keeping people waiting; make their reception friendly and constructive. The more relaxed people feel the more useful information they will transmit and the easier, therefore, your eventual choice of candidate.

Applicants with criminal records

The law states that a 'rehabilitated' person does not have to disclose to a recruiting firm the fact that he or she has a criminal record, provided the applicant's conviction has been 'spent'. And it is unlawful for an employer to deny someone a job solely on the grounds that the applicant has a spent conviction. If an applicant is asked to declare on an application form whether he or she has a criminal record, or is questioned about this during an interview, the applicant is entitled to deny ever having been convicted of the spent offence.

A conviction becomes 'spent' following the elapse of a certain time period, although some convictions can never be spent (notably life sentences and other sentences of imprisonment for more than 30 months). Otherwise the period involved varies according to the gravity of the offence. Thus, a prison sentence of up to six months becomes spent after three years; sentences of between six and 30 months are spent after five years; a probation order is spent one year after it expires, and so on.

There are exemptions to the legislation, and candidates for certain jobs do have to reveal past convictions. The jobs involved are: lawyers, chartered accountants, medical practitioners, nurses, dentists, vets, prison officers, firearms dealers, social and health workers, and any form of work with children under the age of 18. If a job applicant has a spent conviction that you know about, you must not reveal this information to anyone else since you could then be sued for defamation and/or the aggrieved person could make a formal complaint to the police, who might then prosecute you.

You may feel that this law is unfair on the grounds that you believe it necessary to ensure that everyone you hire is trustworthy and reliable. Remember, however, that a person's criminal record might have arisen many years previously and involve only a minor offence. Moreover, criminal records are held only by those who were caught and punished at the time. It is hardly proper that such individuals be punished again through not being able to get a job.

Beware of early resignations

Do not 'oversell' the job. Unfulfilled promises may lead to early disenchantment. Be particularly on your guard against early resignations if you used an employment agency to make initial contact with the recruit. Most agencies offer a full refund if you sack a worker within a month of appointment, and a part refund if the worker turns out to be unsatisfactory and hence is dismissed after a month but before the expiry of (usually) one year. Check the details of the contract offered by an agency to ensure similar provisions apply to staff *resignations*. Otherwise you might hire someone, pay a hefty agency fee, and then lose both the fee and the worker through the recruit becoming dissatisfied and quitting after a short period.

Motivating your workers

Employees are motivated in part by the need to earn a living and partly by:

- psychological and social needs for job satisfaction
- occupational dignity
- job security.

As a small business you cannot offer your workers 'promotion' as such; indeed, even their job security might not be guaranteed. Nevertheless, you can:

(a) design jobs to generate the maximum amount of variety and interest for the worker;

(b) devise performance related incentive schemes that enable you to pay decent wages without bankrupting the organisation.

Job design

Avoid giving workers single, repetitive and boring tasks which they have to complete for excessively long periods, and do not ask employees to work in social isolation, spending all their time away from the company of other people. If the work to be done is necessarily monotonous, try to arrange the circumstances in which it is undertaken in such a way that the worker can easily communicate with others, and can frequently exchange various aspects of the routine job. Employees are usually better motivated if they personally control working methods and take significant decisions, since then they feel they have a personal stake in the survival of the business. Thus, wherever possible:

- combine single tasks into a composite whole
- allow workers discretion over how they achieve objectives
- make workers responsible for the quality of their output
- allocate to employees challenging duties which stretch their abilities.

Make jobs interesting

If you are to design jobs effectively you need to know which aspects of the firm's work are least and most interesting, since only then can you know what to do to make jobs more varied and absorbing from the employee's point of view. Hence you should regularly experience the work personally, and consciously analyse the factors which cause certain tasks to be boring. Then perhaps you can regroup activities, alter the pace of work, allocate broad rather than specific targets, encourage workers to participate in decision making, etc., in order to improve interest and motivation.

Satisfied workers are easy to supervise: they are co-operative, productive and profitable. Sometimes people feel better if they have an impressive-sounding job title (especially if it incorporates the word 'manager') and there is no reason why a small firm should not have employees with grandiose titles – 'chief accountant' for the part-time assistant who (among other things) does the books, 'head of marketing' for the person who takes customers' orders, and so on. Seek to compliment employees on the calibre of their work, and if you have to criticise, direct your remarks towards criticism of an *action* rather than an individual person. Try to involve staff with final customers – much satisfaction can be gained through observing a customer's pleasure in a high quality finished product.

6

Incentive schemes

Few employees are today prepared to accept piece rate wages without having a guaranteed fall-back minimum income. Unfortunately, you might not presently be in a position to offer employees the levels of time rate wages they deserve and need, therefore, to devise some form of output-related remuneration package which contains, nevertheless, a guaranteed minimum level of earnings. Possibilities include:

(a) awarding higher time rates to anyone who exceeds a predetermined target output;
(b) output-related bonuses paid on top of a basic wage;
(c) giving workers a certain proportion (e.g., half) of the money saved through completing a job early so that, for instance, an employee who completes in one hour a task that normally takes an hour and a half receives a bonus of a quarter of an hour's pay at his or her standard hourly rate.

Note, however, that over-reliance on piece rate systems allows employees to determine the firm's level of output, since with piece work operatives themselves decide how much effort they will expend at work – they fix target remunerations and produce as much output as is necessary to achieve those incomes. Thus, they might work harder whenever they happen to be short of money, while reducing output when they are not short of cash. Consequently, your levels of output could fluctuate according to the spending habits of employees, and you could face unexpectedly productive, and hence high labour cost periods (in November or December, for instance, as workers try to get money for Christmas).

You must insist, therefore, that certain minimum output levels are maintained from week to week as a condition of making bonus payments available. Bonuses need to be:

- substantial – at least ten per cent of the basic wage – otherwise they offer no significant incentive
- linked to quality or output levels that workers can *themselves* control
- not too complicated or time-consuming to estimate.

Profit sharing

Profit sharing is a further possibility, especially where individual contributions to output cannot be measured exactly. This may encourage employees' commitment to the business, although pay-outs are not directly connected to immediate effort so that workers might not associate the eventual payment with the hard work they put into its creation during a past period.

You must establish a criterion for allocating the profit to be distributed (e.g., length of service, basic wage or whatever), and decide whether to pay the profit shares in cash or fringe benefits (which may in fact be extremely tax efficient for the workers). Profit sharing will not motivate employees unless the amounts involved are substantial and seen as additions rather than alternatives to basic pay. A major problem here is that workers often come to regard profit distributions as integral parts of their normal incomes, and resent withdrawal of the benefits when the firm is passing through a rough trading period. Note also that a low status worker may feel angry at the prospect of higher paid colleagues receiving bigger profit shares, which he or she believes they do not deserve since the higher paid employees worked no harder than the worker in question.

High staff turnover?

If workers remain with you on average for only short periods you need to question the basic causes of their leaving. A high staff turnover is one of many indicators of flagging morale within the business. Other signs include:

- shoddy output
- persistent latecoming
- frequent absenteeism
- unco-operative and couldn't-care-less attitudes.

Perhaps you are recruiting people to do work that is beyond them (extra training might solve this problem), or maybe you expect employees to achieve absurdly high targets, or are starving workers of the resources necessary for them to perform effectively, or possibly you have personal bad habits which cause employee dissatisfaction (e.g., regularly arriving for work after your employees have started but always complaining if they do not turn up on time).

Exit interviews

Always ask people why they are resigning. Valid reasons include a better job elsewhere, lack of job security, moving house to another area, wanting more time to devote to young children, and so on. Other, undesirable reasons are boredom, personality clashes, frequent arguments with colleagues, lack of self-confidence, poor physical working conditions or marginally inadequate pay. During the conversation ask whether there is anything you can do to persuade the worker to stay, although explain that your purpose in conducting the interview is not to pressurise that person into doing something he or she does not want to do, but rather to discover mistakes you have made in order to correct them and hence avoid his or her replacement being similarly affected. Be as friendly and informal as you can. Encourage the worker to speak freely, to express opinions, describe work experiences, and state how he or she perceives the business and your behaviour as a good or bad employer.

The law on health and safety at work

The law on health and safety matters is complex and voluminous. Currently, the most important statute is the Health and Safety at Work Act 1974, which imposes on employers a general duty to ensure so far as is 'reasonably practical' the health and safety at work of all employees. Breach of this duty can lead to a *criminal* (rather than civil) prosecution. Any firm employing more than four workers must, under the Act, prepare a written statement of its policy on health and safety and bring this to the attention of employees. Plant, machinery and other equipment must be safe and well maintained, and all arrangements for handling, storing and transporting articles and substances must be safe and free of health hazards. Importantly, employers are obliged to provide the supervision, instruction and training needed to ensure health and safety. Firms are statutorily obliged to check that all aspects of the workplace are safe, including means of entry and exit, machinery and equipment and the working environment (fumes, dust, etc.).

Section 7 of the Act states that employees must take 'reasonable care' to ensure they neither endanger themselves nor others at work. Thus, your workers are legally required to co-operate on health and safety matters, though note that it is *your* responsibility to ensure that instructions are carried out. For example, if protective clothing is necessary then not only must you provide it, free of charge, but you must also make sure that it is worn.

Safety representatives

If you recognise a trade union then if it so wishes it can appoint 'safety representatives' at the place of work. The union does not need your permission for this, but it must be 'recognised' by you for the purpose of collective bargaining. Unions themselves decide the procedure for selecting safety representatives, whose functions include:

(a) investigation of hazards, accidents and dangerous occurrences, and making representations to management on matters arising from these investigations or on any other safety issue;

(b) meeting outside inspectors and receiving information from them;

(c) making formal inspections of the workplace every three months or following accidents or dangerous occurrences;

(d) inspecting and taking copies of any relevant information (accident reports, for example) that the employer is statutorily obliged to maintain.

Safety policy

Regardless of statutory and common law duties, you should always pay meticulous attention to health and safety matters. Do not be afraid of being accused of over-fastidiousness in these respects; your good example is bound to influence others and hence reduce accidents in the longer term. Accidents are expensive. Not only do they disrupt production, but also they incur the costs of sick pay, investigations, training of temporary replacement workers and so on. Seek consciously to identify hazards, and to inculcate in others a respect for safe methods of work. Never authorise or even condone unsafe working practices, try instead to incorporate safety checks into the systems and procedures of the firm. Be seen to investigate all accidents, and regularly inspect machinery and equipment. Insist on 'good housekeeping' within the business, and that all accidents, no matter how trivial, be reported.

Other safety legislation

Although the HSWA is intended as a piece of umbrella legislation that eventually will incorporate all other health and safety statutes, it does not replace existing health and safety laws, which continue to operate in parallel with the 1974 Act. The major statutes are outlined below.

The Offices, Shops and Railway Premises Act 1963

This Act applies to offices everywhere, even those on premises normally used for other purposes (factories, for example), although temporary offices or those operated for less than 21 hours a week are excluded. Among the Act's major provisions are the requirements that:

(a) premises, furniture and fittings be kept clean, and that floors be washed weekly;

(b) each person have at least 40 square foot of space;

(c) rooms be properly ventilated, lit and heated (i.e., to at least 16 degrees centigrade after the first hour);

(d) washing facilities with hot water, soap and towels be provided, and that lavatories be accessible and properly maintained;

(e) no worker be expected to lift dangerously heavy weights;

(f) floor, passages and stairs be kept clear and safe, and that all machinery and equipment be guarded;

(g) first aid boxes be provided, the contents of which conform to the requirements of the Health and Safety (First Aid) Regulations 1981;

(h) seating must be available, and staff must be given facilities for keeping clothing not worn at work.

The Fire Precautions Act 1971

The essential requirement of this Act is that certain classes of premises (including those covered by the Offices, Shops and Railway Premises Act 1963, factories, and buildings to which the public has access) possess a 'fire certificate' issued by the local fire authority, which must be satisfied that the means of escape from the building and other fire precautions are adequate.

Shop premises require a certificate if:

(a) more than 20 people are employed in the shop, or;
(b) more than ten people are employed at any one time in an upstairs room.

Your firm should register its premises with the local fire authority, await an inspection, and then adhere to the fire authority's advice. Over and above this, however, you should encourage your employees to be fire conscious and to remove fire risks. Ensure that all your staff know how to use fire appliances, the location of fire exits and how to operate the alarm system. Under the Act, staff *must* be given training in evacuation procedures and the use of fire-fighting equipment kept on the premises. Moreover, written records of all equipment, inspections and training sessions must be kept, stating the topics covered during the session, who supervised the session and who attended.

The Factories Act 1961

This contains similar provisions to the OSRPA, but for factories. However, additional regulations are included on the maintenance of hoists and lifts and, importantly, it specifies maximum working hours for young persons (restrictions on women's working hours were abolished in 1986), and that all young persons working in factories must be medically examined within two weeks of starting work. A firm may request exemption from the Act's restrictions on working hours for young persons if it needs to meet exceptional demand for output, provided the firm can demonstrate that adequate welfare facilities will be provided. Exemptions are not issued for more than one year.

Miscellaneous legislation

The Employers' Liability (Defective Equipment) Act 1969 provides that when a worker is injured because of a defect in the equipment provided by his or her employer and the defect is the fault of a third party (the equipment's manufacturer, for instance), then the injury is deemed to be also attributable to the negligence of the employer even if no actual negligence has occurred. The employer can, of course, sue the third party for any loss suffered.

Under the Employer's Liability (Compulsory Insurance) Act 1969, every employer must insure against liability for bodily injury or disease sustained by employees in the course of their work, and a copy of the insurance certificate must be displayed on the premises. Another important piece of legislation is the Occupier's Liability Act 1984 which requires the occupier of premises to take 'such care as in all the circumstances is reasonable to see that visitors will be reasonably safe in using the premises for the purpose for which they are invited by the occupier to be there'. Visitors are defined as persons on the premises for the benefit of the occupier (customers, for example), guests and those entering under contract. Note that under the Unfair Contract Terms Act 1977, notices warning of dangers or hazards will not necessarily relieve an occupier from liability for injury to visitors; notices proclaiming that 'Persons entering these premises do so at their own risk' have no legal effect.

The Disabled Persons Employment Acts 1944 and 1958 seek to help disabled people secure employment through requiring employers of more than 20 persons (unless the employer's business involves certain types of physically demanding work – merchant shipping, for example) to employ a quota of three per cent registered disabled people.

Vicarious liability

Employees who take decisions that may be in breach of a statutory requirement or other legal obligation are normally (but not always) protected by the doctrine of 'vicarious liability', which holds that if a person is an employee of an organisation, then his or her employer is liable for civil (but not criminal) wrongs committed in the worker's course of employment, and not the worker personally. The phrase 'in the course of employment' means acts *authorised* by the employer or, where they are not formally authorised, where actions are so closely connected with employment that they are incidental to the employee's work. Only if an action is clearly outside the scope of employment will the employee be personally liable.

Thus, if an employee sacks a subordinate wrongfully then it is the firm that might be sued and not the individual worker. The same applies to negligence at work, with the exception of certain aspects of the law on health and safety, since the Health and Safety at Work Act explicitly imposes a duty on all managers to take such steps 'as are reasonably practicable' to protect workers from injury. If an employee fails to take 'reasonably practicable' steps and as a result someone has an accident, then he or she could be personally liable.

Note that while it is technically possible for you to try and pass on to a negligent employee the losses you incur through his or her negligence (e.g., by suing for damages), a court is unlikely to accept your claim. Moreover, the court will expect you:

(a) to have made explicit to the employee the fact that he or she was exposing him or her self to the possibility of such an action prior to the time the negligence occurred;

(b) to have paid the employee a wage increment specifically earmarked for the purpose of taking out insurance against this eventuality, and to have advised the employee of the intended use of the payment.

Much litigation has concerned the question of what exactly constitutes the 'course of employment,' since:

- vicarious liability applies only to employees hired under a *contract of services*, and not to independent contractors (or self employed consultants);
- employees must be doing what they are supposed to do (albeit carelessly, fraudulently or disobediently) at the moment the unlawful act occurs.

Note, however, that you *are* liable for acts committed by an independent contractor if you authorise them (perhaps indirectly) or order the contractor to do dangerous work. Also, many ambiguities surround the situations where:

- employees are using their own equipment or other property while pursuing the firm's business
- a worker commits a crime that benefits the firm
- an employee is mixing his or her own business with that of the employing organisation
- employees take unauthorised action to protect the employer's interests (attacking would-be thieves, for instance) but commit offences while so doing, e.g., by causing physical damage to other people or their property.

Summary

A good employee is possibly the most valuable asset a small firm can possess; a bad one could ruin the enterprise. You need therefore to take great care when recruiting and managing workers; never discriminate unfairly, and always pay your staff in full and on time. Recognise that an employee might not be as committed to the business as yourself, but that he or she could still be a first-class worker. Generally, however, employees of small firms are better motivated than workers in large organisations because of the wide range of duties they are typically called on to perform and their close relationship with their bosses.

Occasionally, owners of small businesses mistakenly hire workers who are lazy or incompetent. No small firm can survive in the long term if it employs indolent staff. If you find yourself in this position you must grasp the nettle and confront the offending worker, taking care not to violate current legislation on redundancy and dismissal.

Firms experiencing severe financial difficulties might need to consider making people redundant. Certain procedures must be followed when implementing redundancies: you must not discriminate unfairly when selecting the workers who are to go, and redundancy payments must be given to workers with more than two years' continuous service. And before declaring someone redundant you are legally obliged to seek alternative work for that person.

Nowadays you cannot sack workers simply because you do not like them – *substantial* reasons are necessary to support a fair dismissal. Normally, the burden of proving that a sacked worker was grossly incompetent, or misbehaved so badly that dismissal was justified, will fall on you.

Dismissal of workers should always be avoided. Try instead to motivate them through job design, delegation of interesting work and performance-related incentives.

There is today much legislation concerning the rights of employees, especially in the fields of pregnancy and maternity, working conditions and the health and safety of people at work. As the owner of a small business you need to be familiar with this legislation, at least in outline.

6

Checklist

---

1. How willing are your employees to undertake any job you give them rather than just the duties outlined in their formal (or informal) job specifications?
2. Have you consciously tried to vary the range of tasks undertaken by your workers in order to make their jobs more interesting?
3. Are your employees actually doing the types of work you originally hired them to do, and if not why not?
4. What proportion of a typical working day does each of your employees spend on unproductive activities?
5. Have you ever asked an employee to undertake tasks that you really ought not to expect of them (doing your shopping, for instance)?
6. How much training has your workforce received during the last three months?
7. How often do you delegate interesting managerial duties to your employees?
8. Do you understand the procedures you must follow before dismissing a worker?
9. How much did it cost to recruit the last worker you employed?
10. When you interview job applicants, do you prepare a checklist of points to raise during the interview?
11. Have you ever hired a worker who turned out to be totally unlike the person you expected following his or her recruitment interview? How do you explain the difference?
12. What are the three most interesting jobs undertaken by your employees, and which are the three most boring?
13. Can you honestly say you have done everything humanly possible to ensure the health and safety at work of your employees?

---

7 Computerise or perish?

Choosing a system □ What word-processing is □ What data bases do □ Spreadsheets □ Stock control □ Accounts packages □ Do-it-yourself systems analysis □ Hardware and software □ System maintenance □ The Data Protection Act 1984 □ Summary □ Checklist

With complete business computer systems available for less than £1,000, computerisation is now a practical proposition for even the smallest business. The general acceptance of the IBM standard and other cheaper computer systems conforming to it have brought this about. But, before taking the plunge, read through this chapter and decide which of your current business systems could be computerised. If your current manual systems are in a mess then forget the idea of buying a computer for the time being. Get yourself straight by applying the 'organisation and methods' procedures suggested in Chapter 4 to your existing business systems. Having done this you may find you can manage perfectly well without a computer! If you do decide to look further into the benefits of computerisation, realise that little technical knowledge of computer technology is required on your part, but you do need to *know your own systems* to ask the right questions of computer salespeople and the like. My advice is to begin your involvement with computers with a *simple, easy-to-use* (and inexpensive) system. You should realise that the benefits of computerisation are by and large intangible – efficiency should improve with time and capacity for expansion will be enhanced – but do not fall into the trap of budgeting overheads savings against the installation of computer equipment.

Systems can be purchased outright, leased or rented. Having made the decision to acquire the asset, payment could be spread over several years by leasing the equipment. This may also offer benefits in that more efficient maintenance service might be available.

Choosing a system

Some consultants advise small firms to buy relatively powerful machines at the outset in order to ensure the availability of lots of space, flexibility and the capacity to handle larger and more complex programs as the business expands. A system that is perfectly adequate for, say, a payroll program may be hopelessly inadequate for more substantial tasks.

I take the opposite view. I believe you first need to master a small and simple system, hence gaining skill, experience and self-confidence as you proceed. In consequence, you will know what you are talking about when you do come to upgrade, and will be competent to put together an expensive configuration appropriate to your newly discovered needs. And if you buy a costly and sophisticated system in the beginning there exists the danger of being misled by an unscrupulous computer salesperson who persuades you to purchase an inappropriate system which you will never fully understand, which has mismatches between printers and keyboards that require specialist programming skills to untangle, and which saves you hardly any money in the longer term. Indeed, it might cost you more since existing manual procedures and the badly-functioning computerised system may have to operate in parallel until problems are sorted out.

Start with a simple machine

Too often, businesses purchase as their first computer a machine that is far too powerful and complex for their objective needs. Then the owner finds he or she cannot understand the instructions attached to the system and the machine thus lies idle in a storeroom, costing not only the price of its acquisition but also the forfeited efficiency improvements that it could, but does not, provide. And the lost benefits: speed, cost, savings, accuracy, reliability, huge data storage and manipulative abilities, are enormous. Of course, you must consider possible future increases in the demands you are likely to make on the system, but you really should tread carefully in the early stages. Buy a cheap, uncomplicated, well-established model and get to know it intimately. As you acquire experience you will rapidly lose your fear of computers and thus become competent eventually to select and operate a more sophisticated machine if you require it. The simple machine can still be used for routine word-processing, invoicing or some other straightforward application.

In the rest of this chapter I explain some elementary business computing applications, assuming you have no previous knowledge or experience of computers or associated jargon. After reading this material you should be able to understand the instruction books that accompany a basic desktop machine and standard commercial programs. Let's begin with the most elementary of applications: word-processing.

What word-processing is

Word-processing replaces conventional typewriting in businesses that have a computer and a printer. The system consists of the computer, a visual display unit, a QWERTY keyboard (set out in the same way as a conventional typewriter) and a program carried on a 'floppy disk'. After switching on the power you slot the floppy disk into your 'disk drive', and the instructions for operating the program then appear on the screen. The computer has its own memory which then takes over the program you have fed in, so that you can now remove the floppy disk containing the program and replace it with a blank 'data disk' on which you store newly created documents. You then type your documents (letters, invoices, etc.) and print them out. Your work appears on the screen of the VDU as you type. If you make a keyboarding error you just press a button to delete the mistake and type new letters or words as required.

Advantages of word-processing

The other great advantage of word processing over old-fashioned typing is that you can store standard documents, paragraphs, phrases and layouts, and insert them in any new document you create. And you can add or delete material at will. Thus, if you need to send a similar letter to several customers you need not type a completely new document for each address, you simply alter the details on the first letter you keyboarded and print the result.

Mail merge

Word-processing programs include a 'mail merge' facility which enables an identical letter to be dispatched to any number of recipients, with the recipient's own name and address being printed on each letter sent. Similarly, using a word-processor avoids having to retype standard paragraphs, contract details, price lists, product descriptions, etc., since all these may be permanently stored on your disk and then employed repeatedly. Programs differ in their speed of operation and in the variety of fonts and type sizes available. The more fonts and type sizes the program contains the more attractive the page layouts and document headings that can be created.

Once you are familiar with word-processing you will become accustomed to its benefits – its speed, ease of editing, high quality output and low document cost – as a matter of course and start to feel frustrated when confronted with the inefficiency of non-computerised operations (record keeping in conventional filing systems, for instance). You are now ready to acquire a 'data-base' program to carry your business's records.

What data bases do

Data-base programs store, manipulate and retrieve information. They sort data into various categories, select and display items according to one or more criteria, perform mathematical operations on numerical data, cross-tabulate, and print out the resulting information in some chosen form (lists, bar charts or pie diagrams, various report formats or graphs). The simplest data bases hold at least 75,000 items, so capacity is not usually a limiting factor in program choice (and you can always put additional records onto another data-base program if you run out of space). Rather, the functions the data base will perform determine the cost, complexity of operation and hence the usefulness of a particular package.

Records and files

Information on, say, all a firm's customers can be put into a customer 'file'. Similar files can be created around other aspects of the business. The data base itself is the aggregate of these files. A 'record' is a self-contained set of information within a file. Suppose, for example, that the firm has a file of names and addresses of customers, then each name and address constitutes a separate record. The records themselves are made up of 'fields'. Thus, in a name and address, the name is one field and the postcode another. Fields must be defined carefully because they are used to identify particular records. If, for instance, there is a separate field for the town in each address then the computer will be able to extract all addresses within any specified town.

Relational facilities

The most expensive data bases have a 'relational' facility whereby one file is related to another. For example, customers' names and addresses could be related to how much each customer purchased from the firm during the previous year, or a file for salespeople's orders could be related to a file for the expenses they claim. A 'search' of a data base is undertaken across one or more fields, such as, 'All customers in London with names beginning with the letter A and who spent more than £200 with the firm last year'. The cheaper the program, the fewer fields can be examined at any one time.

Organisation of data

There are two ways in which a data base can organise information: 'dimensionally' or 'hierarchically'. With a hierarchical mode of data organisation, items are first listed according to one criterion and then searched for any which possess a second characteristic, then for any exhibiting a third, and so on. Dimensional systems, conversely, enable the user to go directly and immediately to all the items required. The relevant criteria are specified simultaneously and the items satisfying these criteria are instantly identified. Consider, for example, a stock control system in a garage which repairs and services several different types of car. A hierarchical data base might identify stock *first* by assembly type (bodywork, electrics, brake system, etc.), then by sub-assembly (doors, lighting, ignition, and so on), then by particular make of vehicle, and finally by specific component. Use of a dimensional system avoids this tedious information gathering procedure. You simply ask for the location and stock position of a certain part of a certain function of a certain kind of vehicle, and the answer appears within a few seconds, (or perhaps longer if a complex problem is involved).

Spreadsheets

Increasingly, data-base information is inputted from 'spreadsheets'. A spreadsheet is simply a grid, containing data and formulae, which processes data. It performs tedious and repetitive functions that are so extensive that they would take enormous amounts of time to complete using manual methods, even with calculators. The common analogy is to compare spreadsheets with accounting ledgers, except that the spreadsheet does all the addition and subtraction, juxtaposition of entries, etc., instantly and automatically. Spreadsheets can be used, moreover, for nearly all other management information applications. The concept of this management-devised, standardised, specially lined paper was to assist inexperienced clerks who prepared accounting statements, but the hard arithmetic then had to be done by hand. Following the arrival of personal computers it soon became possible to purchase electronic spreadsheets which not only organised data in predetermined ways, but which did the arithmetic as well.

Advantages of electronic spreadsheets

A computer-based spreadsheet comprises a matrix of cells (entries) located by horizontal and vertical grid references. Data can be moved around and arithmetically manipulated. Sub-totals can be extracted at will. A particularly useful attribute of the modern electronic spreadsheet is its ability to complete 'what if' projections at the touch of a button, i.e., users can change their assumptions about various factors and observe the effects.

'What-if' questions

For example, if a spreadsheet has been programmed to calculate the manufacturing cost of a certain item, the question 'What if labour costs increase by five per cent and the cost of raw material falls by two per cent?' can be asked and answered instantly, since the computer will automatically recalculate all the relevant figures. Output from spreadsheets can often be used as input to files in other programs, and information may be presented graphically, as well as in other lists and tables and pre-formed reports. Spreadsheets are today widely used in industry and commerce: for accounting, statistical analyses, financial modelling, cash flow forecasting and business planning generally.

Stock control

Next you might acquire a stock control package which enables you to code and quickly locate the various items in your inventory, monitor stock levels, and print out stock reports whenever required. Moreover, the program will advise you when to re-order stock and how much to re-order at each replenishment, depending on such variables as average weekly stock usage and the average costs of stock holding and acquisition. The aim of stock control is to minimise the amount of working capital you tie up in stock, while avoiding stock-outs that prevent you satisfying customers' orders.

There are no easy ways of determining how much stock you should seek to hold and how frequently you should reorder – sudden and unanticipated increases in demand can disrupt the best of intentions. And the problem is compounded if your products are perishable, or there are significant seasonal variations in demand. However, it is possible to establish broad guidelines based on past experience, and the program will do this computation on your behalf.

Most stock control programs contain an invoicing facility whereby withdrawals of finished goods from stock for despatch to customers automatically trigger the printing of the invoices associated with those goods. Stock valuation reports are available on demand.

Inventories might be valued at their cost to you or at current purchase prices, or according to some other specified criterion. The records fed into the package will include fields for:

- a brief description of the item
- acquisition cost
- location and quantity in stock
- selling price
- re-order level, quantity on order and average delivery period.

If the stock file is linked to a file containing suppliers' names and addresses, supply prices and delivery details, etc., you can arrange for re-order documents (e.g., order forms or requests for quotations) to be printed automatically whenever some pre-specified minimum stock level is reached.

Accounts packages

Many small businesses begin computerising their accounts when they start employing people and hence must begin calculating workers' National Insurance contributions and PAYE. This can be tedious (especially if you are not particularly good at figures), yet the computations have to be 100 per cent correct.

All standard payroll packages will deal with:

- overtime
- bonus payments
- statutory sick pay
- Class 1 and Class 3 National Insurance
- tax.

A package will be pre-programmed to do all the calculations once you tell it each employee's tax code, provided it knows current tax rates and threshold levels (which you have to feed in annually following the budget).

The payroll program might be a sub-unit of a general accounts package with separate files for various aspects of the firm's work (sales, purchases, creditors, expenses, etc.). Entries in the accounts can be sub-divided by cost centre (departments, for instance) and, in more expensive systems, entries in certain accounts can be linked to events elsewhere, e.g., when an entry in the sales ledger simultaneously updates the stock control file and prints an invoice with details of the sale and the customer's name and address.

Advantages of computerised accounts

Advantages of computerised accounts include:

- faster invoicing
- tighter credit control (information on outstanding accounts is available instantly)
- more frequent analysis of cash balances, debtors' records and current liabilities, leading to better use of working capital.

Profit and loss accounts and balance sheets are automatically constructed from the files for the various classes of transaction and printed out on demand.

Differences between packages (and their cost) relate not only to the volume of transactions they can handle but also to their adaptability regarding accounting periods, credit periods, payment terms and other variable factors. The range and quality of outputs from accounts packages may also differ; cheaper versions provide simple summary statistics, more expensive programs offer bar charts, pie diagrams, trend graphs and so on.

As businesses differ, so too should the accounts system of each business. Thus, flexible packages that can be customised to meet the particular requirements of each firm are seemingly the best. Typically, however, the more versatile the package the greater its complexity, and there is no point in spending a lot of money on a sophisticated package if you are inexperienced in software use; so go for a cheap and cheerful, well-established and user friendly system as your first buy.

Other benefits

In a limited sense, an accounts package provides its own restricted data-base system. Sales ledgers, for example, offer information on customers' names and locations, on the value of sales, discounts given, cash receipts, credit balances, plus other data. Reports may be commissioned on the basis of any one (or perhaps more) of these criteria, and similar exercises may be performed on any of the other ledgers.

Do-it-yourself systems analysis

A system consists of computer 'hardware' (the machine, disk drive, keyboard and printer) and 'software' (i.e., the packages you use) plus a set of procedures for completing jobs. A payroll system, for example, has procedures which convert pay rates, overtime records, PAYE and National Insurance contributions into pay slips and direct debits into employees' bank accounts. The costs of computer hardware and software have fallen so dramatically in recent years that it is frequently financially advantageous for a small business to develop its internal administrative routines for stocktaking, invoicing, record keeping etc., around the facilities available through using cheap standard software packages.

First, specify the information you require from each of the activities (marketing, production, etc.) your firm undertakes, and then state the formats (lists, reports, data summaries, customer account profiles, charts and graphs, summary statistics) you believe will be most useful for meeting these information needs. For example, you may want your stock control system:

(a) to inform you whenever the inventory of a certain product reaches a predetermined minimum level;

(b) to compute warehousing and acquisition costs;

(c) to generate lists of suppliers' names and addresses with details of their current prices, delivery periods and so on.

In effect you have undertaken a systems analysis which you can now take along to local hardware and software showrooms in order to search for the machine and/or packages that best satisfy your particular requirements. If no simple and inexpensive systems are available to meet your specific needs, then re-examine the outputs you initially specified and see whether you can amend them to fit in with the standard packages that are available. Often, it is possible to specify compromise outputs that satisfy most, if not all, of your demands.

Having chosen a system you will now determine the input data you will need to collect, how it must be stored and manipulated, and the clerical and administrative routines involved. For instance, your stock control system has to be fed with facts on stock issues, receipts of supplies, requisitions, current supply prices, resale values, etc. You have to organise your business in such a way that these input requirements are quickly and easily met.

Hardware and software

The more complex and extensive the duties which the system must perform the greater the space necessary within the computer's memory. This is divided into 'read only memory' (ROM) containing permanent stored instructions read by the computer's central processor, and 'random access memory' (RAM), wherein stored data may be added to, deleted from and generally manipulated (RAM contents are lost whenever the computer is switched off). Each generation of microcomputer contains far more memory than its predecessor, while the efficiency of software packages (measured by the amount of memory they occupy while operating) continues to improve. In consequence, there are now few business functions for which software exists which *cannot* be run on a cheap system. Space no longer represents a major constraint.

Selecting business software

Increasingly, hardware is less crucial to the choice of system than the availability of ready made or easily converted business software packages. Such packages are regularly reviewed in computer magazines and in your own trade journal. These reviews are well worth reading before you invest in a particular package. They report whether the program is 'user friendly', how much training (if any) is required prior to its use, the quality of the instructions, the range of its facilities, special features and any problems or drawbacks associated with its operation.

In choosing a package for a certain application, you should examine the following factors:

(a) The program's ability to handle the volume of data entries (e.g., the number of customers' names and addresses that need to be held on file) expected to be necessary in the new system.

(b) Speed of operation. How long the program takes to load and operate.

(c) Quality of output, especially if the output is in the form of written documents that will be seen by outsiders.

(d) Ease of use. Ideally, a program should be capable of operation by an inexperienced person. Increasingly, standard programs are menu driven: instructions appear on the user's VDU immediately the program is loaded and the user merely selects various options from menus of alternatives that periodically show on the screen. Unfortunately, some of the instruction books that accompany packages are so badly drafted that even the loading of a program can be difficult for the untrained user.

(e) Flexibility. Good packages allow the user to modify, via menus, the basic structures of their operations and output. Note, however, that a package purchased to run on one system (IBM compatible, for example) will not normally run on another – a different version of the same package will be required.

(f) Availability of support services from the program manufacturer. Many software suppliers offer free advice (over the telephone) on how to use their programs, including the correction of errors found in the program itself. The facility is normally available for three or six months from the date of purchase, on payment of a supplementary fee.

Another relevant variable might be whether the package is new or well-established. A new program may be technically superior to its antecedents, yet contain numerous minor errors and logical inconsistencies that will only be ironed out over time. Experienced computer users can usually identify and handle such errors, but novices might be completely bamboozled by such mistakes.

System maintenance

You really *must* take out a supplementary maintenance contract (for which you pay extra) when you purchase or lease a system. These contracts ensure that if the equipment breaks down a service engineer will immediately visit your premises and attend to the problem. Ignore the temptation not to bother with this during the first year of use while the equipment is under guarantee: a breakdown necessitates returning the machine to the shop where it was bought, which in turn sends the machine to the manufacturer for repair – a process that takes several weeks, during which your business is without a computer! And the firm may by now have become totally dependent on computerised administrative systems, so that the machine's absence causes chaos throughout the organisation.

Maintenance contracts typically cost ten to 15 per cent of the purchase price of equipment, but are certainly worth having. Instant attention is guaranteed and temporary replacement equipment is provided if the breakdown cannot be repaired immediately.

Software maintenance

Certain types of software might also be covered by maintenance agreements. Payroll packages, for instance, operate on the basis of particular tax rates, tax liability thresholds, National Insurance rates, etc., which change annually (at least). Sometimes the program manufacturer will, on payment of a small fee, exchange your existing package for an updated version incorporating these amendments: you simply send the disk containing the program to the manufacturer, who dispatches a replacement by return post. Also, software maintenance contracts may offer a certain amount of person to person telephone advice on how to operate particular programs.

Care of equipment

Care for your equipment, and it will care for you. In particular:

- operate your system in a dust-free environment, and use dust covers for protection when equipment is not in use for long periods
- handle disks carefully, always store them in plastic cases and boxes; do not touch their surfaces, bend them, sit on them or use them as table mats
- do not eat or drink anywhere near the equipment: a cup of tea spilt over a keyboard or, even worse, the central part of the computer, can ruin a system
- copy your disks regularly (at least once a day) and store the copied disks securely – otherwise a power-cut may occur or someone may inadvertently pull the plug on you! You will then lose your day's work!

Efficient use of a computer system requires a certain amount of self-discipline. The best way to acquire this is to adopt tidy and sensible computing habits from the very beginning of your involvement with computers, so set out a disciplined operating regime, including:

- frequently copying disks
- printing out key documents
- labelling and indexing files
- placing disks into protective boxes (and keeping these boxes well away from direct sunlight, food and drink, and magnetic fields associated with certain electronic equipment)
- regularly cleaning your units

and stick to these rules rigidly.

The Data Protection Act 1984

This Act (which came into force in November 1987) requires computer users who store 'personal' data to register with the Data Protection Registrar. The fee is £30 for three years; registration forms and further information are available from the Post Office.

When you register you must declare what information you hold on people, its sources, its uses and purpose and to whom you provide information taken from your system. Data subjects (i.e., the individuals about whom data is held) are legally entitled, on payment of a £10 fee, to demand a copy of any data held on them and this must be provided within 40 days of a written request. However, you can refuse to disclose information if:

(a) the £10 request fee has not been paid;

(b) the data subject has not provided sufficient details for you to trace his or her records;

(c) requests are made too frequently by the same individual (bearing in mind the nature of the data) or if the requests are frivolous or vexatious in nature;

(d) you cannot relay the information without disclosing further information that relates to another person who has not given his or her permission for its disclosure.

If your computer records contain information that can be linked to a specific living individual then you must register your use of that data. Thus, file copies of word-processed letters containing the addressee's name and address, or a list of customers with the products they have purchased in the past, or personnel records on staff, must be declared.

There are certain exclusions in the Act. Computers that are used only for personal, family or household affairs are exempt, as are:

- mailing lists of names and addresses, provided no supplementary information is included (past customer purchases for example)
- company payrolls, as long as there is no intention to make the information available to other people and provided the only information listed is the name, address, date and amount of payment in respect of each employee
- information on employee pensions
- data held for national security purposes.

Only data held on 'automatically' processed systems is covered by the Act, so that manually operated systems (card indexes, for example) are not affected. 'Personal' information is defined as data relating to living people who 'can be identified from the information'. A sole trader is classified as a living 'person', but a limited company is not.

Failure to register leaves you open to prosecution. And registration itself is not automatic; it can be refused if the authorities consider that your reasons for wanting to hold the data are improper. Moreover, you are expected to observe eight internationally agreed principles on data protection, namely that the data be:

1. obtained lawfully;
2. used only for the purpose for which it is registered;
3. disclosed only as specified at the time of registration;
4. relevant to the purpose for which it is intended;
5. accurate and up to date;
6. available to data subjects on request;
7. removed from files when it has served its purpose;
8. adequately protected against loss or disclosure.

Note that if you pass computerised records to other organisations you are *not* obliged to inform the individuals detailed in the data transferred. Subjects can demand erasure or correction of information they know to be wrong, and are entitled to compensation if they suffer damage from inaccurate or inadequately protected data.

A data subject who feels unfairly treated may complain to the Data Protection Registrar who, following investigation, can issue to a data user an 'enforcement notice' demanding compliance with the provisions of the Act, or a 'deregistration notice' preventing the user from continuing to process personal data using an automatic system.

Summary

Business computers today are so inexpensive that it is worthwhile for every small business to investigate what they can offer. Software for desktop business computers is increasingly user friendly, and, if you have not done so already, you should make the effort to acquaint yourself with computer technology and hence be in a position to be aware of all the benefits that the computerisation of business procedures can provide.

Choose a cheap and cheerful machine for your first purchase. You can acquire more sophisticated systems later (buying a computer more powerful than you need may turn out to be a costly mistake). Consider the benefits of leasing equipment rather than purchasing outright.

Conventional typewriters are redundant in today's business world. Not only is word-processing cheaper, faster and more convenient, but also it allows you to design your own letterheads, to create a bank of standard letters, paragraphs, contract clauses, etc., and to update price lists and other essential documents effortlessly and whenever required.

Once you have experienced word-processing and all the advantages it offers you will want to experiment with other computer applications. Start with a database, moving on to packages for stock control, payroll and accounts, and then perhaps a spreadsheet system.

7

Checklist

---

1. What efforts have you made to learn about business computer applications during the last year?
2. What proportion of your existing administrative routines is undertaken using a computer or word-processor? What proportion *could* be undertaken in this way?
3. Does your leading competitor operate computerised accounts?
4. How often do you unexpectedly run out of stock?
5. Do you read reviews of new software packages in the trade press?
6. Do you feel competent to discuss your business's hardware and software needs with a local supplier? If not, re-read the chapter.

---

8   Selling your output

A new marketing strategy □ Positioning the product □
Targeting the customer □ Selecting a price □ Selecting
promotional methods □ Choosing products □ Product choice
and business strategy □ Branding your output □ The image
of your business □ Public relations □ Selling face-to-face □
Research □ Summary □ Checklist

Long-term survival requires regular reassessment of marketing
methods and the incessant search for new markets and additional
ways of attracting custom. This chapter discusses the process of
marketing in general, leaving the specific techniques of low budget
advertising and sales promotion until Chapter 9, where they are dealt
with in depth.

   When you started the business you perhaps assumed that, provided you offered a first-class product at a reasonable price, customers would fall over themselves to purchase your goods. While it
is true that excellent and competitively priced output does help to sell
itself, far more is required to achieve for your product the maximum
volume of sales.

What is marketing?

Marketing is not the same as 'selling', although obviously an
increased level of profitable sales is always the ultimate aim. Rather,
'marketing' is a whole range of activities:

- advertising
- packaging
- salespersonship
- public relations, sales promotions
- providing after sales service
- deciding on prices
- planning and introducing new products

all of which complement each other and, hopefully, contribute to
expanding your market share.

   Try not to think of marketing as simply the process of finding
customers for products or services you have *already* decided to

supply. The output your firm produces may be of high quality, but it might not be output that consumers wish to buy!

Questions you need to ask

- Who is likely to purchase the product, and why?
- What features does your output possess which are not available in competing products?
- Where are potential customers located and how best can you get through to them?
- What product attributes are most *needed* by consumers, to what extent and how does your output fulfil these needs, and how high a price is the typical customer willing to pay?

Answer these questions frankly and comprehensively (resources permitting) and then gear your marketing efforts to supplying those products which best satisfy consumer needs.

Particular attention will have to be devoted to certain aspects of marketing, depending on the nature of your firm. If, for example, you produce a consumer good sold by retailers then you may need to concentrate on:

- packaging
- display and sales promotion
- maintenance of favourable price differentials
- devices for bringing the product to retailers' (as well as final consumers') attention.

If, conversely, you sell an industrial good through the trade you might be better off focusing on trade advertising, on transport arrangements, after-sales service, image building or some other marketing activity especially relevant to your specific line of work.

A new marketing strategy

It is essential that all links in the chain – from production of output to its final sale – operate efficiently and interrelate. Recognise, for instance, that advertising unsupported by a well-packaged product and an adequate distribution system is bound eventually to fail. Dispatch and transport arrangements should guarantee that goods are available to consumers on time, where and when required. At the far end of the chain, after-sales service, where appropriate, should encourage repeat orders and generate recommendations to purchase your product to third parties.

The five major steps in formulating a marketing strategy in a small business are as follows.

1 Positioning the product

This means:

(a) deciding how you want the customer to think of your product, e.g., as high-class top-end of the market (and expensive) output, or as a 'cheap and cheerful' good offering excellent value for money at a low price, and

(b) taking appropriate measures to influence consumers' perceptions of the good.

The decision has many implications: for product price, quality levels, selling methods, choice of distribution channel, promotional strategies and so on. In making the decision, carefully examine the state of market demand and how this might evolve. From which sources do you expect most new business to develop, and why? How easily can you create a 'brand image' (see below) that fits in with a top, middle or bottom end of the market position? Other relevant considerations include:

- production costs (and hence feasible selling prices)
- the extent and quality of competition in various market segments
- specific features of the product, its selling points and to which types of consumer these are likely to appeal.

2 Targeting the customer

What *type* of person is most likely to buy your firm's output? Specify the target consumer's age, sex, income, social class, family size and situation, social habits and geographical location. Other 'market segmentation' variables that could be relevant include religion, marital status, political orientation and nationality, plus any other criterion you feel might be important for marketing the product.

Gear your products and their presentation to the particular needs of various target segments. This might involve changing product names in order to enhance their appeal to certain consumer types, or altering colours, order sizes, packages, specifications, or perhaps even the product price.

Efficient market segmentation is essential for small businesses. You must identify the sub-groups that constitute the total market for your output and then vary the features of your product(s) in order to make them attractive to the most lucrative market segments. Note that different advertising media and messages will normally be appropriate for each part of the market.

Analysing segments

Aim to distinguish specific consumer groups (e.g. high income middle-aged women with no children living at home, who work in offices, have received a certain level of education, and who cook using electricity) within which potential customers are as homogenous as possible and then devise advertisements and sales promotions (see Chapter 9), and select styles, prices, package designs, quantities and quality levels particularly suitable for those markets.

Frequently, it is more profitable to supply a large share of each of a small number of niches in a big market than to spend lots of money gaining just a small share of the wider market. Accurate segmentation enables you to pinpoint selling opportunities and to tailor your marketing activities to satisfy consumer demand.

Consumer lifestyles

Once you have identified a possible market segment in terms of the previously mentioned variables, write out a brief account of the typical lifestyle of a member of that particular group. Imagine you are that person and ask yourself the following questions:

- What does he or she do on a typical day from rising in the morning to going to bed at night?
- What are this individual's opinions and prejudices on various issues?
- To which kind of lifestyle does he or she aspire?

Answers to these questions help determine the forms of advertising and promotional messages most suitable for reaching target groups. Consumers often select goods that correspond to their perceptions of what they *should* purchase in order to follow chosen lifestyles (or lifestyles to which they aspire) rather than to satisfy an objective physical requirement. Identify the lifestyle involved and you can present your product(s) in appropriate ways.

3 Selecting a price

Pricing is difficult because it requires not only the estimation of the costs of supplying products (which itself is problematic in view of the numerous ways you can allocate overheads), but also requires that you consider the effects of the chosen price on the image of your output. If your product is similar to products already being sold then you will normally use the 'market price' already established for that product type to guide your pricing decision. Otherwise you have to consider consumers' perceptions of the quality of the product, its 'desirability', and how easily it satisfies their particular needs.

People sometimes judge the worth of an item by its price. They may assume that a very low price means shoddy output regardless of whether this is objectively true. And packaging can significantly affect the feasibilities of various pricing options: high priced goods in low grade cartons could destroy a product's credibility in consumers' eyes.

Expensive packaging can repay its initial costs several times. Consumers today demand packages that are aesthetically pleasing as well as functionally convenient. They want packages that:

- are easy to open, pour and reseal
- have adequate instructions
- are durable, disposable and so on.

If your output is currently sold loose or in the cheapest possible containers then consider seriously the potential price rise benefits (i.e., the ability to raise selling price) that an appealing package may provide (even for groceries, hardware products and other traditionally non-packaged items).

Skimming the market

If target consumers are affluent, innovative, well-informed and educated then consider adopting a high-price approach in order to 'skim the cream' off the top end of the market. Here you offer an expensive but high quality and well-presented item with 'all the trimmings'. Quality images are essential for this to work and there has to be a sufficient number of high income consumers ready to pay top prices.

However, you can earn big profits through this strategy provided supply costs are relatively low. Note, however, that other firms will be attracted to the top end of the market if you are too conspicuous in your success.

Penetrating new sectors

Alternatively, low 'penetration' prices might be best for your business. These involve aggressive advertising and sales promotions in conjunction with visibly low prices that aim to increase your firm's share of particular market segments. The strategy is suitable where bigger outputs enable you to reduce unit supply costs by bulk purchasing (at discount) of raw materials and other input supplies; through integration of processes; making the fullest possible use of machines and labour, etc.

Low price policies will not succeed, however, if your competitors drop their prices in line with yours, since then your market share remains constant even though your revenues are reduced because of the price cut. Also, the low price may cause customers to believe that you are selling inferior output.

Other methods for determining prices include the following:

(a) Setting a target level of profit for the coming year, estimating how much you can sell and then pricing output in order to achieve the stated profit objective.

(b) Charging high prices when introducing new products and systematically lowering them thereafter. Here you attempt to recover startup and development costs immediately following the launch of a new product, but recognise the need to lower the price as competitors emerge and in order to reach wider market segments.

(c) Selling certain items at less than their production or procurement costs to attract custom for other, higher priced products through which losses are recovered. (This practice is sometimes referred to as 'loss leading'.)

(d) Varying prices according to the state of trade. When order books are full you raise output prices, cutting them when spare capacity occurs. This can damage your business eventually, because customers frequently resent being charged different prices for the same goods at different times.

No outsider can definitively state what is the best price policy for your firm. This depends on circumstances, though in choosing much hinges on the product's unique selling points. Unless there is some particular reason to do so, consumers will not normally buy highly priced goods considered identical to competing products offered at lower prices. And the existence of selling points will substantially determine the responsiveness of consumer demand to changes in price. If sales increase by a large amount following a price cut then total income from sales will rise because the extra sales more than compensate for the lower unit price.

4 Selecting promotional methods

Whatever your line of business you need devices to attract attention to your products, your business, and to the fact that the firm is alive and well. Advertising is obviously important; so too are special promotions – coupons, competitions, distribution of free samples, premium offers (i.e., where you offer a larger quantity for the same price, or a free gift or cut-price item following the receipt of so many proofs of purchase), and so on. Such promotions (or gimmicks, if you prefer to call them that) can achieve several objectives; in particular they can:

- increase sales (via stimulation of impulse and repeat purchases)
- enhance consumers' knowledge and awareness of products
- gain retailers' goodwill and encourage them to display your firm's goods prominently
- help fight off competition.

Promotions should be 'genuine' in the sense that they represent value for money in consumers' minds; yet they must not be too costly to implement! They will not usually arrest declining sales of existing and 'tired' products that have been on the market for some time *unless* you simultaneously repackage, redesign and/or improve the product by adding new features or selling points in some way. Promotions, moreover, have only a temporary effect on sales; their effects are short lived and useful only for achieving immediate tactical goals. Yet they may be just what are needed to generate extra sales when you experience deficits in short-term cash flow.

Reasonable intervals must elapse between promotions, and they should reinforce and complement the more general advertising you undertake. Remember that promotions cost money: extra quantities, special price cuts, free samples and so on all have to be paid for, so budget carefully and plan your promotions well ahead. Good promotions are those which are:

- cheap and simple to administer, and
- do not involve your giving away too much.

You should test your promotions on a small scale before applying them market wide in order to assess responses and hence forecast aggregate net returns. So important are sales promotions to the small business that they are considered separately in Chapter 9 below.

5 Choosing products

Think of a 'product' as *anything* the business might be able to sell, not just as a physical object or service. A window cleaner, for example, can offer several products for sale, albeit using the same bucket and cleaning leather. There are window cleaners who specialise in high-rise buildings, those who will only do domestic households, some who give generous discounts for shop and office window cleaning work, and so on. Certain window cleaners provide ancillary services such as waste disposal, minor repairs, drainpipe and gutter clearing, etc., all of which provide unique selling points to the firm.

A window cleaner could operate under an evocative business name. A brief look at *Roget's Thesaurus* reveals the following words and phrases that might be included in the firm's title: wipe-clean, bright and shiny, spit and polish, spotless, stain-free, plus many others. Use of an eye-catching business name ('Bright 'n' Shiny', for example), together with the evocation of particular selling points, e.g., the provision of certain supplementary services and/or easy payment terms, creates a unique 'product' in consumers' eyes.

Product choice and development are crucially important for the overall strategy of your firm, and are thus worthy of further attention.

Product choice and business strategy

What business are you in? The answer to this seemingly banal question is not as obvious as it might appear. For example, is a window cleaner in: the glass washing business; hygiene; maintenance and repairs; the appearance enhancement business; or what? Or consider a building firm that can move into several alternative (and perhaps mutually exclusive) lines of activity: house repairs, roofing, shopfitting, new house building, maintenance of buildings, dry rot and timber treatment etc., each requiring somewhat different approaches to marketing, specific advertising media, differing raw materials input, employee skills, and so on. If you manufacture and/or sell stationery, are you in the paper business, or graphic design, or the written communications business? Suppose you repair mechanical products – do you restrict your activities to repairing metal and plastic objects, or do you start learning about electronics in order to be able to repair electrical and information technology-related products, (e.g., word processors or computer printers) as well?

The scope of your business

In answering these questions you determine the scope of your business, its orientation and its style. The stationer, for instance, might conclude that his or her firm is in the office communications business and is not concerned merely with the purchase, processing and resale of paper. In this case he or she will become interested in *all* aspects of office communications and related equipment – photocopying methods and systems, telephone equipment, E-mail (electronic mail), electronic diaries, relevant computer software, dictating machines – indeed anything to do with office communications. The product range of this firm will differ markedly from that of a stationer who simply designs letterheads and prints and sells various packaging materials and qualities of paper.

Selecting activities

To select your range of products and activities examine carefully the profitabilities of various market segments, their possibilities for further expansion and the ease with which new markets may be entered. Then list – honestly and comprehensively – your firm's particular strengths and weaknesses as they relate to these markets. Are you in fit shape to tackle the most lucrative of the available market opportunities, and if not, why not; and what must be done to remedy the situation? Basically, you have to choose between:

- concentrating on activities you know from experience you can do really well, or
- initiating new products in completely new areas.

This choice – which amounts in effect to your answering the question 'What business *should* you be in? – can be extremely difficult. On the one hand, if you opt to carry on with your current activities you implicitly assume that you will be able to continue to undertake existing lines of work without hindrance, interruptions in supplies, predatory actions by competitors, equipment failures, strikes among distributors, etc., and that unexpected technological innovations will not render your product, or means of creating it, technically obsolete.

Seeking out new and entirely different business opportunities, on the other hand, requires that profitable openings be available and that you possess the means for identifying their locations. Research is necessary, and you must constantly assume risk.

Answering the following questions might help you to take the correct decision:

- How fast is the pace of technical change in the industry in which you operate and how easily can you match your rivals in the technical field? Unexpected technical change can put you out of business, so consider carefully whether long-term investment in capital equipment in a rapidly changing high-tech industry is really worthwhile. Perhaps alternative, less technologically sensitive niches more suitable for a small business are available.
- How does your output differ from that of competitors, and what must you do to take full advantage of these differences?
- How safe is the firm's access to continuing supplies of the raw materials and other inputs needed to continue present activities?
- Is it possible to improve existing products; if not why not; and how would the introduction of a new competing product affect your firm?

Products, however selected, should be branded. And this applies to even the smallest of small firms (including the single-person, single-product business such as a window cleaner or self-employed motor mechanic working from home).

Branding your output

Branding means giving a particular trade name or logo to your product(s) and then seeking through advertising and other promotional methods to associate certain attractive characteristics with the branded goods. This enables customers to *recognise* your goods. And having once purchased one of your products and been satisfied by it the customer need not re-evaluate its worth prior to buying it again – he or she can choose a brand which is already known and trusted! For example people buy Tippex, not whitener or correction fluid, as the brand name has become synonymous with the product.

Having created a branded good your advertising and other promotions may then be directed towards establishing 'brand loyalty' via the reinforcement of existing favourable images. People will immediately identify the branded product: you need not provide fresh information about it in each and every advertisement.

Logos

Business logos are perhaps the commonest means of branding outputs. Either you can design your own logo or commission one from a local printer (most printers keep stocks of 'standard' logotypes which they adapt and cannibalise to meet specific customer needs). The logo might relate to your name or initials, or consist merely of a distinctive symbol unconnected with the business (a drawing of a certain species of bird or animal for example). Your logo should be shaped, lettered or coloured in a form that attracts attention and which projects a favourable image of the firm.

Importance of branding

8

Note that neglecting to brand your product(s) can mean that much of your advertising is wasted. Suppose, for instance, that you operate a one-person window cleaning service and decide to leaflet an area advertising your firm. If you head the leaflet with the words, 'Window Cleaning', or similar mundane title you might simply remind householders to use the services of other local window cleaners. In effect, you are advertising partly for the benefit of your competitors.

Rather, you must *particularise* your specific offer of service by itemising the product's selling points (low price, no-smear guarantees, money back if the customer is dissatisfied, special discounts for longer term contracts, etc.), and relating these to a clearly identifiable brand image embodied in an attractive and distinctive logo and other symbols of the firm.

Building-in a brand image

Successful branding normally requires that products retain their unique brand identity right up to the moment of sale. Hence, brand names and logos must be securely attached (preferably built in) to your output. Otherwise, mixing up or repackaging of products by distributors or retailers may render your goods indistinguishable from other brands – the final customer is denied the opportunity consciously to select your output. There are exceptions to this rule, however, for example where you supply goods knowing they will be sold under someone else's label or name. Thus, a shirt (or other garment) dealer typically purchases shirts from several different manufacturers but sells them all under the dealer's own name.

Own brands

Likewise, many supermarket chains have developed 'own brand' products, obtained from several sources, which sell in-store in direct competition with well-known manufacturers' brands (Sainsbury's own brand 'breakfast biscuits' versus Weetabix, for example). The supermarket's own brands sell at relatively low prices in order to attract price conscious consumers and generally generate traffic 'in-store'. Such arrangements might enable a small business to sell part of its output under its own name and the rest anonymously under another label.

It is important to note that the practice of own branding can cause a business to become liable under the Consumer Protection Act 1987 (see Chapter 10) for defects in the products to which the own brand is attached, and this fact might significantly reduce the benefits of own branding.

Family brands

Brand images encapsulate whole collections of product attributes and special features. Consumers come to know what the brand represents and may thus satisfy their requirements without careful thought or research. And they can avoid re-purchasing unsatisfactory branded items. If you sell several products you must choose whether to allocate separate brand names to individual products or establish a generic 'family' brand covering all your output.

Advantages of family brands

The latter approach can be highly cost-effective, especially if the various products are closely related through associated usage (toiletries, for example) or a common channel of distribution, a common customer group, or similarity of prices. This is because the entire product range may then be advertised jointly under a single brand name thus cutting the cost of advertising individual brands separately. Moreover, additions to product lines are introduced easily and inexpensively since no extra advertising or promotions need be incurred. The new product is simply incorporated into existing advertising literature – you do not have to establish a completely new individual brand image. Separate brands are essential, nevertheless, if you wish to appeal to different market segments or where products are markedly dissimilar.

Once a brand had been brought to customers' attention, selling costs diminish because:

(a) advertising attracts custom to your own brand rather than to that class of product generally;

(b) distributors and retailers are more willing to handle your goods on account of known demand for your particular branded output.

Branding contributes to the general image of your firm. Image building is an important aspect of marketing, worthy of separate attention.

The image of your business

We need to distinguish carefully between your business's *image* (i.e., the mental impression it projects to outsiders) and the 'identity' of the firm, which serves to create the image. A firm's *identity* is visually recognised through its:

- letterheads
- logo
- fascia of premises
- typography of leaflets
- price lists and brochures
- by the manner and dress of its owner and employees
- layout and style of reception area
- tone of receipt of telephone calls
- name display, etc.

These are the physical manifestations of the business which generate its *image* to the external world.

Outsiders base their image of the business on their awareness of its identity and on direct experience of the firm's activities and behaviour. Thus, you should always be concerned that the various aspects of your business identity (name, letterheads, etc.) are congruent and generate a favourable image of innovation, quality, dynamism, reliability, success, or other desirable attribute.

Your business name

Your business name is important because it contributes significantly to the general image your firm creates, and in particular to customers' perceptions of the quality of your products. It is no longer necessary to register a business name and provided:

(a) you do not imply you are connected with the government or a local authority;

(b) your business name does not include words prohibited by the Board of Trade (which publishes a pamphlet listing prohibited words); and

(c) you give your own name and address on all business documents;

then you can choose whatever business name you desire. If you trade under your family name or if the existing name of the business is dull and uninspiring, you should seriously consider how it could be altered. Thus, for example, 'Bright 'n' Shiny' sounds much better than 'R Bennett: Window Cleaner'; 'RHA Management Consultancy Limited' is a more impressive letterhead than the name and address of an individual person.

The persona of your firm

Like it or not, your business has several 'audiences' – customers, bank managers, suppliers, local authority trading standards officers, community neighbours, employees – who you need to impress and who will respond, albeit unconsciously, to the aura of the firm. The outward disposition your business projects will create thoughts about and feelings towards the firm that will encourage outsiders to behave positively or negatively when dealing with the business, without their necessarily being fully aware of why this is so.

Names and images

Certain words in a business name possess favourable connotations and imply high standards (reliability, honesty, integrity, sound after-sales service, etc.). Search your thesaurus for words that relate to the theme of your business. The conventional *Roget's Thesaurus* (which is based on ideas and concepts rather than listing words alphabetically) is better for these purposes than more recent varieties. Note too how positive images are sometimes best projected through motifs, logos and other *visual* means (multicoloured letterheads, for instance). People often intuitively understand the messages embodied in visual representation better than written words, so well designed and printed letterheads, leaflets and brochures are essential ingredients of the promotional mix.

Need for a professional approach

Visit local printers and inspect samples of their work. Printers are pleased to offer advice and to suggest logos and other designs suitable for your line of business. It is essential you realise that consumers today are immersed in professionally created advertising messages, and will hence assume that all firms – even small ones – will wish to project themselves as favourably as possible. Consumers (and others) may thus be extremely suspicious of a business that does not bother to display itself in attractive ways. To ignore external appearances is to invite people to perceive 'couldn't-care-less' attitudes, neglect, shabbiness and unreliability within the firm.

Try to see your business through the eyes of outsiders. Whether outsiders are objectively correct in their perceptions is neither here nor there – impressions, not objective reality, may substantially determine how external audiences behave towards your firm.

Selecting an image

Great care is needed when selecting an image because techniques for projecting one type of image might not be appropriate for projecting others, and once established an image may be extremely difficult to change. The first important decision is which of the firm's potential activities to emphasise and which to leave out, since the business name, letterheads and other promotional material cannot possibly refer to all potential market opportunities. For example, a small business whose target customers (householders) wish to replace some guttering or have other relatively minor repairs completed will be put off approaching this firm if it has created for itself an image of being concerned mostly with large scale house extensions or major shopfitting. A business that is technically excellent can fail through having the wrong image. Impressions of ability can be as important for winning orders as actual competence to produce and deliver goods.

Public relations

Public relations (PR) is about creating and maintaining feelings of goodwill towards the business among outsiders. The resources available for this within a small business are necessarily limited, although much useful PR can in fact be undertaken at low cost. The first and most obvious possibility is the news release which you write yourself (in not more than 150 words) for circulation to local newspapers, including the ever-increasing number of free local papers distributed door to door. Very many items in local papers, especially giveaway papers, originate in press releases issued by local firms. Suitable topics for a news release include:

- your grand reopening
- the launch of a new product or service
- a change of name (plus details of the new orientation of the business)
- a personal achievement
- your first major order
- unusual uses for the product
- a contribution to community affairs (e.g. job creation)
- a visit from a well-known personality.

Mundane news items do not appear in newspapers by accident; someone has taken the initiative to put them there. If you doubt the relevance of business news to local papers just look through next week's issues and count up how many brief items refer to local businesses or products! Most of these paragraphs will have begun as a press release.

Writing a press release

Even a minor modification to an existing product can be made 'newsworthy' by presenting it in certain ways. Thus, when announcing the modification you could describe:

- how it improves the goods or service you offer
- its low cost and instant availability
- how favourably it compares with other products (especially if safety is involved)
- what gave you the idea for the modification
- its usefulness to particular consumer groups
- discounts available, etc.

Always include details of where and how the product can be bought. Write a release in the style of the paper in which you want it to appear, and detail

- *What* is happening
- *Who* is involved
- *Where* and
- *When* an event is taking place, and
- *Why* the event is important.

You need an eye-catching headline which instantly identifies what the item is about, and body copy which *justifies* the newsworthiness of the story. The subject should be specified in the first few words. Put the most important information first (often, only the first couple of paragraphs of a press release is printed) and be careful not to make the release read like an ordinary advertisement. Avoid technical jargon and unusual abbreviations throughout.

Photographs – interesting, 'newsworthy' pictures – can cause editors to accept items they would otherwise reject. Illustrations must be sharp to allow printed reproductions, and send in large prints of photographs to give the editor the option of 'cropping' them as required. Offer captions to accompany each photograph. Find some samples in your local paper and use them as a guide.

Other low-cost PR activities

Here is a list of some other low-cost PR activities you can undertake.

(a) Arrange a reception to re-launch your business in a new format, and invite the desk editors of local newspapers, neighbouring businesses, major suppliers and leading customers to attend. Issue a press release to the journalists who turn up (and they will turn up if there is free food and wine) and get their telephone numbers for further PR work.

(b) Organise a display of your products/sales literature in the entrance to another business (to which you offer a fee) that services a lot of passing trading.

(c) Sponsor a local charity and ask it to issue a press release announcing your support.

(d) Make your premises available to local charities for their own press conferences and other media relations exercises (photo call sessions, for instance).

(e) Have some T-shirts printed with your business name and give these away or sell them at low cost to customers and visitors to the firm.

(f) If you live in a densely populated area containing non-English speaking ethnic minorities, contact the local ethnic language newspapers (possibly consisting of little more than broadsheets or monthly newsletters) which cater for those groups and invite the editors to do special features on your firm. Offer a special discount to readers of these newspapers on presentation of a coupon which was printed in the papers involved.

Selling face-to-face

Personal selling is dealt with definitively in Peter Allen's excellent book *Selling*, already published in this series, and you should read this for a comprehensive account of sales techniques. Here I merely outline some tips on how your personal selling competencies may be improved.

You do not need academic qualifications to be good at selling, but you must be able to see things from other people's points of view and to identify and understand their requirements. Effective sales people are those who are capable of *sensing* customers' perceptions of their needs and of convincing customers that a certain product will satisfy particular wants. A typical sale can be broken down into stages as follows.

Contacting the customer

Gather as much information about the prospective customer as you can before making contact. If the prospect is a firm, find out about its products, organisation, key personnel, future plans and prospects. In the case where customers are members of the public who visit your premises, acquaint yourself with the *type* of person that is likely to enter the showroom or other selling area, so that you can avoid making introductory remarks which might offend potential customers. The aim of the initial introduction is to establish a comfortable relationship with the prospect based on mutual agreement, avoiding dissent wherever possible. Thus, casual observations – about weather, transport, sport, etc., are generally preferable to contentious statements.

Interest arousal

Now engage the prospect in conversation. Seek to discover as much as you can about his or her special requirements. The customer will talk to you easily, provided you were able to establish an amicable relationship through your initial comments. Aim at this stage to increase the customer's awareness of the selling points of the product.

Product presentation

The next objective is to form in the customer's mind a distinct preference for your goods in comparison with competitors' products. Where appropriate, demonstrate the product or illustrate its use with photographs, sales literature and perhaps a glossy brochure. Systematically increase the amount of product information presented. Explain how various aspects of the product satisfy the customer's particular needs. List the attributes of the product: its performance characteristics, reliability, quality, aesthetic appeal, and so on. And describe how your firm will meet the consumer's requirements better than competitors – how you offer quick delivery, money-back guarantees, technical advice, after-sales service, special discounts, etc.

Dealing with objections

Inevitably, the customer will experience misgivings and will raise objections to your characterisation of the product. Treat objections as opportunities for exerting even more pressure on the customer (a frequently used rule of thumb is to answer each objection with three further benefits associated with the product). In order to have enough arguments ready for production at the appropriate moment, you must hold back some selling points during earlier stages. Often, the main objection is the high price of the goods. In response, aim to 'particularise' the item with respect to its *unique* features. Encourage the customer to think that this product has unique attributes not possessed by any other. A consumer who is convinced there is no comparable substitute for the product offered will not make mental comparisons of its price with the prices of competing items.

Closing the sale

Assume the customer has decided to buy, and phrase closing remarks accordingly. Questions such as 'Which colour do you want?' or

'When shall we deliver?' can prompt positive responses. If despite all your efforts the prospect still refuses to buy, be sure you leave on friendly terms – he or she might consider purchasing the product later.

Maintain detailed records on the numbers and values of sales achieved relative to the number of enquiries and contacts in various sales categories. Establish a reminder system for repeat follow-up calls and for recording the outcomes of calls. And analyse all your sales extremely carefully. Prepare a form for completion after every contact itemising:

- the source of the enquiry
- whether repeat or new business
- time spent with the customer
- whether a follow-up is likely to prove worthwhile
- method of approach (e.g., technical or personal emphasis, how familiar you were with the customer, any sales technique you consciously applied and the customer's response)
- value of order

plus any other details particularly relevant to your products and line of work. Did the prospects you initially thought most promising actually convert into sales? And if not, why not?

Analyse your effectiveness

Analyse the time you devote to face-to-face selling. How much time is spent in travelling and administration relative to time spent making a sale? Other matters worthy of investigation include:

- selling costs per sale and per customer
- the value of discounts necessary to attract custom in various market segments
- changes in the ratio of enquiries to sales.

The latter is worthy of detailed attention since if this can be reduced (say from five to one to four to one) the effect on sales is phenomenal.

Consider the feasibility of doing a telephone survey among those potential customers who enquired about your product(s) but who did not actually buy, in order to discover the reasons for their deciding not to purchase. The cost of this exercise might be recovered several times over in the longer term through the information it generates on your promotional/distribution inadequacies. And you might even pick up a few orders from the people included in the survey.

Lost customers

The loss of existing customers is especially disturbing, and each major loss should be analysed in depth. How easy was it for the customer to change its source of supply (you should always try to have customers 'locked in' to your products with long-term contracts and trade deals so that they gear their production or distribution systems to supplies of your goods), and why do you think the customers abandoned your business? Do not be afraid to ask customers for this information – you have nothing to lose.

What went wrong?

Where did you find the customer in the first instance? Can a replacement customer be obtained from the same source? Perhaps the customer is experiencing cash flow problems and is thus seeking a cheaper, albeit inferior, alternative to your product. Consider the feasibility of offering a special price in exchange for a long-term contract (though avoid giving credit) if this is so. Check to ensure that you provided the back-up, maintenance, and after-sales service you promised in the contract.

How profitable are your sales?

It is vital that you analyse sales according to their contributions to *profit* as well as to sales volume. Small value orders, for example, while perhaps contributing little to aggregate sales, might contribute a lot to total profits. Equally, very small orders might not be worth servicing. Either way you need to know the exact position.

The bulk of your profits might be derived from just a few orders. If so, ask *why* this situation exists and seek to apply the factors contributing to high mark-ups to the less profitable of your sales. Many considerations explain differences in unit profitability:

- selling costs
- packaging and delivery charges
- method of distribution (mail order versus personal sale, for example)
- cash or credit settlement
- discounts given on various order sizes
- administrative costs, etc.

The frequency of delivery of supplies appertaining to a large order, e.g., twice rather than three times a week, can make a big difference to its profitability.

Develop your skills

Work hard at your selling skills; there will always be new things for you to learn. Keep notes on your selling successes and failures, with statements of why you succeeded or failed in particular instances. Experiment with various styles of dress and modes of behaviour (relaxed, assertive, formal, familiar, etc.) until you find the one that works best for you. Enter selling situations in a positive frame of mind, determined to achieve a sale. Be friendly, sincere and respectful; make sure you are fully briefed and, unless there are special reasons why this should not be the case, acquire a comprehensive technical knowledge of the product(s) sold by your firm.

Telephone sales

Where appropriate, experiment with telephone sales. This is a useful way to follow up customer enquiries, and enormous amounts of time and travelling expenses are saved if it succeeds. Plan the telephone call carefully, specifying the objective you hope to achieve and the major points to be made during conversation. Some people find it useful to sit before a large mirror when making a telephone sales pitch. They consciously smile at themselves and use the mirror to observe their own emotions while speaking, especially emotions that could quickly transfer into negative voice intonation and which, therefore, must be avoided. Have all relevant information before you prior to the call; be brief, keep to the point, and if the prospect responds in a hostile manner simply apologise for having been a source of disturbance and ask if you can ring again at a more convenient time. Voice is obviously important for successful telephone selling. Through your voice you project impressions of enthusiasm, knowledgeability, integrity and the fact that you are sincere. Experiment with your voice; intonate, speak clearly, and more slowly than you would in other social situations.

Research

Marketing research is problematic even for the very large firm, let alone for the small business which does not possess the resources necessary for major investigations. Difficulties arise from environmental uncertainties and from the simple fact that human behaviour can and does change suddenly and unpredictably. Ideally, you should:

- test market new products before introducing them to the market as a whole
- assess the psychological impact of your business image and advertisements on consumers
- statistically forecast the effects of a price change on sales and revenues, and so on.

In reality, however, such aspirations are pie-in-the-sky as far as small firms are concerned: there is no way you can undertake sophisticated research on a strictly limited budget and you are forced to rely, ultimately, on your personal intuition and judgement. Nevertheless, some useful small-scale low-cost 'research' can be undertaken by a small firm, and the fundamental *principles* of marketing research are the same no matter what the size of the business.

8

The information you need to gather

Good research is as much to do with the spirit of enquiry as with particular investigative techniques, which are bound to be imprecise anyway. All firms need to ask the same questions when conducting market research, including the following.

(a) What sort of customer is likely to buy from the firm – business or personal, large or small, old or young, rich or poor?

(b) Where are customers located and how can they best be reached?

(c) What causes consumers to buy the firm's particular type of product?

(d) How extensive is the competition and what is its quality: how do competitors set their prices, advertise and generally market their products?

(e) How much are customers willing to pay for the firm's output?

(f) Is the market likely to expand, contract, or alter in character, and how does it react to new products and/or changes in price?

Several conventional market research techniques can be adapted for small businesses, particularly those outlined below.

Market surveys

As the owner of a small firm you have the advantage that you come into direct personal contact with customers and thus can ask them for their views on your products, how they are presented, about desired quality levels, customer reactions to product prices, after-sales service required (and how much customers are prepared to pay for this), etc.

Define your market

Avoid defining potential markets too broadly, since this might cause you to ignore the need for different marketing methods in various market segments. For example, local customers might be best serviced with retail outlets and/or a direct delivery network, whereas national customers could require an expensive mail order system.

You cannot afford to undertake much primary field research, so you must become adept at finding whether anyone else has already investigated certain markets. It may be, for instance, that local population surveys have been conducted showing the number of people in the business's catchment area, their income per head and age and sex distribution. Trade journals (which you should read avidly) might survey particular markets; local competitors may be quickly identified from *Yellow Pages*.

Multiplication of the number of potential customers (identified according to age, income, occupation, social status and so on) in the firm's catchment area by target sales per customer gives the financial value of the maximum market size. Divide this by the number of competitors plus one and the result can be used as the target market share for your next year of operation. Do not assume the firm's market share will exceed this, because substantial periods might elapse before customers become aware of your business's revival.

Observation

Observing a product in use can provide much information about its value to customers and the characteristics that need emphasis in marketing campaigns. You could, for example, personally follow an item of output from the moment it leaves the premises right up to and including its final use by a randomly selected customer. Hence, the adequacy and appeal of packaging, the clarity of instructions for assembly or use, operating difficulties, etc., can be witnessed first hand. If you supply to retail outlets then visit outlets and buy a unit of your product to see how well it is presented to customers.

Sampling

Small businesses cannot afford large-scale surveys of customers' tastes and responses to products. (Note, moreover, that doubling a sample size might improve its accuracy by only a few per cent). Normally the small business must rely instead on a small sample comprising truly representative respondents. Great care is needed in segmenting potential customers with respect to age, location, manner of dress, etc., before sampling begins.

Use of questionnaires

Valuable information can be obtained from simple questionnaires asking for customers' views on various aspects of your firm and its product. These can be handed to customers when they buy, or enclosed in invoices or other mailed business documents.

Postal questionnaires are cheap to distribute, and people who respond normally do so quickly. But response rates may be low, and replies are constrained by the wording of questions – respondents do not usually elaborate on their immediate responses. Keep your questions short, clear, simple, logical and capable of speedy (and cheap) clerical cross-tabulation of answers.

Telephone surveys

Some marketing research can be done by telephone. The method is cheap, convenient (no travelling is involved) and a wide geographical area can be covered. It is particularly suitable if you do not personally come into contact with customers. Problems will arise, however, if (i) you find it difficult to sound pleasant over the telephone, (ii) respondents are busy when the call is made and thus do not want to answer questions, and (iii) secretaries and/or switchboard operators rebuff your approaches.

Interviews with customers

Ask selected customers for views on your product and its presentation. Most customers are willing to be interviewed provided the exercise is short and simple. Also, the exercise will create in customers a sense of involvement with your firm.

Although face-to-face interviews can elicit answers to questions appearing on questionnaires or checklists, less structured approaches – whereby customers are encouraged to talk openly about the firm and its products – are also worth undertaking. In the latter case, open-ended rather than 'yes-no' questions should be asked, and you should not seek to direct the course of the interview.

Summary

Marketing is more than just 'selling', although higher levels of profitable sales are obviously the ultimate aim of all marketing pursuits. Simply providing a good product at a reasonable price is not sufficient to achieve the best possible sales.

You have to be an all-rounder where marketing is concerned. Evaluate market opportunities *before* you decide your selling strategies, relating your product's attributes to customer needs. Different aspects of marketing will need to be emphasised according to the particular circumstances of your firm.

Marketing activities must be integrated and consistent: there is no point spending lots of money on one marketing activity (advertising, for instance) if you do not have support facilities (a distribution system, attractive packaging, point of sale literature, etc.) to back it up.

There are five major steps involved in formulating a marketing strategy:

- product positioning
- market segmentation
- choosing a price
- selecting promotional methods
- deciding when to introduce new products and when to withdraw old ones.

The tactics associated with your marketing strategy should include policies for branding output, creating suitable business images, and for public relations as a whole.

Personal selling is an important marketing skill and you should constantly seek to improve your selling skills. Work on your sales techniques: experiment, improvise, and keep careful records of the effectiveness of various approaches to prospective customers.

Checklist

1. When did you last ask a customer what he or she thinks of your output without revealing that you are the owner of the firm?
2. List six reasons why a consumer should buy your output rather than that of your leading competitor?
3. Have you a system for identifying changes in consumers' needs?
4. When did you last devise an attractive new display of your goods?
5. Is your packaging sufficiently attractive?
6. If you operate at the top end of the market, could you develop an economy version of your product, and vice versa?
7. What brand images attach to your output?
8. Have you consciously attempted to segment your markets?
9. Can you describe the lifestyles of your last three customers?
10. How frequently do you vary your advertising messages to make them attractive to various market segments?
11. How many more units do you believe you could sell if you cut your prices by ten per cent?
12. Have you considered using a loss-leader, and what would be the implications of loss-leading for the total revenues of the firm?
13. When did you last consider using the following forms of sales promotion for your output:

    - coupons
    - free samples
    - a competition
    - free gifts?

14. List five attractive new names for your firm?
15. What are the average unit profitabilities of each of your products? To what extent are differences in unit profitabilities explained by price differences rather than differences in production cost?
16. Does your leading competitor operate in a market that you have not entered, and if so, how long would it take you to enter that market?
17. Does your firm possess a distinctive logo? If so, how recently did you consider altering it in order to enhance its appeal?
18. How do you think your last three customers recognised the 'corporate identity' of your firm?

8

19. How many items that are obviously based on business news releases appeared in last week's edition of your local giveaway newspaper?

20. Do you feel self-conscious when selling face to face? If you do, why is this?

21. How much did you know about the backgrounds of your last three customers prior to contacting them?

22. Have you prepared checklists for helping you develop a sales pitch?

23. What is the ratio of enquiries to customer orders for your products?

24. What caused your last three lost customers to withdraw their trade?

25. How closely do you monitor market trends, and how do you do this?

9 Advertising and sales promotions

Advertising □ Sales promotions □ Types of promotion □ Sales promotions versus discounts □ Trade deals □ Sales promotions law □ Display and merchandising □ Direct mail □ Summary □ Checklist

The importance of effective marketing for the growth and development of a small firm cannot be overemphasised. Advertising and sales promotions (special offers, discounts, coupon distributions, competitions and so on) are the cutting edges of marketing practice, and failure to take them seriously is one of the commonest causes of underperformance among small businesses. This chapter tells you how to draft advertisements and how to devise and organise inexpensive, but profitable, promotions. It explains the key elements of attractive display, and how to write your own sales literature.

9

Advertising

Small businesses usually cannot afford television or radio advertising and thus reply primarily on local newspaper advertisements, on entries in *Yellow Pages*, and direct mail leaflets distributed door to door. You can draft these yourself and need not employ expensive professional advisors. Every penny you spend on advertising should be made to work hard on your behalf, so great care is necessary in segmenting markets (see Chapter 8), targeting potential customers, and selecting appropriate messages. This section presents a do-it-yourself guide to writing copy for advertisements. Proceed as follows:

- List the desired *outcomes* to your advertising activities. Messages that succeed in creating awareness of your business and its products effectively might not be so good for inducing people to visit your premises or write to the firm. Other aims could be to generate enquiries, counteract competitors' advertisements, compile names and addresses for direct mail, etc.
- List and briefly describe the *selling points* of your product, e.g., low

cost, high efficiency, easy installation, availability of credit, a new flavour, a special offer, an attractive package, that the product conserves energy, uses less space, etc. Select from this list just two or three attributes you consider especially important to customers, and highlight the most attractive as your *major selling proposition*. This should define why your version of the product is superior to any other available.

- Write a headline based on the major selling proposition stating that, for example, the product works efficiently, is cheap, attractive, or has some other desirable feature. The headline should be eye-catching, interest arousing, perhaps even provocative in style. If you get stuck thinking up a suitable headline look for inspiration to the hundreds of advertisement headlines that you see around you every week in newspapers, magazines, on direct mail advertisements and on posters. Select a model and improvise on the chosen theme. Cannibalise various headlines until you have something you think fits. Otherwise, look at a good book on advertising practice (see Note 1) for further hints.

- Devise an illustration for insertion below, above or superimposed over the headline. This can be a photograph (possibly of the product in use or of a typical consumer) or a line-drawing commissioned from your printer. Its purposes are to reinforce the headline message and to present the product attractively, so it must be visually appealing and large enough to impress.

- Draft 'body copy' for insertion in one, two or three columns immediately below the illustration (or headline if this itself follows the illustration). Stick to the following rules:

- avoid technical and unintelligible jargon that consumers will not understand

- explain the headline, using short simple sentences, usually with just one sentence per paragraph

- justify claimed advantages, mentioning extra selling points and, where appropriate, the costs and disadvantages of being without the product

- be brief and accurate, and make the points sound interesting. Inform readers of things they need to know. Again you might look at existing press advertisements for other products to inspire and guide your thoughts.

- Position your business name and logo prominently in a lower corner of the advertisement. Put supply details alongside your business name, i.e., state how, when and where the customer can obtain or experience the product, e.g., phone a certain number, fill in a coupon, visit your showroom or write to the firm.

- End the advertisement with a 'tag-line' (or 'exit line') running across all or part of the bottom of the advertisement. A tag-line is a brief summary statement reinforcing the advertisement's basic theme or summing up the character of the product. Most press advertisements have tag-lines. Examples are the lines 'The Lion goes from Strength to Strength' that appears beneath Peugeot advertisements, or 'Number One Across the Atlantic' as used by PanAm, or the line 'Metro Gets You Going' which appears in Austin Rover advertisements for Metro cars.

None of these rules are hard and fast, and you will observe many variations in the structures of advertisements that appear in magazines (the *Radio Times* and *TV Times* are good places to look) and in newspapers. In general, however, aim for a balanced appearance to the advertisement, with a single focal point – located half-way across the advertisement and perhaps one third the way down its length – to fix the reader's attention. A good advertisement:

- informs the reader
- creates within him or her a desire to possess the product
- makes it easy for the customer to convert this desire into action through directing the reader to behave in an appropriate way, e.g., by making a telephone call, filling in a form, visiting the firm, etc.

Code your advertisements

Each campaign should carry a code enabling the easy identification of response (use differing department references in the address you quote, slightly different response form designs, etc.) and hence the effectiveness of advertising expenditures. And be sure to relate the number of enquiries an advertisement elicits to the volume of orders eventually received. Many enquiries may result from an advertisement, but hardly any actual sales, indicating perhaps that the advertisement overstated the objective worth of the product hence causing disappointment among consumers who inspected the goods.

Outdoor advertising

Posters can be difficult to design, costly to print, and poster sites are expensive to hire. Unless there are particular reasons for using posters (if you run a hotel, for example, you probably need a conspicuous poster near the local railway station, or you might require additional point-of-sale advertising alongside retail outlets), you should think twice before committing yourself to this expense.

Mobile advertisements

More useful to the small business, perhaps, is an attractive display

9

specifying your line of business and telephone number on the side and back panels of vehicles operated by the firm. Back panels face the drivers of the cars behind you and thus can usefully contain a lot of detail because the advertisement will be read carefully by following drivers in slow-moving traffic. Side panels, coversely, need large, bold letters for your firm's name and description of its business because onlookers will have only a brief glance at the vehicle as it passes.

If a particular bus route passes through an area containing a high density of potential customers then it may be worthwhile hiring an advertising space on an upper or lower deck interior side panel.

Sales promotions

Every business needs a promotional strategy for its products. Begin with a statement of who you want your material to reach, and what you want consumers to do or feel as they receive the messages it conveys. Thus, for example, a competition or sweepstake can be used to create consumer awareness; money-off offers, free gifts or coupons, on the other hand, might be useful for encouraging customer loyalty. Depending on the nature of your business you can devise special refunds, 'buy one, get one free' offers, cut price samples, cross-couponing and banded packaging (i.e., a big price reduction on one item is available if another product is purchased at the same time), etc.

Perhaps you haven't previously considered employing these devices, but just think of their potential advantages; they can be used to:

- reach entirely new markets
- further penetrate existing markets
- retain custom
- expedite the launch of a new product
- smooth-out seasonal demand
- stimulate repeat purchases
- secure impulse purchases
- shift slow-moving stock

and generally draw attention to your firm and its products.

Promotions need not be expensive and, because of their immediate impact, may provide precisely the shot in the arm your business requires. They may be adapted to attract specific target groups (particularly at the point of sale), and they enhance the brand images you have already created.

Which promotion?

Choice of a particular promotional technique should depend on your promotional objectives. Are you aiming primarily to stimulate impulse purchases, penetrate new markets or encourage loyalty to the product? Concentrate on the areas you are *least* good at. If consumer loyalty to your product is already strong there is little point in devising a promotional strategy aimed at enhancing repeat purchases; rather you should be seeking to attract completely new customers in different market segments.

Types of promotion

The main types of sales promotion are:

    (a) linked-product discounts or gifts,
    (b) cash reductions (possibly through coupons),
    (c) competitions (subject to certain legal requirements),
    (d) free samples and gifts, and
    (e) self-liquidating premiums.

Linked-product offers

These may involve cross-couponing or banded packs. The idea is to persuade consumers to sample one product having already purchased something else.

Banded packaging

Banded packaging means connecting the packages of two items with glue or tape (as happens when a toiletries manufacturer bands together soap and toothpaste packets, for example). The two items are then put on sale for a total price lower than they would cost if purchased individually. Essentially, you offer the consumer a *sample* of one of the items, but do not have to give it away. Banding encourages impulse purchases and is extremely useful for shifting slow-moving stock. You need to ensure, of course, that outlets do not split banded packs and resell the items at higher prices.

    Note that banded products do not have to be physical goods;

services can also be offered at a reduced rate when accompanied by others. Use your imagination to think up ways of applying the concept in your own business.

Cross-couponing

Cross-couponing refers to the practice of issuing a money-off coupon for a product when a different product is purchased. It aims to encourage customer sampling of the coupon product and thus to create entirely new consumer demand.

Cash reductions

Cash reductions occur directly via price cuts marked on flashpacks (i.e. specially printed packages which prominently display the price cut or increased quality) or indirectly through cash refunds to customers who furnish proof of purchase after buying the goods. The latter method encourages repeat purchases and, importantly, the customers who send in proofs of purchase provide you with names and addresses for subsequent use in future direct mail activities. Refunds may be paid in the form of a money-off voucher for the customer's next purchase – thus further increasing his or her loyalty to your firm – rather than in cash or by postal order.

Redemption rates

The problem with this type of promotion lies primarily in forecasting the redemption rate. Goods that are frequently purchased normally involve higher redemptions because the requisite number of proofs of purchase (package tops, for example) is easier to obtain and this increases the total cost of the promotion. The more attractive the offer the higher the redemption rate, yet the greater the number of redemptions the more expensive the offer becomes. (Vouchers rather than straight cash refunds are, in fact, more economical because not all vouchers issued to customers will actually be traded in.) It is essential, therefore, that you assess the likely redemption rate by conducting a small scale test of the offer's appeal prior to launching the full promotion.

Note that refunds may be graduated to accommodate varying levels of consumer loyalty, e.g., a 50 pence voucher might be offered in exchange for ten proofs of purchase, whereas £1 is given for 20. The proofs of purchase need to be identifiably related to the items on special offer, not to existing retail or consumer stocks.

Coupons

Money-off coupons may be printed on a product's package, enclosed with the item, or incorporated into newspaper advertisements or leaflets distributed door-to-door. They serve many purposes: market penetration, encouragement of repeat purchases, sampling by new customers, higher levels of consumption, impulse purchases, and so on. Coupons are more appropriate for small value items sold by one business to another, though even here some equivalents of couponing may occur.

Coupon redemptions

Not all the coupons issued will be used so you need to estimate the redemption rate. This will depend primarily on the value of the coupon, its aesthetic appeal, and the extent of its distribution. Numerous secondary influences exist: method of delivery, redemption period, frequency of purchase in shops, etc., and you will certainly need a trial run. As a rule of thumb allow for two or three per cent redemption from coupons in newspaper advertisements, ten per cent from leaflets distributed door-to-door, and 30 per cent from mailshots and coupons contained on a package.

9

Problems with coupons

There is certainly no shortage of coupons currently circulating upon which you can base your own coupon design – they arrive through the letterbox daily, and note how readily you can weave an advertising message into the coupon. However, if you sell through retailers they will demand compensation for handling the coupons, and retailers might redeem your coupon against *any* item purchased by the coupon holder. Regular issue of coupons creates further problems: customers may become accustomed to the effectively lower sale price of the product and thus resent subsequent withdrawal of the coupon offer. Moreover, regular users – who would buy the product anyway at the regular price – also benefit, thus reducing your aggregate returns.

Distribution

Target the distributions of your coupons at carefully selected consumer groups (blanket distributions are expensive to administer and potentially wasteful) and select the media for carrying the coupons with the target consumer groups in mind. Choose 'on-pack' coupons if you wish to stimulate brand loyalty and repeat purchases, but recognise that redemption rates (and hence the cost to your business) will be higher through this medium. Use leaflets containing coupons if you wish to make direct consumer appeals. And always make sure you can identify the sales resulting from a particular channel.

As a small business operating on a strictly limited budget, consider the feasibility of producing (with a word processor and photocopier) your own coupon promotion material and distributing it personally door-to-door. This avoids the need for costly newspaper advertisements (which may not be read by target consumer groups) and ensures that the offer goes directly into the potential customer's home. You may be able to do the distribution in your spare time, and might even get the family to help.

Competitions

Competitions are enormously popular among consumers. But there are substantial legal restrictions on the circumstances in which a competition can take place. Under the UK Gaming Act, any competition involving a purchase as the means of entry must include some element of skill. A 'luck-of-the-draw' competition is illegal unless no product purchase is required, yet the absence of a proof of purchase makes the promotion essentially useless from the business's point of view. To overcome this difficulty you must incorporate into the competition some means whereby the entrant exercises judgement, e.g., by stating in not more than a dozen words *why* he or she prefers your product, or by answering some easy questions. The restriction does not apply to trade (non-retail consumer) competitions, although obviously trade buyers are unlikely to purchase goods just to enter a competition.

Uses of competitions

A competition might be used to create consumer awareness of a product, to penetrate a new market, stimulate impulse buying *and* encourage repeat purchase as well. An important advantage is that you know in advance how much the promotion will cost (there is no redemption rate to be estimated, no cash refunds or free gift problems), and administration need not be expensive. News of the competition can be incorporated into your normal advertising literature and/or be disseminated through retail outlets. The effect of a competition on sales will depend on the:

- attractiveness of the prize offered
- level of difficulty of questions asked
- number of proofs of purchase needed to enter
- period for which the competition is open
- how extensively the competition is advertised.

Free gifts

Impulse purchasing can sometimes be stimulated by attaching a small free gift to a prominent part of the outside of a package. The cost of the free gift reduces the mark-up on the item, but sales will increase and administrative costs are minimal. 'Mail-ins' require consumers to send proofs of purchase through the post in order to claim the gift. When the gift is dispatched it is, of course, accompanied by further promotional literature.

Problems with free gifts

The problem is the cost of the giveaway item. Thus, many firms recoup some of their expenditure by offering items at greatly reduced prices rather than giving them away free. Mail-ins generate their own mailing lists for subsequent use in further direct mail activities, and consumer loyalty increases. However, response rates must be estimated (you are legally obliged to supply the offered item or something of equivalent value to anyone providing the requisite number of proofs of purchase), and many people who claim the gift may have bought the product in any case. As a rule of thumb think in terms of one purchaser in a hundred taking up the offer.

Items distributed as free gifts should be:

- appealing
- easily described or illustrated in promotional literature
- conveniently delivered
- safe to use
- in keeping with the product's image (high quality products require high quality promotions to reinforce their attraction).

As a small business you cannot afford to store large quantities of the gift in anticipation of a high take-up rate, so choose something you can obtain easily 'off the peg' from several sources.

Note that under section 46 [1](f) of the Consumer Protection Act 1987 any item given away (or offered as a prize in a raffle or competition) must be safe, and that the firm is liable to pay unlimited compensation to those injured if an item turns out to be defective.

Self-liquidating offers

An important advantage of 'self-liquidating' offers (i.e., those requiring a contribution from customers) is that the degree of self-liquidation can be varied. Thus, you might offer the extra item completely free if the customer mails in, say, ten proofs of purchase, or for £3 plus five proofs, or £6 plus three. This extends the appeal of the offer from regular users (who will opt for ten purchases and no cash payment) to the occasional user who is encouraged to buy the product just three times. Note, moreover, that many people purchase specially marked packs *intending* to send off the money and proofs of purchase, but never actually do so, thus reducing your costs.

Careful costing is essential to the success of this type of offer. First you must do an experimental trial run to estimate the extent of demand for the special packages, then you obtain the purchase costs of various batch sizes of the item to be offered, assess the costs of advertising the offer, and finally compute your administration, handling and postage expenses. A gross miscalculation here can ruin your business.

Support for local charities

Your public image might be considerably enhanced if you visibly support a local charity, evidenced perhaps by your advertising in its publications, shop window or other media. You could, for example, offer to donate money in proportion to the volume of your trade during a pre-specified period (e.g., by paying so much to the charity for each proof of purchase sent to you in a particular month) up to a maximum amount. Supporting a charity demonstrates your commitment to the local community and that your business *is here to stay*. Charity promotions, moreover, can be tailor-made to support other advertising activities and to reinforce the 'corporate image' your firm projects: your business name is widely circulated, and is perceived in a favourable light.

Sales promotions versus discounts

An advantage of sales promotions generally is that they attract new business without the need to offer easy credit or highly expensive discounts for prompt settlement of accounts. Debt collecting is expensive: special promotions typically give customers incentives independent of the system for credit control. Even a device as simple as offering free delivery on large cash orders can be cheaper than the administrative and other costs of extended credit. True, the administration of sales promotions incurs costs (printing or photocopying the literature, postage, refund costs, advertising the offer), but at least they increase sales; easy credit terms usually do not!

Discounts as a means of sales promotion

Certain discounts, however, have promotional value, for example:

(a) quantity discounts, which, if taken up, will enable you to economise on your holdings of finished goods stocks (and the fact that customers are induced to buy in greater numbers encourages them actively to promote the sale of your product);

(b) forward buying discounts whereby goods are ordered today under a contractually binding agreement for delivery on specified future dates;

(c) free delivery or free extra goods on certain sizes of order (e.g., buy six cases and get one free);

(d) straight cash bonuses on quantities sold through particular outlets;

(e) *ad hoc* payments to new stockists and payments to existing outlets which introduce new stockists to you.

The discounts you offer should not mislead customers into believing that the price quoted is lower than it actually is. Otherwise you could commit an offence under the Consumer Protection Act 1987 (see Chapter 10). If in doubt check with your local Trading Standards Office.

Trade deals

People in business are not prepared to do things for free; they require incentives to induce them to behave in particular ways. To the extent you have to rely on other firms to sell your output you need to offer them financial inducements to promote your goods. Trade deals and bonuses are pre-planned payments to retailers or distributors for extra services or favours. Retailers in particular are concerned with the 'shelf-life' of your product, since they dislike having money tied up for long periods in slow-moving stock. Perhaps, therefore, you can devise an incentive which partly compensates the retailer for carrying a slow-moving item and thus encourages larger orders.

In return for the payment (and hence a higher profit margin on selling the product) the retailer should be asked to display your goods prominently and to guide customers towards them when customers seem indifferent as to which brand to select. In consequence:

- your product sells faster
- the retailer obtains a higher unit margin on a higher volume of sales
- your competitors' products are crowded out from key display positions.

Try to link trade deals with forthcoming sales promotions (coupon or money-off offers, for example) that make your product even more attractive to stock. Note, however, that trade deals are not suitable for goods that are well established and which already occupy prominent display positions in retail outlets.

Offering a trade deal is a bit of a gamble. Retailers and distributors might increase *current* purchases in order to obtain the bonus, but in effect may simply bring forward the timing of their orders: aggregate purchases might not be affected in the longer run. Nevertheless, your business receives an injection of short-term funds and if you tie the bonus to increased retail sales and/or enhanced display then the additional goods taken will hopefully be sold quickly and thus lead to further orders for your firm.

Sales promotions law

Certain ethical standards must be maintained in the implementation of sales promotions, which should be honest and legal, with expiry dates and other limitations on the offer clearly printed on the *outside* of the pack. (See the Advertising Standards Authority's *British Code of Practice on Sales Promotions* for further details.) Offers that require proof of purchase prior to your paying out should involve proofs that are unique to the product under offer, which are easily removed from the package, and easy to send through the post. Application forms for redemption should be clearly legible and provide sufficient space for the customer's name and address.

Free gifts can only be described as 'free' if there is no charge for handling, packaging or administration. If postage is required this fact should be stated on the offer. It is illegal to state that an offered item is worth more than its actual value, and you cannot incorporate the logo of the firm that makes the item into your promotional literature without the manufacturer's permission.

Medicinal products, especially those available to the public without prescription, are subject to special legal control. Accordingly, the Medicines (Labelling) Amendment Act 1977 requires that all containers and packages of such products carry the words 'Keep out of reach of children', or other words of similar meaning; free random distribution of medicine samples to the general public is illegal (under the Medicines Act 1968).

Any promotion that might be construed as incorporating a lottery, i.e., a free draw where success depends entirely on chance, creates special difficulties. The Lotteries and Amusements Act 1976 (and subsequent regulations issued under the Act) states that a lottery is legal only if:

- no proof of purchase is involved
- it is not passed off as a competition
- all entries have an equal probability of success
- prizes are clearly defined.

Thus, a money-off coupon distributed door-to-door that is also used as a draw ticket is quite legal, provided the coupon clearly states that entry to the draw is possible without buying the product. Similar considerations apply to sweepstakes (see Note 2). In either case the price of each ticket must be the same, and tickets must state:

- the name and address of the promoters
- the date of the draw and the prizes available
- that prizes will only be delivered to purchasers of winning tickets.

Display and merchandising

If you rely on retailers selling your output, encourage some of them – perhaps via financial inducements – to have special displays of your product(s) away from normal shelf positions, or otherwise to draw special attention to the product.

The display should surround the goods with promotional materials – a poster, leaflets, special offer coupons, invitations to participate in a competition, etc. – that attract consumer interest and encourage them to buy.

Dump displays

A dump display might be appropriate for your needs. This consists of a big stack of units of your product strategically piled up in the middle of an aisle in such a way that consumers cannot avoid confronting the display. Similarly, an appealing layout of the product just where customers enter or leave the outlet may increase sales. These interrupt the normal 'traffic flow' of customers within the store and thus lead to a higher level of impulse purchases.

The problem is that of convincing the retailer:

(a) that you both have a common interest in shifting the product quickly;

(b) that your suggestions about how best to display the product will lead to an increase in sales.

Do-it-yourself merchandising

Study the nature of trade in the catchment area of the retail outlet concerned, and ask yourself what sorts of display are most likely to impress the customer types who frequent that establishment. Now examine the store's layout, its customer traffic flow, position of pillars and doorways, and the current locations of major product categories.

Next, identify the best positions for displaying your product. Normally the most attractive positions are the natural high-traffic areas around:

- the perimeter of the outlet (customers tend to keep to the outer edges of gondola layouts)
- entry doors (which are usually placed to the side of the shop window, so that at least half of all customers must pass the entire window display before entering
- shelves containing high-demand items, where the customer flow automatically slows down and hence where impulse purchases are more likely
- checkouts, which are an obvious source of customer traffic congestion.

Explain to the retailer that a special display of your product – especially a dump display – will give atmosphere to the store, enhance its general appearance, and increase consumer spending to your mutual benefit. Importantly, special displays between gondolas can be used to control traffic flow and thus encourage customers to shop in certain store sections they might otherwise overlook. Also, the existence of an in-store display distinguishes the retail outlet from its competitors, and helps create a progressive and competitive image for the firm.

Direct mail

Direct mail encompasses both mail-order selling and the distribution of advertising and other promotional literature to target consumer segments through the post. All you need to operate a direct mail system are a cheap word processor (even an old-fashioned typewriter will do), paper, a photocopying facility, and a relevant, accurate and up-to-date list of names and addresses. Mailing lists can be obtained in several ways:

(a) from the names and addresses of customers who have replied to your mail-order advertisements in newspapers or to leaflets distributed door-to-door;

(b) by going through appropriate sections in the *Yellow Pages* and other business directories (e.g., national directories of the Chamber of Commerce) available in your local library, or perhaps simply by inspecting the electoral roll;

(c) through using the services of mailing list brokers who sell lists of names and address to other firms. All the subjects on a particular list will belong to a group of consumers who exhibit certain characteristics: owners of expensive cars, people interested in wildlife, members of various types of organisation, mortgagees, members of certain ethnic and religious groups, etc. A list broker might, for example, sell you a list of addresses of black, Catholic owners of a certain type of motor car, living in a certain town, who spend more than a certain amount per month on a particular product. List brokers themselves purchase names and addresses from other organisations (the Automobile Association, financial institutions, churches, sporting and cultural bodies, and so on) that are prepared to disclose their members' whereabouts. Then the list broker cross-tabulates names and addresses according to its customers' needs. Brokers will also administer the campaign (including the design of promotional literature) for an additional fee.

9

Mail order

Mail-order business arises from customers returning order forms enclosed with direct mail, or from completing order forms included in newspaper advertisements or leaflets. This type of selling is ideal for servicing customer groups which are unable to purchase your product through normal retail outlets, say, because of their working hours, lifestyles or geographical location. To reach these consumer groups you may need to organise a targeted maildrop (which if done properly could evoke a substantial response – even a one per cent response can be cost effective), or to advertise in particular local newspapers or special interest magazines.

A problem with press advertising of mail-order items (apart from typically low response rates) is that if you include a money-off coupon, or a name and address panel for the reader to complete, or anything else that needs cutting out (hence disfiguring the printed page), then you will usually achieve a higher response if you position the advertisement at the bottom right-hand corner of the page, where the response form is easier to remove. Unfortunately, some newspapers and magazines charge extra for this location. Full details of these (and other) charges are printed monthly in the *BRAD* press guide (*BRAD* stands for 'British Rate and Data') which covers all UK publications that carry advertisements. *BRAD* is available in most public libraries.

Unique selling points

Mail-order customers are typically attracted to goods that are unique or unusual in some way, so direct your advertising messages at the *unique selling points* of your products: their special features, ease of use, charm, good looks, low price or whatever. A 'no quibble' money-back guarantee on mail order goods (including the refund of return postage) is a useful selling point, which should be prominently displayed in advertising messages.

Note that customers are rarely willing to send high value cheques for goods they have not inspected. Thus, low priced items are more appropriate for mail-order trade. Unfortunately, this means that postage, packing, transit breakages, handling and administration costs necessarily account for a relatively large part of the final sale price of the product. Hence you may be compelled to accept lower profit margins on the output you sell by mail.

Office of Fair Trading Rules

Because mail-order customers are expected to part with their money before seeing goods the OFT specifies precise guidelines for mail-order operations. In response to these, several trade associations have introduced 'mail order protection schemes'. The most important of these are operated by:

- the Newspaper Publishers Association (covering the national press)
- the Newspaper Society (representing local newspapers)
- the Periodical Publishers Association (for magazines)
- the Independent Broadcasting Authority.

Such schemes aim to protect mail-order customers and compensate those who lose money through the mail-order systems. A central fund is created into which all member organisations contribute and from which claims are paid. Each member then imposes a small levy on every mail-order firm advertising in its publications.

The NPA scheme

National newspapers belong to the NPA scheme, and you must subscribe to this before any national newspaper will accept your mail-order advertisement. You apply initially to the paper in which you wish to advertise, pay the appropriate fee (between £60 and £1,000 depending on the total annual value of the advertisements you place with NPA members) and must provide evidence that your business is financially sound, i.e., that is well established (or has substantial assets if it is new), is trading profitably, and employs reliable and experienced staff.

The NPA then takes up credit references and might send a representative to inspect your premises. If the NPA is not fully satisfied it may insist that you offer a substantial bank guarantee or possess appropriate insurance cover before entering the scheme. Other mail order protection (MOP) systems operate in a similar fashion.

Customers who lose money through the bankruptcy, company liquidation or fraud of an advertiser belonging to an MOP scheme is entitled to a full refund, with the following exceptions, which cannot be covered by MOP:

- any kind of foodstuff
- contraceptives or other sexually-related item

- products which appeal to fear or superstition (e.g., lucky charms or horoscopes).

Note that you need to join an MOP scheme *only* if customers are required to pay prior to receiving the goods. If your advertisement merely invites customers to send for a catalogue or low cost brochure, or to visit your premises or to order returnable goods on approval, then you do not have to become a member. Also, each MOP system has its own special exemptions (see Note 3).

Advantages of direct mail

Direct mail has several advantages:

- Unlike most advertising it may be carefully targeted at particular groups.
- It can be designed to carry a personal appeal.
- No salespeople are necessary.
- Responses are quickly, accurately, and easily assessed.
- You can experiment with different types of mail-drop literature, send it to differing consumer categories and observe the response, and you can vary the geographical areas covered.
- Much direct mail work you can do yourself, without recourse to newspaper advertisements, expensive agents, publicity gimmicks, etc.

The cost per customer contact is substantial, but is cost effective provided you target your market segments with care. Ensure that mail drops are easy to reply to, and 'code' the responses (e.g. by using differing GPO box numbers, different 'departments' quoted in the reply address, or through incorporating visible differences in the response forms) in order to measure consumer reactions to various campaigns.

Sales literature

The material sent to potential customers via direct mail might comprise an existing advertisement reproduced on a leaflet plus an accompanying letter; or you could devise a self-contained 'one piece mailer' consisting of promotional messages, body copy and order form all incorporated into a single document. Whichever way you do it, the basic principles are the same. You must:

- firmly establish the identity of the firm and the nature of its business
- explain the claims made in your advertisement and/or document headline
- provide information (e.g., what the product does, how it works, why it should be purchased), and generally reinforce other promotional messages.

When drafting the document ask yourself repeatedly why anyone should want to buy *your* output and not that of competing firms. What are the product's exclusive qualities? What advantages does it offer over other brands? What attributes and benefits does it possess?

The end part of the document should stimulate the reader to take positive steps to acquire the product. Reiterate the major selling proposition, and state – precisely and straightforwardly – how the item may be ordered plus any discount or credit terms that apply. Use short and simple sentences, lots of headings, and paragraphs that consist of just one or two sentences. Most mail-drop recipients do in fact open envelopes containing sales literature, but only spend a few seconds inspecting the contents. Immediate visual impact is thus critically important for a campaign's success.

There are certain general rules to follow when devising a sales letter.

9

- Avoid technical jargon.
- Try not to irritate the reader by excessive repetition of points.
- Personalise the literature. You can use the mail merge facility on a word processor for this.
- Be brief and stick to the point of the exercise. Do not include superfluous material; concentrate on dramatising the *basic* message contained in the literature.

If you experience a mental block while trying to think up appealing messages, seek inspiration from the numerous specimens of direct mail literature that come through your letterbox every week. Much of this will have been professionally, and expensively, produced by large organisations. Base your own material on the best bits of these examples – some are bound to contain approaches relevant to your needs. Cannibalise, reword, restructure, and rework this material until you come up with something appropriate for your requirements (though be careful not to infringe copyright through directly lifting words and phrases from a single source).

Note that grossly inaccurate sales literature violates the Sale of

Goods Act 1979, and possibly the Trade Descriptions and Consumer Protection Acts as well (see Chapter 10). If you are unsure of the precision of your descriptions then qualify them with words such as 'approximate', 'probably', 'generally', and so on. And avoid ridiculously exaggerated claims about your product, especially any implication that it is suitable for a specific purpose when it is not.

Summary

Effective advertising and sales promotions are essential for the long-term survival of the small firm. You need not spend a fortune on these activities: much of the creative and administrative work attached to them you can do yourself. Begin with a statement of the *purposes* of your promotional strategy, listing the specific outcomes you wish to achieve and the target periods involved. Then describe all the selling points attached to your output. You need to be able to define precisely how and why your product is superior to those of your rivals.

People today are immersed in advertising messages and symbols, and as a matter of course they expect a business to present itself attractively. If you do not bother with advertising and promotion, consumers might think your output is defective in some way.

Seek inspiration in the advertisements and promotional methods of your competitors and other firms. Select an appropriate model and improvise on the chosen theme. Be on the lookout for illustrations that could be used to support advertising copy, and note carefully any attractive logos belonging to businesses similar to your own.

Consider the applicability and feasibility of using each of the following types of sales promotion:
- a competition
- a buy-one get-one-free offer
- packaging your product in a money-off flashpack
- a coupon offer
- sponsorship of a local charity linked to levels of sales achieved.
- free samples or gifts.

Use promotions for improving sales performance in the areas in which you are weakest. And above all be innovative in your general approach – experiment, devise new schemes, constantly modify your promotions (and advertisements) to make them more appealing to target consumer groups.

If your output is sold through retailers, visit retail outlets and advise their owners on how best to display your goods. Select the best display positions in each store and suggest that your products be located there. A small cash inducement to the retailer may be worthwhile if the very best display positions are secured.

Direct mail is increasingly important for marketing the output of small businesses. You can write your own direct mail sales literature according to certain predetermined and straightforward rules. There is no shortage of examples of direct mail literature distributed by other firms upon which you can base your own efforts.

Checklist

1. How much of the last £1,000 you spent on advertising can you be sure contributed significantly to achieving a higher level of sales?
2. Do you draft your own advertising copy? If not, why not?
3. What are the major selling points of your output (list at least ten of these), and what are the minor selling points?
4. Why is your product superior to that of your rivals?
5. When did you last revise your firm's logo?
6. Are your business name, telephone number, and line of work prominently displayed on the side and back panels of vehicles belonging to the firm?
7. Which form of sales promotion is most likely to shift your slow-moving finished goods stock?
8. Does each of your advertisements carry a tag-line? If not, think up at least four such lines that you could use for this purpose.
9. Do you code your advertisements in order to assess the responses from various campaigns?
10. How many different ways of promoting your product have you tried during the last 12 months?
11. Are you aware of the major legal restraints on sales promotions? If not re-read page 176 in the text.

Notes

1. The best I know is P. Quinn, *The Secrets of Successful Low Budget Advertising*, London, Heinemann, 1987.
2. See J. Williams, *The Manual of Sales Promotions*, London, Innovation Limited, 1983.
3. For example, the NPA allows certain services such as membership of a club or the sale of magazine subscriptions to proceed without its approval. And any mail order advertisement may be placed in a national paper's 'classified' section regardless of NPA considerations. See Alan and Deborah Fowler, *Mail Order: A Small Business Guide*, London, Sphere, 1986.

10 Keeping within the law

Defective products □ Misleading price indications □ Trade descriptions □ The Sale of Goods Act 1979 □ The Misrepresentation Act 1967 □ Other consumer protection acts □ Consumer credit □ Hire purchase □ Summary □ Checklist

Previous chapters have cited various legal constraints on small businesses, and there are indeed many legal considerations that a small firm needs to take into account.

Laws change frequently: new ones are enacted; existing law may at any time be repealed. And laws have to be interpreted by judges in courts hearing specific cases. Courts regularly alter their interpretations, and vastly different constructions of the same issue are sometimes applied. Decisions of lower courts are frequently overturned on appeal and new precedents are established from time to time. The interpretation of any given legal problem is thus liable to sudden and possibly unexpected change.

Small businesses need to be particularly vigilant in relation to consumer protection (including consumer credit regulations), employee rights and health and safety at work. Chapter 6 deals with employment and safety; this chapter focuses on consumer protection law, ignorance of which has caused many small firms to fail.

Defective products

Different countries adopt different approaches to the question of who is liable for damages caused by defective products. Some countries insist that the producer is liable no matter what the circumstances. Others make suppliers liable only if the injured party can *prove* negligence on the supplier's part. Prior to 1987 the latter situation applied in the UK.

This contravened a 1985 EC directive on the subject, so in order to bring UK practice into line with minimum EC requirements the UK Parliament enacted the Consumer Protection Act 1987 which abandoned the need for plaintiffs to prove the supplier's negligence when pursuing defective product claims. However, the Act does not go so far as to render suppliers absolutely responsible for defects in their products. Instead, a supplier is generally liable, but not if he or she can demonstrate that the 'state of scientific and technical knowledge' at the time the product went into circulation was *not* such that a supplier could be reasonably expected to have known about the defect the product contains.

Nevertheless, the new approach embodied within the 1987 Act is sure to place many small businesses at risk since from now on, not only can they be sued by victims (and there are no upper limits on compensation), but also:

(a) the insurance costs for cover against such liability are rising sharply;

(b) manufacturers will be increasingly reluctant to purchase goods from small businesses which cannot guarantee provision of full product liability insurance cover, because manufacturers are now liable to consumers for the inputs and raw materials they use and thus need to be sure they can pass back financial responsibility for defective inputs to initial suppliers;

(c) as purchasers of inputs from other firms, small businesses must now ensure that their *own* suppliers have adequate product liability insurance, so that they do not end up being made financially responsible for defects in another firm's products.

Under the Act, a 'producer' is not only the manufacturer of a finished article, or its raw materials (or the extractor of raw materials), or the manufacturer of component parts, but may also include any firm or person who imports, processes, distributes or otherwise supplies (e.g., by hiring or lending) the product.

A 'product' is defined as any good (including electricity) or part of another good, or raw material, Producers are liable for their products, as is any person or firm putting a *name*, *trade mark*, *or distinguishing mark* (such as a business logo) on the product. The victim of a defective product must ask the person or firm that supplied it to identify its producer and, if the supplier is unable to do this (i.e., if the last known supplier cannot 'pass back' liability for the defect) then the last supplier is fully liable. If more than one producer is involved then all are equally liable and if some are insolvent then the remainder are responsible for meeting the entire claim. Customer complaints must be registered within three years of the purchase, or within one year of the customer discovering the fault within this three year period.

In deciding whether a product is or is not 'defective' a court will examine:

- what it might reasonably be expected to do
- how the product is marketed, i.e., what the supplier claims it will do (described in the Act as the product's 'get-up')
- any operating instructions, printed warnings and related literature accompanying the product.

Defences

Actions are not possible unless the damage allegedly caused exceeds £275. Confronted with a claim, you may assert that:

(a) you did not supply the good:

(b) someone else produced it and is therefore liable; although if you cannot pass back liability, either because you are in fact the producer or the actual producer has disappeared or is insolvent, then you are fully responsible for the damage caused (unless you are a 'retailer', see below);

(c) the goods are not defective;

(d) the state of technical knowledge at the moment of supply could not reasonably lead you to suspect the goods were defective;

(e) defects arose not within your product but through the way someone else made up or designed the final product into which they were incorporated.

Note, however, that liability cannot be avoided through exclusion clauses in sale agreements or through notices posted around the point of sale denying responsibility. Moreover, you must show that you were 'duly diligent' and took all reasonable steps in trying to avoid committing an offence.

10

Consumer safety

The Act makes it illegal not only to supply unsafe goods, but also to:

- possess them (e.g., by holding them in stock)
- provide inadequate instructions for their use thereby causing accidents
- fail to provide proper warnings of dangerous aspects of the goods
- fail to apply all reasonable measures (having regard to cost and the likelihood of improvement) for improving the safety of goods.

Retailers have a special protection under the Act. They are not liable for the defective goods they sell provided:

(a) they did not know the goods were unsafe, and
(b) that such ignorance was reasonable in the particular circumstances.

It is interesting to note that tobacco is explicitly excluded from the Act. Cigarettes therefore are not a 'defective product' despite the deaths and suffering they cause.

Misleading price indications

The Act states that it is a criminal offence (punishable by fine) to mislead consumers over product prices. A price indication is misleading if:

(a) the actual price is higher than that shown;
(b) the low price indicated depends on facts or circumstances not revealed to the customer;
(c) additional charges are not disclosed;
(d) the supplier makes out that the price will shortly be increased when this is not the case (e.g., the statement 'buy now to beat next month's price rise' when no such price increase is scheduled to occur).

Misleading price indications are unlawful in advertisements, catalogues, circulars and price lists as well as at the point of sale. And the Act applies to services (including credit and banking services) as well as physical goods.

Trade descriptions

The Act strengthens and updates some of the provisions of the Trade Descriptions Act 1968 (the 1972 update to this is replaced in its entirety) which established the general principle that it is illegal to advertise goods in such a way as to give incorrect, misleading or false information about them. In passing the Trade Descriptions Act Parliament sought to prevent sellers from:

(a) publishing advertisements which contain false information about their merchandise;
(b) stating such information orally or in writing;

(c) displaying signs about their merchandise which might give a false impression.

Misleading statements might relate to the physical characteristics of a product, such as its size, weight, colour, etc., or its suitability for the purpose for which it is intended, or to any other relevant characteristic. Goods may be described through a label, a statement on a package, statements in documents (guarantees, for example) relating to the goods, or through signs on, above, alongside or near the goods.

Sellers can avoid liability if they prove that a false description was given due to a genuine mistake, or by accident, provided all reasonable precautions against mistakes and accidents had been taken.

The Sale of Goods Act 1979

Under this Act the seller of goods must:

(a) sell goods which are of merchantable quality, i.e., not defective in any way. If the goods on offer are defective then defects must be pointed out or clearly visible at the time of the sale;

(b) supply goods which are reasonably fit for the purpose for which they are intended;

(c) deliver (or make available for collection) goods which correspond to the way in which they have been described or to a sample previously inspected.

Buyers can claim compensation if goods are not delivered, and have the right to reject them on delivery if they do not correspond with the agreed details of the transaction. Customers are entitled to full compensation if goods prove to be defective or unfit for their purpose.

Under the Act a supplying firm is not lawfully able to impose a condition on a sale saying that the supplier does not accept responsibility for their quality, suitability or delivery. Such a statement is of no effect and the buyer is still entitled to replacement of the goods or a refund.

The Misrepresentation Act 1967

This Act was intended to prevent retailers making false statements about merchandise prior to its sale. Anyone who is misled can apply under the Act for compensation equal to the value of the loss incurred through relying on false information. Misrepresentation may occur 'innocently' or 'fraudulently'. The former involves statements that are genuinely believed to be true. Fraudulent misrepresentation, conversely, is false statements which are 'recklessly or knowingly' given. Note, however, that false statements about merchandise, even if made unknowingly, may be considered by a court as fraudulent misrepresentation since the person selling the goods is assumed to possess expert knowledge about their quality and features.

Other consumer protection acts

The Unfair Contract Terms Act 1977 deals with the use of disclaimers and exemption clauses, restricting their use to certain specified circumstances. Thus, it is not permissible for a firm to make a general statement 'anyone who enters these premises does so at their own risk', because this statement seeks to avoid responsibility for death or injury to employees or members of the public that might occur through the firm's negligence, failure to implement statutory conditions, or other fault.

Nevertheless, some exemption clauses are lawful, provided they are fair and reasonable. In assessing whether such a clause is 'reasonable' a court will consider:

- the bargaining positions of the parties
- whether inducements (e.g., price reductions) were offered to the customer to accept the term
- whether the goods were specially made for the customer
- trade customs and whether the consumer should reasonably have known of the general existence of exemption clauses in a particular trade.

Service contracts

The Supply of Goods and Services Act 1982 lays down consumers' rights in contracts that involve not only the supply of goods but also their installation and/or servicing. In consequence of the Act, the services (such as installation) supplied with physical goods must be carried out with reasonable skill and care to ensure that the goods supplied fulfil the purpose for which they were intended, and the services must be completed within a reasonable time. What constitutes a reasonable time depends on the circumstances of the situation.

Weights and measures

Under the Weights and Measures Act 1985, it is a criminal offence for suppliers not to specify the quantities of most pre-packed goods on their packets, tins or bottles. The 1985 legislation is but one of a series of Weights and Measures Acts passed over the years. These have determined that:

- it is a criminal offence to give short weight or measure when supplying goods
- responsibility for short weight packages falls on the manufacturer or packer of goods rather than on the retailer
- it is not necessary for each packet to be *exactly* the prescribed weight so long as the *average* weight of a batch of packets achieves the prescribed level.

Unsolicited goods

The Unsolicited Goods and Services Act 1971 states that where goods are delivered to someone who has not ordered them then the customer is entitled to keep the goods after six months, provided:

(a) the sender has not exercised his or her right to reclaim them within this period, and

(b) the recipient has not undertaken to return the goods.

10

Consumer credit

Credit arrangements in Britain are regulated by the Consumer Credit Act 1974, under which retail businesses that formally 'lend' (normally at interest) to their customers, e.g., through 'budget accounts', via a finance company, credit card charge accounts, personal loan accounts, payment by installment agreements, etc., are subject to the Consumer Credit Act 1974 and thus require a licence (from the Office of Fair Trading) to grant credit. Licences are only given to 'fit people', and trading without a licence is a criminal offence. However, the licencing provisions of the Act only apply to credit agreements between £50 and £15,000 in value. The Act forbids the charging of 'extortionate' interest, and lays down many rules about how credit may be advertised. Note that normal trade credit expected to be settled within three months is not affected by the Act.

Customers are entitled to the following information at the time of the transaction:

(a) the cash price of the goods, the amount of the deposit required and details of any security demanded;

(b) the value of the credit extended and its total cost, including the true annual percentage rate of interest;

(c) the timing and amount of repayments.

The customer must receive within seven days a copy of the credit agreement he or she has signed. If the customer entered a contract anywhere other than the firm's premises, he or she must receive two copies – one on signature and one by post within a further seven days, and the customer may then withdraw from the agreement without penalty within five days of receiving the second copy. Both copies must state the customer's right to cancel the agreement.

Any deposit must then be repaid and the goods collected by the supplying firm within three weeks. These provisions do not apply if the agreement was signed on the premises of the supplying firm.

Hire purchase

Under the Act, a hirer has the right to terminate a hire purchase agreement at any time once installation charges plus half the total purchase price has been paid. If less than half the price has been paid the hirer can be required to make up the balance to 50 per cent before cancelling the agreement, or face a penalty. Hirers who settle early are entitled to a rebate on credit charges accrued under the deal.

Once a third of the purchase price has been remitted the owner cannot repossess the goods without a court order. Note that these rules apply only to hire purchase and not to credit sales.

Exemptions

The Consumer Credit Act does not cover:

• borrowing by limited companies
• mortgages
• accounts that must be totally cleared each month (e.g., debts accrued on an American Express Card)
• loan arrangements involving less than five repayments.

The Act draws a crucial distinction between on the one hand 'debtor–creditor–supplier' agreements, i.e., where a finance company makes a loan for a specified purpose such as buying a television set or motor vehicle, and on the other 'debtor–creditor' agreements under which money is lent but for *no specific* purpose.

Under the former arrangements (sometimes called a 'purchaser agreement') the company lending the money can be held equally liable with the supplier of the goods for any defects in them. This is why credit card companies such as Access or Barclaycard may be liable for the quality of the goods purchased using a credit card facility, whereas they are not liable for goods bought with cash drawn on a credit card. Hire purchase is a further example of a debtor–creditor–supplier deal. Bank overdrafts and personal loans are examples of the debtor–creditor relationship.

Licences

It is a criminal offence for unlicenced creditors to make loans, and only licenced salespeople can make unsolicited calls on potential customers and offer credit terms. It is illegal to induce anyone under the age of 18 to enter a credit agreement.

Licences cost between £80 for sole traders and £210 for larger firms. All debt collecting businesses, credit reference agencies, debt counsellors, plant-hire enterprises and credit brokers (i.e., firms that introduce customers to hire purchase or leasing companies) require licences.

Extortionate agreements

If a court decides that a credit bargain is 'extortionate' (as sometimes happens in transactions with loan sharks, see Chapter 11) it may reschedule the repayments, alter the terms of the agreement, or even set aside all or part of the debtor's obligations. In determining whether an agreement is extortionate a court will examine:

- the 'principles of fair dealing'
- prevailing interest rates
- whether the borrower was under pressure when the loan was agreed
- the debtor's age, business experience, capacity and health
- the degree of risk assumed and the lender's relationship with the borrower.

Debtors are entitled to repay any loan covered by the Act at any time and may be able to claim a rebate of interest (though this is not necessarily the case).

Creditors cannot take action against a borrower who fails to repay on time unless a 'notice of default' has been served on the debtor giving seven days in which to pay up, and outlining the consequences of not clearing the debt. Only if the debtor fails to respond to the notice of default may the lender then ask a court for an enforcement order (see Chapter 5) against the debt, and even then the court might give the debtor additional time to repay the loan.

Credit references

The Act stipulates that if you receive a written request from a customer to disclose the name and address of any credit reference agency you consulted for information about that customer's credit standing then you *must* reveal this within seven working days – whether a credit agreement resulted or not! However, the customer's request must be made within 28 days of the discussions (called 'antecedent negotiations') preceding the intended credit deal. If you receive a bad report on the customer from the credit reference agency you are not obliged to disclose this; merely to provide the customer with the agency's name and address.

Having been given the details of the agency used the customer is then entitled to demand from the agency full particulars of the records on that person which the agency holds. No time limit is imposed; the customer simply makes a formal written request and pays a small fee.

The agency must send the applicant a copy of his or her file within seven days, plus a statement of the customer's rights. These are the rights to have all incorrect information on his or her file amended and have details of the corrections sent to everyone who consulted the agency about that person within the previous six months.

Summary

The law on product liability has changed drastically in consequence of the Consumer Protection Act 1987. Suppliers are now generally liable for defects in their products, though how exactly the new law will operate has yet to be fully ascertained. You *must* be extremely vigilant where product liability is concerned, in respect both of your own products and those supplied to you by other firms.

Under the Act, a 'producer' can be a manufacturer, an importer, a distributor, extractor of raw materials, a firm that hires or lends the product to users, or indeed *any* supplier of the item. Merely putting your business name or logo on a product might itself cause your firm to become liable if the goods turn out to be defective. And not only must you not supply unsafe products, neither may you even possess them. Existing trade descriptions legislation has been updated and strengthened, and it is now generally illegal to mislead consumers with respect to product price.

As the owner of a small business you need to be aware of the major provisions of the Sale of Goods Act (which requires firms to sell goods that are of merchantable quality and fit for their intended purpose) and of the Misrepresentation Act, which seeks to prevent business from making false statements about their goods.

Consumer credit is regulated by the Consumer Credit Act. According to this, most businesses which offer credit terms to their customers need to be licenced. And there are specific restrictions on how firms may offer credit to customers who are asked to sign credit contracts anywhere other than on the premises of the supplying firm.

10

Checklist

1. Have you checked to ensure that your product liability insurance is adequate, considering the implications of Consumer Protection Act 1987?
2. Do you ask major suppliers whether they are properly insured in respect of liability for defective products?
3. Do you realise that you could be held liable for a defect in a product you sell even if you did not manufacture the item? If not, then re-read this chapter.
4. What steps have you taken to incorporate into your sales literature the fact that you are well insured for product liability?
5. Have you examined your catalogues, price lists and other price indicators to establish that none of the prices you quote could be regarded as 'misleading'?
6. Does your storeroom hold any unsafe products?
7. If you are a retailer, what have you done to find out whether any of the goods you sell are unsafe?
8. Is the way you describe your products in advertisements and other promotional materials accurate and not intended to misrepresent them to customers?
9. If you sell on credit and do not have a licence, are you quite sure you do not require one?

11 Restructuring for survival

Legal structures □ The single person business □ Partnership □ Limited liability □ Company formation □ Running a company □ Acquiring other firms □ A revival plan □ Summary □ Checklist

Already you have seen how you can cut costs and generally improve the efficiency of the operational aspects of the business. And you should by now have adopted a fresh and better attitude towards marketing, distribution, operations, and promotional activities overall. The next thing you must do is apply this newfound spirit of adventure to the overall composition of the firm. Next you need to ask some pointed questions about the adequacy of your existing legal structure and to consider the alternatives that exist.

Legal structures

So far you will have traded as a single-person business, as a partnership, or as a limited liability company or co-operative. This chapter asks you to re-examine the suitability of the existing 'legal structure' (i.e. form of ownership) of the business, and perhaps to change to an alternative, more cost-effective and protective arrangement.

Some small businesses naively believe that becoming a private limited company is the be-all and end-all of legal structure. But this is certainly not the case; limited liability is not necessarily the best way to conduct trade. On the other hand, the owner of a single-person business operating without limited liability (the technical term for such a firm is 'sole trader') stands to lose his or her personal assets if the business fails. Choosing an appropriate legal structure is not always as straightforward as it first seems. Basically the choice depends on the:

- state of your cashflow
- extent of your outstanding liabilities
- costs and inconveniences of incorporation (i.e., the process of

becoming a limited company) in relation to the protection limited liability offers.

To understand these issues we need to consider the advantages and disadvantages of your existing structural form.

The single person business trading without limited liability

If you are a sole trader you will not have had to bother with the legal formalities of forming a company or limited liability co-operative, and your business affairs are entirely private except for your tax return. Moreover, you are free to diversify as and when you wish without being bound by company memoranda or articles of association (see below), so that you can instantly exploit any business opportunities that emerge. Unfortunately, however, your liability for the business's debts is unlimited: if you go bust you must settle all these debts from your personal estate (house, car, furniture, money in your personal bank account, etc.). Some of these difficulties can be overcome by altering your business's legal form, especially through forming a limited company and/or bringing in other people as stakeholders in the firm (creating a partnership for instance); but there are many problems here of which you need to be aware.

Partnership

Bringing in a partner can save an ailing business, since a partner(s) might contribute skills or capital you do not possess. There are, however, several potential pitfalls, and entering into a partnership is not something to do without careful thought. The intended partner should be a person you get along with easily *at work*, not necessarily someone you know well socially, since a good social relationship need not automatically translate into good working relations. And you really must have a formal written partnership agreement which clearly establishes the precise obligations and rewards of each partner. Usually, partners will not want to invest in your business unless they have a say in how it is run, but this is not necessarily the case: sometimes people with money are prepared to invest in businesses without becoming involved in their management. You can advertise for partners through the trade press, local newspapers, enterprise agencies, Chambers of Commerce, or through discrete enquiries with existing business contacts.

Responsibility for debts

Partners in a business are jointly responsible (to the extent of their personal assets) for its debts. Moreover, a contract entered into by any one partner on behalf of the firm will bind the rest. If your partners have no assets when the business goes bust the firm's creditors can come after you for the full amount they are owed.

Sleeping partners

There is an exception here: a partner who takes no part in management and does not enter contracts or sign cheques on behalf of the firm can obtain limited liability by registering the business as a 'limited partnership' with the registrar of Companies at Companies House (see Note 1). Such a partner loses only the money he or she has invested in the partnership if the business fails. Remaining debts are the responsibility of other partners, at least one of which must, by law, have unlimited liability.

The Partnership Act

Disputes within a partnership can arise over such things as:

- who is responsible for which activities
- how much work each partner is to undertake
- policy matters
- the returns on money invested by partners in the business
- distribution of profits

and many other things.

A written agreement clarifying such issues is, therefore, essential, although many partnerships do not actually bother with this. In the absence of a written document then – like it or not – the Partnership Act 1890 will apply to the firm. The major provisions of this Act are as follows:

(a) All partners shall share equally in the profits and losses of the business, and take equal shares of the partnership's capital assets upon its dissolution.

(b) Partners are equally liable for the business's debts.

11

(c) Contributions of capital over and above those which partners initially agreed to pay should attract interest at the rate of five per cent.

(d) Partners shall share equally in management, and be rewarded via shares in the profit of the enterprise (no salaries are paid).

(e) New partners may not be admitted unless all the existing partners give their consent.

(f) Disputes must be settled by majority vote, unless a change in the nature of the partnership's business is envisaged, in which case a unanimous decision is required.

Note, importantly, that since a partnership is a relationship between people it automatically ceases on the death of any one partner. If the business is to continue following a partner's death, an entirely new partnership must be formed.

Be sure you understand the legal implications of partnership *before* you take a partner. That person becomes an agent of the firm and can bind it contractually without your knowledge or prior consent, and you are personally liable for debts thus incurred. Your partner can buy goods for the business, sell its assets and borrow money on its behalf. And if you leave the partnership or retire you are *still* responsible for the debts accumulated while you were a member of the firm.

Sometimes, sole traders take as partners existing employees whose past contributions to the firm have been particularly valuable. Note, however, that personal qualities excellent for being a good employee – working under someone else's direction – are not necessarily identical to those found in successful entrepreneurs. Perhaps, therefore, an ex-employee should begin as a 'junior' partner, with restricted powers and responsibilities, prior to his or her promotion to a 'senior partner' role.

You can have up to 20 partners for a non-banking business; ten if banking is involved, and any number if the partnership is 'professional' in nature, solicitors, for example. The extent of your partners' powers should be embodied in a written 'partnership deed' specifying:

(a) the precise duties of each partner, whether they can sign cheques, and if so to what amount;

(b) the basis on which partners shall contribute capital, and their returns on such investments;

(c) rules for admission of new partners and the age at which partners shall retire;

(d) how profits shall be divided.

The deed can be tailor-made to side-step some of the inconveniences of partnership (e.g., that partnerships automatically end on the death, resignation or retirement of any one partner). Moreover, a retiring partner need not be liable for previously accumulated partnership debts provided a special 'contract of novation' exists between him- or herself, existing partners, creditors, and a new partner entering the firm. Novation means the substitution of a new legal obligation for an old one with the consent of all parties. Here, the new entrant contracts to 'take the place' of the retiring partner as far as existing debts are concerned.

A problem confronting retiring or resigning partners is that in certain circumstances they can be *deemed* liable for debts incurred after they leave the firm, since a creditor who continuously does business with a partnership is entitled to assume that all its 'apparent' members are still there until formally notified of the change. Thus, it is essential that if you leave a partnership you notify all existing customers and suppliers at once. Also you can advertise your resignation in the *London Gazette*, which officially gives notice of your withdrawal to anyone who has not previously dealt with the firm.

Ultimately, a partnership will succeed or fail depending on the energy, skills, mutual trust, competence, commitment and co-operation of the partners. A good partner is an invaluable asset. He or she can be a source of emotional support as well as financial assistance. Bad partners can ruin the firm.

11

Limited liability

The overwhelming disability attached to trading in ordinary partnership or alone is that, so far as your creditors are concerned, you cannot separate your firm's assets – the premises, equipment, stock, cash in hand, vehicles, etc., of the *business* – from your own private property, which you must use to meet the firm's debts if the business fails.

Normally a solvent small business with a *high cash flow*, or which enters the occasional *ad hoc* high value transaction, should seek limited liability. Suppose, for example, that your monthly income is £70,000, with outgoings of £65,000 per month, giving you £5,000 per month profit, i.e., £60,000 per year. Obviously, you have a profitable business; but suppose something happens to prevent you realising, albeit temporarily, your sales (e.g., a strike among input suppliers, liquidation of a major distributor, an exceptionally severe seasonal decline). You have *already* entered contracts for the supply of inputs such as labour, raw materials, rent on the premises, etc., and are legally committed to settling these debts, yet your income has ceased! After four weeks you owe £65,000, after eight weeks, £130,000; and nearly £200,000 after three months! By now your creditors are issuing writs and the business is collapsing – leaving you saddled with a vast amount of debt which you are personally obliged to clear up.

What limited liability is

To avoid this possibility you could form a limited company (or co-operative registered under the Industrial and Provident Societies Act, see Note 2) which enables you to restrict your personal liability for the business's debts to the amount you have invested in the company (usually a nominal £100), provided the company was formed *before the debts were incurred*.

Effectively, you become a shareholder in your own firm, and are liable for its debts only to the value of your shares. Creditors can claim from the firm's assets (of which your £100 share capital is a part) but they cannot take any of your personal goods because, in law, the business is an entirely different *person* to yourself – you happened to invest in it, and you were its employee; but apart from your shareholding you are not responsible for its debts!

Debts previously incurred

Do not imagine you can avoid liability for debts already run up while you were a sole trader or in partnership simply by forming a company. Debts assumed in your own name (or business name) remain in your own name and are not taken over by the company, which in law is a completely different and independent business to the one that existed before. Only debts invoiced to the company *after* its formation are covered by the principle of limited liability.

Personal guarantees

Note also that banks (and sometimes even trade creditors) ask directors of limited companies to give personal financial guarantees for loans or major credit contracts. If you have signed such guarantees and if the bank or one or two large creditors constitute the great bulk of your outstanding debt, then there is very little point in forming a limited company in the first place. Indeed, you could actually be worse off under such an arrangement because the guarantee could involve a particular personal asset (your house, for instance) which, if seized, could cause your family great emotional as well as financial distress. Nor will your death cancel the guarantee; the asset must still be surrendered even if its loss results in your surviving relatives becoming destitute (typically your spouse has to sign the guarantee as well if there is any question of joint or family ownership).

Another common misconception about limited companies is the idea that their directors are not personally liable for damage caused through allowing trading to continue despite knowing the company is already, or about to become, insolvent. The 1986 Insolvency Act has considerably strengthened creditors' ability to claim from company shareholders' personal estates.

Fraudulent and wrongful trading

There is an important distinction between shareholders who take no part in the management of a company and those who do. Most private limited companies have just two shareholders: one is the director and the other the secretary of the company, and such individuals are necessarily involved in 'management' as implied by the 1986 Act. Personal liability arises in either of two circumstances.

Wrongful trading

A shareholder who helped manage a company is liable for its debts if the company continued to trade prior to liquidation while he or she knew, or ought to have known, there was no reasonable prospect of avoiding insolvency. Wrongful trading is not fraud (i.e., *deliberately* trading in order to obtain benefit despite knowing the business is about to fail). Rather it is the consequence of 'poor judgement'. Courts will ask, 'What should a prudent, knowledgeable person have done in the circumstances?' If a court considers that continuation of the business for a few extra weeks or months might have enabled settlement of a few more debts, no personal liability arises.

Fraudulent trading

This means deliberate bad judgement, i.e., carrying on the business *intending* to put its creditors in a worse position. A court might then seek to identify the individuals responsible for the company's fraudulent trading.

Personal liability can be avoided in such circumstances if you can prove you took 'all reasonable precautions' to avoid potential problems. In practice, this might require your demonstrating that you:

- regularly checked the financial state of the business
- checked the accuracy of management control information, including accounting data
- planned future activities
- did not give preferential treatment to any one creditor (who might be connected to the director in question) at the expense of others
- took proper professional advice, e.g., from a qualified accountant.

Objects of the company

You have to ensure, moreover, that all your business transactions are covered by the Memorandum of Association (see below) of the company you form. If you buy a company 'off the peg', (usually costing about £100) check the 'Objects' clause in the Memorandum. This states the purpose of the business and the activities it exists to undertake. A garage business, for instance, needs an objects clause specifying activities such as the purchase and sale of vehicles, petrol, motor accessories, servicing of vehicles, and so on.

If your off the peg company (acquired perhaps via mail order through the trade press) has an objects clause designed for a business selling fish and chips then you might not be able to enforce contracts which relate to the garage! Such contracts are called *ultra vires* contracts, meaning that a fish and chip shop (the legal personality and purpose of which is established in the objects clause) has no contractual powers to be dealing in anything other than fish and chips (unless the company's objects have been drafted in such general terms that virtually any trading activity is covered – if you have a company check whether this is so in your own case).

Other problems with companies

Two further problems exist.

1. You must prepare annually a profit and loss account and balance sheet audited by a qualified accountant (to whom you will have to pay an auditing fee) and deposit these with the Registrar of Companies.
2. When the business becomes a limited company you become an *employee* of the company (which has its own separate legal identity) and thus liable to PAYE and Class 1 National Insurance

contributions. Additionally, the company must also pay *employers'* NI contributions as an employer in its own right! Note, however, that you become entitled to unemployment benefit if the company fails.

Corporation tax

A payment by the company to you as a director is a tax deductible business expense as far as the company is concerned, but counts as taxable income for you personally. Profits earned by the company attract corporation tax, but for small businesses (with annual profits currently less than £150,000) the rate of corporation tax is the same as the basic rate of personal income tax (presently 25 per cent). However, this concession is only available for one company. A company earning £300,000 profit cannot be split into two in order that each may pay at the lower rate, unless the second company has different owners. Note that a sole trader earning nearly £150,000 per annum would pay tax at much higher marginal rates.

There are no restrictions on how much a sole trader may withdraw from his or her business. Limited companies may pay wages to directors, but company law generally prohibits directors receiving company loans. Note, importantly, that companies are now allowed to sell and buy back their own shares in certain circumstances, thus enabling venture capital financing (see Note 3) to occur (though the company's articles of association must clearly state that this may take place). Companies with five or fewer shareholders (or which are controlled by any number of directors who are also shareholders) are called 'close companies'. The tax authorities might attribute the investment income of a close company to shareholders, i.e., tax officers will assume that investment income is the result of shareholders using the company as a 'money box' for the purpose of paying only 25 per cent corporation tax (whereas if they invested similar amounts as individuals they might be liable for much higher personal rates of tax).

Company formation

Many sole traders are put off the idea of forming a company by the legal jargon involved. Do not be afraid of legal terms: costs and benefits regarding risk, tax and National Insurance contributions and cash flow considerations should determine your choice of legal structure, not the fear of legalistic terminology.

Having read this section you should already understand the

fundamental issues involved and feel reasonably confident about buying a company off the peg. Such companies are usually satisfactory provided your business does not undertake unusual or highly specialist activities and you check to ensure that the objects clause of a company so purchased actually meets your trading needs. A ready-made company is instantly available and cheap; and even if the Memorandum of Association is not exactly to your liking it can easily be altered (by a special resolution at a shareholder's meeting). The name of a company can be changed on payment of a small fee (currently £40) to the Registrar, provided the Registrar does not consider the name chosen to be obscene, offensive or illegal, and provided no other company with that name has already been registered.

Otherwise, the details of company formation need not be your concern, since the registration agent will do most of the work. I assume that as a small business you would not want to consider becoming a public company, which needs £50,000 of share capital at least, and that you wish to maintain your personal and direct control of the firm. Thus, a 'private' company is probably appropriate for your needs. These require only two shareholders (so that you could hold £99 of a total £100 worth of shares and a friend or your spouse have the other £1), one director (normally yourself) and a secretary who might perhaps be the other, minority shareholder. A company secretary is an important officer of the company – responsible for transmitting various documents to the Registrar of Companies, for communicating formally with shareholders on the company's behalf, and for enabling the company to operate in accordance with the law – and not a shorthand typist as the name might suggest.

Briefly, companies are formed by depositing certain documents with the Registrar of Companies and paying a registration fee (currently £50).

Company documents

These documents: the memorandum of association, articles of association (i.e., the internal 'rules' of the company regarding shareholders' voting rights, etc.), a statement of how many shares the company can issue (usually £100), plus details of the company's name, address, shareholders, directors and so on, can be obtained through the post from a registration agent who will already possess hundreds of ready formed companies on file. The agent finds a company suitable for your business and sells the package of its documents to you for currently £100 to £200. Articles of association are not normally included in the package because there is no legal requirement that they be deposited. If they are not, courts simply assume that the specimen articles contained in the Companies (Tables A to F) Regulations 1985 (issued under the Companies Act 1985) apply to the company. All you have to do is complete – together with one other person – two forms in order to change the director and secretary of the company and the company's registered address from those already on file.

Buying a company 'off the peg' is suitable for new businesses or where the firm being converted into a company owns very little property. If, however, the business already possesses land or other substantial assets that are to be passed on to the new company, or if complex leases on premises are involved, then expert advice from a lawyer or chartered accountant is usually required.

Running a company

There is, inevitably, some administrative work attached to running a limited company. On its formation you receive from the registration agent (or your accountant or solicitor) the following items, in addition to the company's memorandum and articles of association:

- a Certificate of Incorporation (a sort of 'birth certificate' for the company)
- 'statutory books' i.e., registers for lists of shareholders, directors and company secretaries, share transfers, details of share allotments, debentures, directors' interests in the company, and mortgages and charges (see Chapter 5)
- the company seal, i.e., a die press used to emboss important company documents
- some share certificates that can be used to issue or transfer company shares.

If the company is purchased off the peg you also receive the letters of resignation of the first director and secretary (i.e., the agents who set the company up) plus draft minutes of the first meeting of the company's board of directors.

The company must hold at least one board meeting per year, and the following rules apply:

(a) One of the meetings must convene the company's annual general meeting.

(b) Each director must receive seven days' notice of every board meeting.

(c) Minutes of board meetings must be kept in a separate 'minute book'.

To run the company you (or the company secretary) must record changes in directors, share transfers, debenture issues, mortgages and charges, and transmit this information to the Registrar at Companies House. An AGM of shareholders must be held within 18 months of incorporation, and annually thereafter (though up to 15 months can elapse between one AGM and the next). Twenty-one days' notice must be given of the date of the AGM.

At the end of each financial year the company must submit its final accounts (approved by the company's directors and externally audited) to the Registrar. These accounts must be accompanied by a directors' report outlining:

(a) any major events occurring during the previous twelve months,

(b) lists of directors' names, addresses and financial interests in the company, and

(c) any political or charitable donations made by the company in excess of £200.

The report must be circulated to all shareholders prior to the annual general meeting.

Exemptions

'Small' companies with (a) annual turnovers not exceeding £2,000,000, (b) assets of less than £975,000 and (c) less than 50 employees, need not file directors' reports, but must still produce these and send copies to shareholders, and the reports must inform shareholders that the company has utilized the exemption. A business satisfying the above mentioned criteria is also exempt from filing its profit and loss account with the Registrar.

Being a director

As a director of a limited company you incur certain legal obligations. And restrictions exist on who may become directors in the first place, in particular:

- a person cannot be a company's sole director *and* its secretary
- undischarged bankrupts may not become company directors.

Directors are legally responsible for ensuring that accounts are prepared, that AGMs are convened and that these and board meetings are properly minuted.

Loans to directors

Companies may not lend more than £2,500 to any one director. Other specific requirements are that:

(a) directors' spouses and children must declare their holdings of the company's shares and/or debentures, and the annual accounts must show company loans to directors' spouses and children (there are substantial legal restrictions on the circumstances and amounts of such loans);

(b) directors must declare any directorships in other UK companies;

(c) if a director has an external business interest in a contract that the company is considering entering into, then he or she must declare this to the board meeting at which the contract is discussed;

(d) directors' contracts of employment (including details of remuneration) must be available for inspection by shareholders;

(e) on a director's resignation, any compensation paid to that person for loss of office must be approved by shareholders.

11

Acquiring other firms

Many factors may cause you to want another firm: control over supplies, integration of processes, acquisition of extra plant and equipment, access to distribution channels, build up of transport facilities, etc. If a competitor is the major source of your difficulties you may want to consider submitting an offer for taking over that business (the deal being financed by a loan secured against the assets of the acquired firm). A common stimulus to expansion by takeover is the need to diversify into new products and market segments. The business you acquire may possess the equipment necessary for producing new (as far as you are concerned) products and already employ staff with the relevant skills. And it might own brand names, logos, etc., already familiar in the markets you intend to enter.

Problems with acquisitions

There are, of course, many potential pitfalls attached to acquisitions, and you must carefully analyse the products, markets and competitors of the firm you have in mind. Common difficulties include the following:

(a) Lack of experience and technical knowledge of the line of business of the firm you intend acquiring. Possibly you can take over existing employees when you buy the firm, but they might soon leave, or your working methods and approaches to problems might differ.

(b) Sudden changes in market conditions or the emergence of new competitors following the acquisition.

(c) Inability to co-ordinate the work of two businesses at the same time. Running two, or more, firms simultaneously requires considerable managerial expertise and attention to the detail of a wide range of issues. Techniques applicable to one of your businesses might not be relevant to the other. At worst, all the problems you have experienced in your first business will be repeated in the second.

(d) The need to gather management control information (rates of return, operating data, information on environmental conditions, etc.) for two businesses instead of one.

Specialist advice may be needed on particular issues, especially if anyone is to be made redundant at the time of the takeover (normally the vendor is responsible for making redundancy payments, although you need a written indemnity from the vendor confirming his or her liability in this respect) or if patents, registered trademarks, service contracts or licences have to be transferred. The dismissal of a worker is automatically unfair (see Chapter 6) if the transfer of ownership of a business is the sole or main reason for the sacking.

Need for caution

Whatever you do, never sign an undertaking that you will honour the acquired business's previously accumulated debts: these are entirely the responsibility of the owner(s) of the old firm. In purchasing the business you have effectively created a completely new firm as far as creditors are concerned; make clear the change of ownership to suppliers as you receive invoices. All existing liabilities should, of course, be settled at the time ownership is transferred.

Remember too that if you choose not to conduct the acquired

business under your own name (e.g., by continuing to trade under
the business's previous title) you are legally obliged to state your
name clearly on all business documents and correspondence.

Danger of new competition

Note that the person who sold you the new business is normally
quite free to set up in competition against you. This possibility might
perhaps be pre-empted by insisting the vendor sign an agreement not
to compete with you within a certain area for so many years, but such
contracts are complex in their interpretation and could be challenged
in court. Generally, courts dislike such agreements (although they
are not illegal) on the grounds that they are 'contrary to the public
interest' and liable, therefore, to be declared void if one of the parties
so desires.

Need for indemnity

If the business you acquire is already a limited company then,
because a company is a legal 'person' in its own right, its liability for
debts, faults in past output, pension schemes for employees, etc.,
continue regardless of who is the majority shareholder. In this case,
however, you are protected by the doctrine of limited liability and
are not personally responsible for the company's debts beyond the
value of your shareholding. Ensure, nevertheless, that all liabilities
have been settled before taking a majority of shares. And it might be
wise to have a solicitor obtain a personal indemnity against previously accumulated company debts from the last majority shareholder. Otherwise you might discover to your horror that the previous owner had run up large debts in the company's name
immediately before the share transfer, resulting perhaps in creditors
forcing liquidation of the company just after you take possession.

11

A revival plan

Detail your intentions for revitalising the business in a written plan.
This will be useful for negotiating with bank managers, creditors,
landlords, local authority business development officers, etc., and
the discipline of writing forces you to clarify your thoughts and
properly investigate key issues. Banks in particular will want to see
objective written analyses and plans for action before lending you
money. Written plans make it easier for outsiders to understand and

evaluate your proposals, and they provide a basis for further discussions. Also, you can use the plan to monitor your progress as you develop the business in its new form.

Layout

The plan should have a beginning, stating *why* you are initiating change; a middle that outlines *how* you intend improving the business; and an end specifying detailed objectives. Start the plan with an introduction outlining the origin of the business, what impelled you initially to set it up, how it has developed, and the barriers and problems that have temporarily (you hope) interrupted its successful expansion, e.g., a technical change, emergence of a new competitor who has perhaps unfairly slashed prices thus forcing you to look to other markets, labour shortages, and so on.

The body of the plan

Then you need headed sections explaining the changes in production methods, supply arrangements, labour procurement, organisation structures, etc., which you intend to implement, plus outlines of any major cost-cutting exercises already undertaken. Follow this with some headed paragraphs on how you will market your new, altered, modified or existing products. List their selling points, who will buy them, where, and why. Describe the following:

- the present state of competition
- any market research undertaken (however basic)
- which market segments you intend to tackle
- your pricing strategy, specifying discount structures and credit policies, with full justifications.

Emphasise the strengths of your plan rather than its weaknesses, although recognise that if major shortcomings exist, outsiders will almost certainly spot them so you might as well point them out from the beginning, but do spell out how you intend to overcome the difficulties. Now state your basic assumptions about the nature of future environments, including:

- tax regimes
- consumer protection and other laws
- production techniques
- public tastes and fashions
- how significant environmental change might affect the business.

Outline intended promotional programmes, mentioning the techniques (coupons, premium offers, competitions, etc.) to be adopted.

The plan should detail your intentions for dealing with existing inadequacies in distribution channels (breakages, deterioration of goods, high packaging costs and so on) specifying the measures you mean to apply to improve the system, e.g., security systems to prevent pilfering, new warehousing arrangements, different outlets, introduction of a mail-order service, purchase or sale of delivery vehicles, etc. Other important matters to be dealt with in the plan are:

- changes in key employees, and the qualifications, skills and experiences of new entrants
- locations of competitors, and how many new competitors you expect in the future
- a recent or proposed change in legal structure, (e.g., from a partnership to a limited company) and the reasons for this
- contingency plans stating alternative sources of supply (following a strike in a major supplier, for example), who will take control if you fall ill, how you will cope with bad weather, and how you will handle other emergencies that might detrimentally affect your firm.

It is important that you have a contingency plan for dealing with serious equipment breakdowns. You might, for example, enter a mutual arrangement with another firm whereby you each agree to make your plant and machinery available to the other for night shift working for a limited period in the event of a dire emergency. (Your employees must, of course, be informed of and agree to such an arrangement.) Regularly check the current costs and availabilities of leased equipment that could be used in these circumstances. And keep an eye open for possibilities for short-term sub-contracting.

Actual or proposed changes in premises require prominent attention in the main part of the document. Outline the predicted benefits of the alterations. the extra facilities available, lower costs and so on.

Financial matters

Outsiders are primarily interested in the financial worth of the business and its future trading prospects. List the firm's:

- assets and liabilities
- key financial ratios
- break-even points for various output prices.

Mention major contracts presently being undertaken, the current state of trade and where your custom is mainly located. Append to the plan a comprehensive 12-month cash flow forecast and an estimated end of year profit and loss account. Then specify the additional resources (machines and equipment, new premises, extra working capital, etc.) necessary for successful operations and from where you want the money to come.

If you are looking for a substantial bank loan the bank will want to ensure the revitalised business can generate sufficient revenues to repay loan capital and interest at appropriate intervals. And the bank will need to know the extent of your personal means and of your own investment in the business. Accordingly, a business revival plan used to raise money must contain a list of your personal assets – property, vehicles, house contents, stocks and shares, insurance policies and so on, that could act as security against a loan.

The section on objectives should state definite sales targets, cost reduction programmes, gross and net margins, and target cash inflows. If you intend introducing new products, specify timetables for their launches. Whenever possible support your objectives with evidence of the likelihood of their success; append documents, statistics, lists of potential buyers, etc.

Detail *precisely* how you expect targets to be attained, but express cautious realism when assessing the probability of their achievement. Quote figures for expected market share, turnover, profit contributions by market segment, product line, customer location, etc.

Summary

Businesses cannot operate effectively in the longer term unless they stand on firm and appropriate organisational and legal foundations. If you are a sole trader, consider the feasibility of taking a partner. And seriously consider whether limited liability would be appropriate for your firm. If you already trade as a limited company, yet still have to provide personal guarantees for all major loans and credit transactions, then ask yourself whether the costs and inconvenience of operating a limited company are really worthwhile.

Advantages and disadvantages are attached to each of the various forms of business ownership. Which to choose depends on the circumstances of the enterprise and how you want it to develop, Note, however, that it is not possible to avoid personal liability for a business's existing debts simply by converting the firm into a company half-way through its life: all debts incurred prior to the conversion remain with you.

Possibly your business can be improved through acquiring another firm. This might enable you to integrate production processes, to obtain much needed plant and equipment, rationalise distribution channels, and so on. Yet many difficulties are attached to mergers and acquisitions and you must take great care not to bite off more than you can chew.

All your proposals for revitalising the business should be embodied in a written revival plan, with lots of headings and a comprehensive statement of the various aspects of your firm's present and likely future operations.

11

Checklist

---

1. How many people do you know who might be prepared to inject fresh capital into your firm?
2. If you go bust tomorrow how much will your business owe, and to what extent are these liabilities covered by the realisable assets of the firm?
3. Do you understand the difference between wrongful trading and fraudulent trading? If not, go back to page 205 in the text.
4. Can you list three benefits of your acquiring another firm?
5. Do you feel you have the experience, technical knowledge and energy to run two businesses at the same time?
6. Have you prepared a formal plan for reviving your business?
7. What are the three major business objectives you wish to achieve within the next three years?
8. What are the major barriers which might prevent you achieving these objectives?
9. List two significant technological developments that may occur in your industry over the next five years and state how they will affect your firm.
10. What would happen to your business if its senior employee were to quit next week?

Notes

1. The address is: Registrar of Companies, Companies House, 55–71 City Road, London EC1Y 1BB.
2. For details see R. Bennett, *Organisation and Management*, Pitman Publishing, London, 1988.
3. Venture financing means that an outside body (e.g., a merchant bank) buys shares in your business in order to inject capital, takes a big share of the profits in return, and then sells the shares back to the company for an agreed price at a predetermined future date.

12 The wolf at the door

Taking stock □ Premises □ Rent and rates □ Mortgage arrears □ Dealing with creditors □ Loans from banks □ Security □ Selling out □ Valuing assets □ Summary □ Checklist

So far I have concentrated on practical measures for turning around businesses which, although they have experienced problems and thus achieved only modest rates of return, are nevertheless fully solvent in the medium, if not the short, term. But how should you proceed when confronted with *really* serious financial difficulties – when you haven't any money at all and are being hounded by creditors?

This chapter is intended to help you cope with an immediate and desperate cash flow deficit. It outlines a plan of emergency action for use when you simply cannot honour your outstanding bills. Drastic measures are involved, typically requiring the surrender, at a loss, of capital assets. Yet the forfeit of assets, in association with other crisis policies, may be the only way to save the firm; indeed, the only way you can avoid personal bankruptcy and the consequent seizure of your private estate.

Taking stock

In this situation you should list all the amounts you owe in order *not* of when they fall due, but rather in terms of the seriousness of the *consequences* of various creditors taking action to recover outstanding balances. For instance, the detrimental effects of a supplier putting you onto a 'cash with order' basis until you settle your credit account might not be as severe as, say, having your gas or electricity cut off during the winter. Conversely, you might be able to do without gas-fired central heating for a month or two in the summer, but it is unlikely (though not entirely impossible) that you could do without a telephone.

Ruthless realism is required. Impose a strict embargo on all capital expenditure and look for fast ways of raising cash. If you operate a very small single-person business you might be able to take a paid job for a few weeks and run the business part-time. This is exhausting, but might just be feasible in the very short term, and at least it keeps your business alive.

Set all your surplus assets (including unused stock) and wherever possible replace purchased capital assets (vehicles, equipment, etc., which you can liquidate for cash) with leased items. Make sure you are fully informed of all revenues the moment they arrive, of needs for immediate expenditures (minimum gas or electricity payments needed to avoid being cut off, for example), and the expected dates of other necessary spending.

Specific policies are needed in each of the following areas.

Premises

While sale and leaseback (see Chapter 4) is obviously an appropriate medium-term capital raising measure for businesses that own their premises, it takes time to organise and itself involves substantial expenditures (solicitors and valuation fees, etc.). In buying your premises you will almost certainly have financed the transaction through a mortgage, probably through a bank or building society (see Note 1). A bank will have lent to you – against the security of the business's premises and/or other assets – for anything up to 20 years. Building society loans are available for business premises, and are similarly secured, but usually they are only available to people who have already paid off most of their private household mortgages.

Increasing an existing mortgage

If to date you have a good mortgage repayment record the best solution may be to approach the mortgagor of the premises and request an increase in the size of the mortgage, and/or an extension in the period of the loan, with the bigger mortgage being secured against the building's higher current market worth. Such an injection of finance might even enable you to pay off all your outstanding business debts and totally reconstitute the firm; and the need for alternative, more draconian, measures is overcome. Note too that if presently you run a large overdraft, then your borrowings are *extremely* expensive in view of the high interest rates on overdraft loans. It will pay you, therefore, to swap overdrafts (and any other high cost short-term borrowing) for higher mortgage repayments but at a significantly lower interest rate. Indeed, a substantial lengthening of the repayment period might stretch out the repayments on a higher mortgage to the extent where the monthly amount payable actually falls. And you will, of course, have realised a substantial capital sum.

Talk to the lender

Mortgagors will usually listen to small business owners who wish to enter this type of arrangement, because most lenders realise that a freshly constituted firm is far better able to repay a mortgage (and is therefore a safer lending proposition) than a run-down business constantly struggling to cope with high priced debts! Banks and building societies can, and do, reclaim property in the last resort, but generally wish to avoid the legal and administrative costs, inconvenience and unpleasantness associated with this. Thus, they might respond sympathetically to a request for a higher mortgage that helps prevent such an eventuality. Remember, however, that you can do this only once. If you squander the benefits of a higher mortgage you will not be given a second chance.

Subletting

Subletting part of your premises provides a quick source of income, though certain costs and inconveniences are necessarily involved – separate telephone lines must be installed, office partitions erected, and there is the additional expense of advertising for tenants. Note that extra planning permission may be needed before conversion occurs.

12

Property conversion

Significant economies of scale are available from property conversion: it might be little more expensive to subdivide an entire large building into small lettable units than to undertake all the work necessary just to fit out your own firm. And the rent from subletting the units thus created might pay not only for the conversion work itself but also for the essential maintenance and repairs that you would have had to undertake in any event.

Even if your premises are leased and the lease does not permit subletting it may still be worth approaching the landlord to ask for special permission to convert the premises and sublet. After all, you are offering to undertake the conversion into smaller, possibly more marketable units at your own expense, and you would not be doing this if the demand for smaller units did not exist.

Make room to sublet

If you have recently expanded the business you may feel that you cannot possibly make room to sublet. But expansion does not inevitably lead to greater space utilisation provided that:

(a) you have efficient systems for dealing with goods inward, stock control, and finished goods awaiting dispatch (so that large areas are not tied up accommodating excessive amounts of idle stock) and

(b) that you take the trouble to reorganise, tidy up the existing premises, and generally conserve the floor space needed for your operations.

Check local rents

Of course, conversion and subletting should only be considered if local rent levels and user demand are sufficient to make the exercise financially worthwhile. Accordingly, you should regularly collect information from local estate agents and others on current rentals for nearby premises of varying quality and size.

Rent and rates

A business that rents its premises will have a lease or a licence (see Note 2) that determines the precise conditions of its tenancy. Most rented premises are let under a lease of between 3 and 20 years, although shorter term agreements are possible, providing, perhaps, for as little as a week's notice to terminate the contract. However, these very short-term leases are not common because of their unpopularity with tenants, who dislike them on account of their inherent lack of tenant security.

Rent arrears

Posssibly the most tempting thing to do when you cannot pay all your outstanding bills is miss paying this month's rent. Unfortunately, arrears can soon build up to the point where they become a major threat to the survival of the firm, and if you fall too far behind the landlord will seek to repossess the premises.

Danger of eviction

Legally, it is much easier to evict someone from business premises than from a household; indeed, if you are well behind with the rent on business premises then a court has *little option* but to grant the landlord an eviction order, which if it is not obeyed will be quickly followed by forcible eviction by court officers.

This rapid eviction need not occur, however, if you are 'in dispute' with the landlord regarding a lease 'covenant'. Lease covenants involve matters such as:

- who is responsible for the maintenance and repair of property (for instance, you might be justified in withholding rent if necessary repairs have not been undertaken by a landlord who is contractually liable for their execution)
- who is responsible for the payment of rates
- the details of procedures for repossession.

The lease

Three aspects of a lease are especially important for a small business in financial difficulties: rent reviews, subletting clauses, and surrender arrangements. Most longer term leases (in excess of two or three years, say) contain a rent review clause.

Rent reviews

The size of the rent increase associated with the clause is subject to negotiation, normally based on some published index of changes in property prices or a general measure of inflation. A rent review can come as a nasty shock to a recently established business which did not anticipate a big rent increase early in its occupation of a building. Look carefully at your lease to identify any such provision, and budget generously for possible rent increases. Look also for any clause that might prevent you subletting parts of the premises in times of crisis.

Surrender values

The third potential source of difficulty – lease clauses that prevent you terminating the lease quickly or assigning it to another business without penalty – can be most distressing. Landlords normally insist that tenants see out their tenancies or pay full compensation for early

12

surrender. Check your lease to ensure you fully understand its surrender provisions.

Avoiding eviction

If you are evicted for rent arrears you will have difficulties in finding new premises because landlords (or estate agents acting on their behalf) usually want to know your previous location and why you left that building. The physical move attached to eviction may itself disrupt your existing business. Eviction, therefore, must always be avoided.

When you become a long way behind with the rent explain to the landlord or managing agent the reasons *why* you cannot meet your obligations, emphasising the positive measures you are taking to revitalise the business. Landlords are not anxious to incur the administrative and legal costs attached to eviction and the inevitable loss of the accumulated rent already owing. Hence they might react more sympathetically to a reasonable proposal for slowly reducing the arrears than you might initially have expected.

Make an offer

The process of reporting your difficulties to the landlord may take quite a long time, thus giving the business a limited period in which to recover, especially if the landlord uses an agent to collect the rent. Offer to pay your arrears by increasing your monthly rent by a small amount, starting a couple of months from now. This presents the landlord with a tangible alternative to having to write off the debt: arrears cease to accumulate and you demonstrate your good faith to the landlord.

If your premises are too big and the lease forbids you to sublet, point out to the landlord how the business may collapse, leaving the landlord with a large unsettled account if the lease is not altered. Perhaps you could sublet and pay the landlord a percentage of the incoming rent, or simply redefine the boundaries of your tenancy (at a lower rent) thus allowing the landlord to re-let other parts of your existing premises.

The costs of eviction

Emphasise the *costs* to the landlord of not accommodating your needs. Tenants of local authority premises sometimes have an advantage here because local authorities are subject to democratic control and you can appeal directly to your local councillor if the authority threatens to evict. And in fact, few councils will actually put a small business onto the streets (except as a very last resort) provided the firm demonstrates its determination not to allow rent arrears to accumulate further. Indeed, a local council may even help you find cheaper alternative accommodation.

Private landlords will not normally allow large arrears to build up and will quickly seek an eviction order once they suspect that a tenant is insolvent. On receipt of a court summons you must first decide whether or not to contest the action. Either you 'admit' the landlord's allegation of non-payment, or you 'defend' your position. Grounds for defence include:

- disagreement over how much is owed
- counterclaims for emergency repairs you needed to undertake at your own expense despite their being the landlord's responsibility
- the landlord's failure properly to maintain the building.

Following the delivery of a contested summons, go to the landlord with another offer. State how much you can afford to pay each month and contrast this with the possibly substantial legal costs and inconvenience of proceeding with the eviction.

Rate arrears

Failure to pay business rates is a criminal, rather than civil, offence and the amount you owe is not subject to negotiation. You *must* pay your rates, since rates are a form of taxation. The local authority will not (indeed cannot) write off rate arrears. However, this does not mean you cannot reach an agreement with the local authority regarding the form and timing of payment. And you can always apply to the ratings office of the local authority for a rates reduction, say because of changed environmental circumstances.

Mortgage arrears

A bank or building society may be prepared to suspend or reduce your capital and/or interest repayments temporarily. It is better to ask than simply await a summons to court in respect of a possession order. Do not think you are better off allowing 'nature to take its course' through a court order, because substantial legal, administrative and valuation costs will be involved in the sale of the property following its repossession. And all these costs are deducted from the sale proceeds before the sum raised is applied to the outstanding balance. Also, the mortgagor will be seeking a quick sale and thus might sell to the first purchaser that comes along, even if only a low price is offered. Remember always that banks and building societies want to avoid unpleasant and administratively troublesome repossession proceedings. Mortgagors invariably prefer to accommodate the unfortunate circumstances afflicting bona fide borrowers than to evict, even when legally entitled to do so, provided the mortgagee demonstrates a genuine willingness to repay the arrears. In assessing your commitment the lender (a bank, say) will consider:

(a) how quickly you came to see them after getting into financial difficulties;

(b) whether the source of your cash flow problems lies in your own negligence or incompetence, or in external and perhaps unavoidable events;

(c) the extent and nature of the measures you have implemented to revitalise the business and the likelihood of their success;

(d) whether you ignored earlier warning letters (other than perhaps the first couple).

The longer you delay discussing your predicament with the lender the worse it is for you. Note in particular that the issue of a court order in relation to premises may lead to your name appearing on a list of general bad payers (many credit agencies collect information on people against whom such court orders have been issued) resulting possibly in your not being able to obtain business, or indeed personal, credit overall.

Services

Gas and electricity can be cut off if you do not pay your bills, without the need for a court order. Then you are taken to court for the amount outstanding. If you cannot settle your gas and electricity accounts then either you must choose to do without these services (and eventually pay substantial reconnection charges), or negotiate with the gas or electricity authorities with a view to settling the arrears over a protracted period. Alternatively, if yours is a one-person firm with tiny premises, you could arrange for slot meters to be installed, pre-set so as to recover some of the accumulated arrears from each coin put in the meter.

Similar considerations apply to telephone bills. It is unlikely that you will be disconnected provided you inform British Telecom about your current financial difficulties, and negotiate a special arrangement to clear your outstanding balance.

Dealing with creditors

You can afford to ignore the first couple of reminders from a creditor, but not thereafter. If you are in real trouble you should write to each major creditor offering an excuse for not paying outlining what you intend doing to settle outstanding balances. Explain that, for example:

   (a) you are awaiting some large payments from your own customers and are *actively* pursuing them for the money you owe, including the threat of legal action;

   (b) you have not been able to produce an important order because of non-availability of raw materials;

   (c) a strike among suppliers or distributors has temporarily disrupted your operations;

   (d) the business depends crucially on your own personal inputs and that you have recently been ill.

Show commitment

Say that you are fully committed to settling your debts, and apologise for the inconvenience your behaviour is causing. Offer whatever interim payment you can reasonably afford and specify when you anticipate being in a position to pay the remainder. Obviously you need to pay relatively more to the most potentially troublesome of your creditors, but do offer something to everyone. If a creditor starts charging you interest on unsettled balances then compare the cost of paying this (though check with an accountant or other professional advisor whether the creditor is legally entitled to charge interest under that particular contract) with the interest cost of a bank loan, bearing in mind the need to offer security against a formal bank loan.

   These letters are guaranteed to trigger telephone calls from creditors. Prepare for this, and use the conversations as opportunities to reinforce your case for deferring payment. Ask for a discount on the sum outstanding. The creditor is unlikely to agree but will at least have something to think about instead of contemplating legal action. Creditors want their money and are usually aware of the costs and

12

inconvenience of court proceedings. So you lose little through asking for special consideration.

Collection agencies

It is sometimes easier to deal with a debt collection agency than with the firm to which you originally owed money. If the agency has 'purchased' the debt it will have done so at a considerable discount (say half the book value of the debt), so it can still make a profit by accepting an offer of partial settlement. Alternatively, the agency might have taken the debt on a commission basis, and thus will normally be willing to reschedule your repayments over a longer period, providing its total commission is not affected.

Payments moratoria

As a last resort consider discussing with your major suppliers the possibility of a payments moratorium, whereby creditors agree to a delay (three months, for example) in the settlement of outstanding balances. Creditors promise not to take legal action in the interim, but do not forgo their right to sue eventually. Payments moratoria are best arranged through a professional advisor (e.g., a solicitor, accountant or branch bank manager) since creditors will usually insist that an independent outside party supervise the arrangement.

Explain your problems

Write to creditors in the manner previously outlined. Explain the sources of your problems and the crisis measures you are implementing. And say that your professional advisor (who might actually draft the letter) will collect and hold all the money you receive during the period of the moratorium. Offer to pay off some part of the debt owing to each creditor after a certain period) the end of the second month, for instance) and suggest an intended timescale for settling remaining balances.

The advantages

This puts the ball firmly in your creditors' court. Asking for a moratorium has several advantages:

- creditors are made aware of your difficulties and the fact that you seriously intend to rescue the business

- they realise there is little point in their taking legal action against your firm
- you demonstrate your integrity and you gain time in which to restructure your finances.

In your letter emphasise your need for *increased revenue*, and include an offer to provide them with goods or services at a special discount and/or to give commission for any business with third parties they secure on your behalf. Of course, a creditor may choose to petition for your bankruptcy, but this will happen anyway if you simply continue to ignore demands for settlement of your debts.

A bankruptcy petition (see Chapter 13) is more likely if you possess many assets that could be liquidated to settle outstanding balances. In this case you may need to mortgage (see below) some or all of these assets to your creditors as a gesture of goodwill.

Hire purchase

Your firm may not sell equipment obtained on hire purchase since it does not belong to you until all instalments have been paid. If you default on payment the goods can be reclaimed (although a court order is needed once you have paid some minimum amount – see Chapter 10). This might be the best thing from your point of view. Also, the hirer may be anxious to negotiate a system of lower repayments over a longer period in view of the difficulty of rehiring second-hand equipment, plus the costs and inconveniences involved.

Loan sharks

If yours is a very small single-person business financed entirely by yourself, and you have been foolish enough to fall into the hands of a loan shark who charges exorbitant interest for short-term loans, the best thing usually is to write to the lender advising that you are unable to repay the loan and suggesting that the lender take action through the County court. Then you can ask the court for a repayment schedule suited to your particular circumstances (see Chapter 10).

Loans from banks

If you are frank and honest with your bank manager then he or she is unlikely to take you to court. Banks greatly prefer to negotiate reasonable arrangements with customers than to enforce court actions. Explain your circumstances, and ask for help. Never ignore warning letters from the bank. If you do the local branch will simply refuse to honour your cheques and refer the case to its regional office, whereupon legal action *will* be taken to recover the loan. And once your cheques begin to bounce your credit rating collapses. Two major options are possible.

Rescheduling of repayments

This might involve converting one type of loan into another, e.g., from a loan with conventional monthly repayments to a loan which requires only the interest (and nothing from the capital sum advanced) to be paid in the first year of the loan's duration. Equally, the bank may be prepared to change an existing overdraft (repayable on demand) into a fixed term, fixed interest loan. You save quite a lot on bank charges here because your current account ceases to be in deficit, although you pay more interest in total.

Further loans

You might take out further loans to clear existing repayment arrears and to provide finance for future operations. Such loans will have to be secured against your own and/or the business's assets. The question of security deserves further consideration.

Security

The bank will want to know the precise purpose for which the requested sum is intended, and will require comprehensive cash flow forecasts that demonstrate your firm's probable ability to repay the loan on schedule. Also, a detailed business revival plan (as outlined in Chapter 10) should accompany the application. As well as studying your firm's immediate prospects the bank will also consider your personal skills and qualities, especially your prospects for paid employment if – despite everything – the business does eventually go under. From the bank's perspective a 'good' security is one that is quickly realisable, keeps its value, and adequately covers the loan. Certain securities have market values. Banks will not advance 100 per cent of the current market values of such assets because market prices fluctuate and the bank will fear falls in market price. The commonest means of providing security against loans are outlined below.

Life assurance policies

You can assign to the bank the rights to which you are entitled under an existing life assurance policy. Thus, you continue to pay the premiums, but if you die the bank and not your next of kin receives the benefits of the policy. If you default on the premiums, the bank liquidates the policy at its surrender value (which the bank will ensure fully covers the loan before advancing any money). Note that you lose heavily in terms of the value of your past contributions if the policy is in fact surrendered.

Banks are usually willing to take life assurance policies as security because of their straightforward nature, relative to other assets. They are reliable, customers understand what is going on, and few legal formalities or administrative costs are necessary. You will be required, however, to furnish the bank with confidential personal information and perhaps to undertake a medical examination, since the bank needs to protect itself against customers failing to disclose to their insurance companies 'material facts', or lying about their health in order to obtain a policy. (Insurance companies will not honour policies in these circumstances.)

Land and buildings

The bank may take a mortgage on your property, or perhaps a debenture secured against certain of your assets. A mortgage is a 'conveyance' (transfer) of an interest in property as security for debt. Mortgages may be 'legal' or 'equitable'. Under a legal mortgage the bank assumes legal ownership of the property which it can sell as it wishes. With an equitable mortgage the bank has claim to the property, but may not sell it. (Equitable mortgages can be used where someone else *already* has an interest in the same property.) Normally the bank will want to have a legal mortgage.

12

Debentures

Debentures usually apply to limited companies. A debenture is a loan to a company conditional on the debenture holder obtaining sufficient of the company's assets to settle the loan if the borrower defaults on repayment. Normally, the bank will require the debenture to be secured against specific named assets (such as equipment or premises owned by the firm), in which case the security is known as a 'fixed' charge against the firm's assets. If the business is a limited company then 'floating' charges may also be used, in which case the loan is secured against all the company's assets. In the latter case, however, the bank has no right to claim specific assets if the business fails. Instead it must take its place alongside the rest of the company's creditors and may receive only partial settlement.

Stocks and shares

If you own stocks and shares you can offer them as security, although the bank will only advance a portion of their current market value because of uncertainties caused by fluctuations in market prices.

Guarantees

Here, a third party agrees to be personally responsible for the debts of another person or business. If you trade as a limited company the bank will normally insist that you personally guarantee the repayment of any loans it makes to the company; and the guarantee will probably have to be secured against your home and/or other personal assets. If you are married your spouse has a claim on half the house, so the bank may further demand that your spouse also sign the guarantee in order to provide the bank with complete indemnity. Before accepting a guarantee the bank will carefully examine your financial status and debt history.

Another means of providing security is to give the bank the right to reclaim and sell the goods which you purchased with the loan should you fail to repay the money. Banks are typically reluctant to enter this sort of arrangement (sometimes referred to as 'hypothecation' of a loan) because they have neither possession nor control of the goods, and they must rely on your willingness to hand them over – complete and undamaged – following your default.

Other crisis measures

Instead of offering a life assurance policy as security against a loan you could cash it in at its surrender value. But think carefully before doing this, and note that the option is not available if the policy has already been used as security for an existing debt. Surrender values are usually low (certainly much less than the amount you will already have contributed), and you might desperately need this money for personal use if your business does eventually go under.

Do you really need a car?

Try instead to economise on operating costs and to raise cash by selling non-essential assets. Do you *really* need a car, for example? The sale of a vehicle can raise a couple of thousand pounds, and public transport – while inconvenient – can be used during an immediate short-term crisis. Consider daily or weekly car hire as a temporary alternative to having your own vehicle.

Credit cards

Interest rates on credit cards are enormously high, and you should never use credit cards for long run financing. Nevertheless, judicious timing of purchasing using credit cards can provide short-term relief to a small business experiencing moderate cash flow difficulties. Credit card companies will reschedule the payments of users whose credit card debts get out of control, but will insist that no further use be made of the facility.

Selling out

If you are approached by an outsider interested in purchasing your business then clearly the firm is not without value. Perhaps you can suggest a merger rather than outright sale, especially if the other party is a competitor, in which case you will already know each other's strengths, problems and business methods. Such a merger might enable you jointly to tackle new or bigger projects and markets previously inaccessible because of your limited resources and lack of experience and expertise.

Note also the possibility of approaching a very large company which might welcome the opportunity of incorporating your firm into its overall supply or distribution system. The buyer will impose its own administrative routines on the business, and you will probably become an employee (subject to PAYE and Class 1 National Insurance contributions) of the takeover company, subject to its day-to-day control. But at least you have an income and continue to manage the firm.

A going concern

In the case of a straight sale, you want if possible to sell your business as a 'going concern', since the market value of an ongoing business is invariably higher than one which is not operational. The firm has

12

existing products (each with its own unique attributes and selling points), machinery and/or office furniture and equipment, customers, a distribution system, suppliers, a business image, product brands and premises. The purchaser of the firm is thus saved considerable start-up expenses, the costs of acquiring capital assets, and the need to establish new business and product images.

How much is a business worth?

Valuing a business is not easy, yet you need to be able to establish a provisional valuation figure before negotiations can even begin. Also, you might wish to consider winding up your present business and buying another, more profitable, firm which you will have to value to establish whether it represents a good purchase. Ultimately, the only way to value a business properly is to put it up for sale and observe the offers that result. It is possible to auction a business, simply accepting the highest bid, but the procedure is not common. Usually, therefore, you must compute an initial benchmark figure and advertise the business at this price; or perhaps along the lines of 'offers invited from' a stated minimum value.

There are two fundamental approaches to valuation. One assesses value from the assets the business possesses, the other from the earnings it can create.

Valuing assets

The true values of a business's owned assets are not necessarily reflected in its books. Fixed assets are depreciated annually at the rate which is most tax efficient, not the rate which most accurately reflects their loss in worth. Thus, valuable fixed assets can remain within a business long after they have theoretically ceased to exist (i.e., when they are completely written off in accounting terms). This is frequently the case with motor vehicles, machines and certain items of furniture.

Equally, certain assets might be massively overpriced, so you should never even consider buying a business merely on the basis of its balance sheet – inspect its physical assets personally, and make sure that all the assets offered for the inspection actually belong to the firm.

Valuing current assets

Valuation of current assets (stock, debtors, cash) is just as difficult. Everyone in business knows that *some* debtors will not settle their bills, yet establishing which *particular* debtors will default and the extent of subsequent losses is extremely difficult. You must examine the structure of outstanding debts, especially the periods for which certain debts have remained unsettled, and why longstanding debts have not been cleared. The 'cash' figure in a balance sheet represents cash available on the date the balance sheet was compiled – it might all be spent a week after!

Book values thus represent little more than a starting point for true valuation. Thereafter you need to assess the business's worth *either* for its 'break-up' value, or as a going concern.

Break-up value

This means the aggregate of the selling prices of the firm's disposable assets on dissolution of the business, after deducting selling costs such as estate agents' fees when disposing of property, costs of transporting goods to points of sale, expenses of salespeople, etc. The past ability of assets to generate earnings within the firm is ignored.

The value of a going concern

Here you examine not so much the sales potential of individual items but rather the firm's total capacity to create new earnings and growth. And 'two plus two' often equals more than four in these circumstances. Land and buildings, for example, may be worth considerably more when plant and equipment is already installed and working than when the land and buildings have to be sold in isolation.

12

Investments

Investments in stocks, shares and debentures might also be worth more when viewed from a going concern perspective. A firm's portfolio of equity investments, for example, will have a low book value immediately after a stock market crash, yet may still offer a sound and potentially lucrative long-term investment for a firm which is able to hold on to its stocks and shares until they recover their value. Similarly, a long overdue debt owing to the firm will raise little if sold to a debt collector, but might be paid in full if the firm continues in operation and can thus wait for eventual settlement. Stock that is just about to be converted into saleable finished products is worth potentially more than stock that has to be auctioned immediately.

Goodwill

The difference between the value of a firm's assets and its sale price is referred to as 'goodwill', which is actually realised only at the moment of the firm's purchase. It represents the worth of the business attributable to it being a going concern, including:

- its good name
- brand images
- existing customers and suppliers
- access to markets and skilled labour
- the state of its order books and similar attributes independent of physical possessions.

Note how the value of goodwill fluctuates as trading conditions alter. An economic recession, emergence of a new competitor, adverse press or other publicity, or a change in public taste or fashion can quickly wipe out a business's goodwill.

Estimating goodwill

Estimating goodwill is problematic. Basically, you have to predict the firm's minimum net profits over, say, the next three years, add to this the expected break-up value of the business in three years' time, and then ask how much you would have to invest today in a safe, interest-earning asset (a building society account, for instance) in order to earn these revenues. Suppose, for example, that I expect a business to yield £20,000 a year net profit after tax for each of the next three years (thereafter I have no idea of likely trading prospects, so I only consider a three-year period) and that I anticipate being able to sell the firm's physical assets for £30,000 in three years' time. The interest rate on building society deposits (after tax) is currently six per cent and I have no reason to expect this to alter significantly over the next couple of years. To generate the £90,000 I expect from the business (i.e., three times £20,000 plus £30,000) I would need to put £75,566 into the building society today and leave it there for three years (see Note 3). I ignore the possibility of investing the business's first year's £20,000 profits in an interest-bearing deposit account for the next two years and of investing the second year's profit intact for a further year. You can take these possibilities into account if you wish, but you then need to do more calculations.

On these assumptions I would be crazy to pay more than £75,566 for this business, because I can achieve the forecast minimum return simply by depositing the same amount in the building society, at no risk. Fifty thousand, it seems to me, is a reasonable figure on which to base negotiations; less if I expect the interest rate to rise (see Note 4).

Summary

Severe financial difficulties require a drastic response. Keep calm, be rational, and tackle your problems systematically. Accept that you may have to surrender capital assets, but realise that there are still many things you can do to save the firm. Establish priorities and initiate crisis measures for coping with serious deficits in your cash flow.

Place an embargo on all new capital spending and look for emergency means of raising funds. Consider taking a temporary part-time job, and if you own your premises investigate the feasibility of a sale and leaseback arrangement. Perhaps you can increase your personal mortgage or otherwise raise money secured on property owned by yourself or the firm.

Extending the period you take to settle your bills might usefully constitute your first line of defence, though beware of the possibility of creditors suspending delivery of vital supplies to the business.

You might be able to get away with not paying your rent or mortgage repayments for a couple of months, but will face eviction in the longer term.

Creditors may be sympathetic to requests for accommodation, provided you make a sincere and sensible approach and demonstrate your intention eventually to clear up outstanding debts. Explain to each creditor the reasons for your financial problems, asking for an extended period in which to pay. In really grave circumstances you might need to employ a solicitor or accountant to request a payments moratorium for unsettled bills.

Your bank could be your biggest friend in this sort of situation. It can offer advice, may be prepared to reschedule the repayment of existing loans, and might even lend you more money, provided appropriate security can be found.

12

Checklist

---

1. Have you a contingency plan for dealing with a serious cashflow deficit?
2. How well do you know personally the creditors to whom you owe most money?
3. Might it be possible to convert your premises into smaller units?
4. How quickly could you sublet part of your premises?
5. Does your lease contain a rent review clause and if so, do you understand its provisions?
6. If you were to stop paying your rent, how soon do you think you would be evicted from your premises?
7. What is the extent of the security you can offer against a loan?
8. Could you do without your firm's car for a short period?
9. For how much do you think you could sell your business in its present state? What is your estimate of the goodwill of the business?

Notes

1. Property 'licences' offer a more flexible means for letting commercial property than is available through the traditional lease. The conditions embodied within a licence are usually similar to those of a typical lease, but offer minimal security of tenure since licences do not imply any legal interest in premises and thus are not covered by the Landlord and Tenant Act 1987. Also, you cannot sell a licence at a premium as you can an orthodox lease.
2. Merchant banks also make loans for premises, but usually only to large and well established businesses. And they often require an equity in the firms to which they lend. A further possible source of finance for premises is 'Investors in Industry' Plc which is a consortium of commercial banks plus the Bank of England. This body frequently lends to small businesses that wish to buy their own premises. Additionally, local authorities sometimes provide finance for these purposes.
3. This is nothing more than 'compound interest' in reverse. The compound interest formula is: $A = P(I+R)^n$, where A is the amount at the end of the period, P is the principal invested today, R is the interest rate and 'n' the number of years of the investment.

$$\text{Thus,} \quad P = \frac{A}{(1+R)^n} = \frac{90,000}{(1.06)^3} = £75,566$$

4. A common rule of thumb for calculating goodwill is to compute the average difference between the profits of the business and the interest that would have been earned through depositing an amount equal to the value of the business's assets in, say, a building society account over the last three years, and multiplying this by three. Then the break-up value of the firm's assets is added to the resulting figure to give the price at which the firm is offered for sale.

12

13 Thinking about the unthinkable

Bankruptcy and company liquidation □ What bankruptcy means □ How bankruptcy occurs □ Discharge □ Company liquidation □ Administration orders □ Summary

If you are up to your neck in debt and there is absolutely no hope of the business succeeding you must confront the unpleasant reality of having to close down. Previous chapters have suggested ways of helping you avoid this predicament: numerous stop-gap survival measures were outlined, and several hints and strategies for repositioning and promoting your product offered. Nevertheless, despite the very best efforts of their owners, some businesses do go under. And it would be improper of me not to tell you about the circumstances in which bankruptcy and company liquidation occur and the procedures attached to the dissolution of a small firm.

Bankruptcy and company liquidation

Sole traders or partners in business without limited liability can be declared 'bankrupt' by a County court. If, on the other hand, you have formed a limited company then it is the *company* that is 'liquidated' – as an independent legal entity in its own right. And you are not personally responsible for the company's debts beyond the value of your shareholding in the company. Bankrupts, conversely, must use personal assets and future earnings to pay off business debts. They stand to lose their houses, furniture, vehicles and other 'non-essential' possessions (although the court ultimately determines what constitutes a non-essential possession). Note, importantly, that most banks will not lend to a limited company unless at least one company director personally guarantees the loan's repayment, if necessary from his or her private estate. Such loans are typically secured against specific personal assets (houses or cars, for example) which are seized if the company fails to redeem the loan.

What bankruptcy means

Bankruptcy law in this country follows the principle that although a bankrupt person must use his or her personal wealth to settle outstanding debt, the bankrupt should be free of these liabilities and thus able to start another business following the expiry of a 'reasonable' period.

You can be declared bankrupt if you run your own sole trader business or share ownership or responsibility of any firm that does not have limited liability. If, as a partner in a business, you have more money than other partners then the firm's creditors will probably come gunning for you before they go after the others: creditors are not concerned that seizing your personal assets and not those of your partners will mean that you make a disproportionately high contribution to settling the partnership's total debts – they just want their money.

The bankruptcy petition

A bankruptcy petition differs from an enforcement order (see Chapter 5) in that whereas the latter seeks settlement of a specific proven debt (e.g., by seizure of particular physical assets), bankruptcy is the requirement that the debtor settle *all* outstanding debts – the totality of the debtor's income and assets being taken from the debtor and managed by a trustee appointed by the court specifically for this purpose. Thus, petitions for you to be declared bankrupt are especially likely in the following circumstances:

(a) Several creditors have not been paid and, realising you are unlikely to settle any of their accounts, they get together to recover as much of the money they are owed as possible.

(b) You have backtracked on settlement of a single (perhaps substantial) proven debt and the creditor uses the threat of the public humiliation associated with bankruptcy proceedings as a means of extracting payment.

(c) Creditors believe you are concealing the true extent of your personal assets.

(d) An enforcement order has not been honoured and the creditor involved wishes to punish you (and recoup at least some money) by having you publically disgraced as a bankrupt.

(e) A small creditor thinks you will use whatever money you have to settle larger debts with what to you are more important suppliers at the expense of the small creditor, and thus petitions for bankruptcy as a means of obtaining compensation.

An important factor in a creditor's decision to try and have you declared bankrupt is that your formal bankruptcy automatically provides the creditor with sufficient evidence that a debt is 'bad' so that it can be written off in respect of tax and VAT.

What you stand to lose

Once you become aware of impending bankruptcy it is unlawful for you to get rid of valuable assets by giving them away or selling them cheaply to close friends or relatives with the intention of recovering them later. Moreover, the official receiver is empowered to seize such assets *regardless* of the name in which they are held. The court, acting on the official receiver's advice, decides which of your goods (including houshold goods) you and your family need in order to survive and confiscates the rest.

Court estimates of 'need' depend on family circumstances: how many children you have, the presence of an elderly relative or other dependent family member requiring special attention and expenditure, and so on. All bank accounts, including joint accounts, are frozen at the point of bankruptcy, and all monies received in bank and similar accounts are thereafter turned over to the trustee. Note, importantly, that if someone (including your spouse) leaves you money in a will, your family cannot benefit because the amounts received belong to the trustee and not to you. Thus, if you are a bankrupt female parent and your husband dies leaving you all his money, then your children might never see any of that money because it has to be used first to settle your debts. Your husband will probably want to will all his assets direct to the children in these circumstances.

Things that cannot be taken

You can retain property which you hold in trust for someone else, and property held in your spouse's name cannot normally be seized provided:

- you did not transfer the property to your spouse intending to defraud creditors
- the transfer did not occur within three months of the date of the bankruptcy petition

- gifts of property to your spouse occurred more than two years before your bankruptcy.

Sales of your assets to other people at low nominal values might not be considered valid in law and the goods involved could be confiscated (unless you can prove you were solvent at the moment the sale was transacted). Goods involved in such deals can be seized if they were sold up to five years prior to a bankruptcy petition (the exact period depends on the nature of the transaction).

Avoiding bankruptcy

You might be able to avoid bankruptcy by obtaining an 'administration order' from your local County court. This enables the court to supervise your affairs while you sort out your debts. An administration order is extremely useful if you are being pursued by several creditors, all of whom are using different debt collection methods. The court protects you from harassment by creditors, who are now unable individually to enforce specific claims without the express agreement of the court. In return you agree to make a fixed monthly payment to the court (which then distributes the money to your creditors equitably) until you clear your debts. You *cannot* be declared bankrupt while an administration order is in effect unless the court agrees, which is highly unlikely as long as the monthly payments are maintained. To apply for an administration order you contact the office of your local official receiver, whose address and telephone number are available from your County court.

Deeds of arrangement

Similarly, you can arrange an *ad hoc* meeting of your creditors at which you try to persuade them to settle for less than they are owed. This saves them the costs and inconvenience of petitioning for your bankruptcy. However, creditors may conclude that:

(a) they have nothing to lose in having you declared bankrupt, thus ensuring that the court administers your affairs, and

(b) that bankruptcy is better because they can then write off your debts in the current tax year.

A more realistic approach is therefore to seek a 'deed of arrangement' with creditors whereby all your business property is legally assigned (registered) to a trustee acceptable to them. The official receiver can arrange appointment of a suitable trustee, who now administers your assets on your creditors' behalf. This is a secure, legally founded arrangement which avoids your being declared officially bankrupt. The deed must be approved by a majority of creditors and is binding on signatories to the deal, but it does not bind creditors who refuse to participate in the arrangement. All the administrative costs of the process are borne by you.

How bankruptcy occurs

It is possible to declare yourself bankrupt (through the County court) in order to avoid being served with an enforcement order from a particular creditor. Equally you can be forced into bankruptcy via a petition from a creditor acting alone or with other creditors. Petitions are not allowed unless you owe at least £750 and have done so for at least three months.

Creditors become aware of your uncertain financial position when, despite threats and reminders, their bills remain unpaid for long periods. However, they cannot initiate bankruptcy proceedings unless there is clear evidence of your inability to settle your debts (see Note 1).

Traditionally, courts have accepted the following behaviour as indicative of personal insolvency:

(a) If a creditor has obtained a court order requiring a debtor to settle a debt and this order has been served and ignored. (In this case a 'bankruptcy notice' is served which, if ignored, enables bankruptcy proceedings to begin).

(b) The debtor informs creditors of his or her inability to settle debts in full.

(c) If a debtor deliberately makes him or herself inaccessible, e.g., by changing address demonstrably intending to avoid creditors.

(d) The debtor fraudulently transfers property to other people to avoid its possible seizure.

Interim receivers

The creditors' first step is to approach the County court and ask for the issue of a 'bankruptcy petition' against you. If the court accepts the request the petition is served on your last known address and a date for hearing the case is determined. Following the hearing the petition is either dismissed or accepted. In the latter case the court appoints an 'interim receiver' to take charge of your affairs (prior to 1987 this stage was known as the issue of a 'receiving order'). This has the effect of freezing your finances and enables the interim receiver to take immediate possession of your property, pending the appointment of a trustee to manage your assets on behalf of the creditors. Note that a creditor's right to seize any of your assets (the right being obtained under, for example, a warrant of execution, garnishee or similar order – see Chapter 5) is lost at this point, *even if* you present your own bankruptcy petition. The creditor holding the warrant becomes just another unsecured creditor who will receive proportionately no more or less than others.

The examination

Next you must prepare a full statement of your affairs, listing all your personal assets and liabilities, and perhaps attend a 'public examination' held in open court. Here you are required to explain the circumstances and causes of your financial difficulties, and answer questions from creditors and/or the official receiver concerning your conduct and the whereabouts of your assets. And you have to satisfy the authorities that the cause of your impending bankruptcy did not involve fraud or improper behaviour.

Composition settlements

A first meeting of creditors now occurs at which you may offer 'so much in the pound' to each creditor (this is sometimes referred to as a 'composition' settlement). A three-quarters majority of proven creditors (and the debts must have arisen *prior* to the bankruptcy petition) is needed for acceptance of such an offer. If accepted, the agreement must be ratified by the court, following a report by the official receiver on your conduct. The court will want to assure itself that all major interests have been satisfied (e.g., the dissenting minority could be one or two creditors owed large amounts) and, if it believes the proposed scheme is reasonable, the settlement becomes legally binding on *all* creditors. On payment of this amount you have no further liability for these debts. Alternatively, a deed of arrangement (see above) might still be negotiated thus avoiding the need for your bankruptcy

Formal bankruptcy

Note, importantly, that so far you have still not been adjudged formally bankrupt. This happens only if your creditors refuse the offer you make, or if you abscond, or if you appear to be hiding your assets or are otherwise deliberately unco-operative. In any of these circumstances your creditors and the official receiver will jointly ask the court to declare you formally bankrupt. When this happens the court issues an order depriving you of your property and placing it with a trustee appointed by the creditors and approved by the court, although initially the official receiver undertakes this role, subject to the court's approval.

Trustees

The trustee (usually an accountant) must be a person considered by the Board of Trade to be a fit and proper person to undertake these duties. His or her task is to realise your assets as quickly as possible and distribute the proceeds among creditors. In return the trustee is rewarded by an agreed percentage of the amount raised. If there are no assets to be realised the official receiver acts as the trustee.

Payment of creditors

Creditors are paid according to the predetermined order specified in the Insolvency Act 1986. 'Secured' creditors (i.e., those with direct claims on specific assets, such as a bank loan secured against the firm's premises) are paid first. If the sale of the particular asset specified in a security arrangement (only fixed charges are allowed to sole traders and partnerships – see Chapter 11) fails to raise enough money to pay off a secured debt, then the outstanding balance is pooled with the debts of unsecured creditors and a 'so much in the pound' settlement is applied to this amount. Next come unpaid taxes and local authority rates, followed by employees' wages, then outstanding National Insurance contributions, and only then the firm's unsecured creditors.

13

Partnerships

In partnerships, each partner is treated individually (because the firm is not a separate legal entity) although the fact that one partner is adjudged bankrupt does not necessarily mean that the entire firm must become bankrupt. Here, the bankrupt partner's share of the partnership's property is handed over to the trustee. If the firm goes bankrupt then of course all the partners (excluding registered sleeping partners with limited liability) necessarily become bankrupt.

Undischarged bankrupts are prohibited by law from obtaining credit (beyond very small amounts) without disclosing their bankruptcy, and are not allowed to trade under any other buisness name unless they simultaneously and openly reveal they are bankrupt under their previous business names. Bankrupts cannot become company directors or be in any way involved in company management.

Discharge

If realisation of your assets raised enough money to settle your debts you are discharged at that moment. Otherwise you have to apply to the court for a discharge some time in the future, having demonstrated serious attempts at settling outstanding balances. There are three ways to obtain a discharge: by 'automatic' expiry of a minimum time period, by 'review', or by early 'application'.

Automatic discharge

Discharge occurs automatically for the first time bankrupt after three years. People who have been bankrupt before may have to wait up to 15 years for automatic discharge.

Discharge by review

The County court registrar may suggest at the moment a bankruptcy order is issued that a date be set when the matter might be reconsidered. In the meantime you have to make regular contributions towards settlement of your debts. If you take a job following your business's collapse, your wages could be subject to an attachment of earnings order (see Chapter 5).

Early application

You can apply to the court for early discharge at any time. On receipt of the application (plus the appropriate fee) the court informs (a) the creditors (who may oppose the discharge), (b) the trustee, and (c) the official receiver. The court may grant immediate discharge, or make the discharge conditional on particular events (repaying a certain amount of money, for example) and/or specify that the discharge occur only after a certain period has expired. You must demonstrate to the court that your bankruptcy is causing you *exceptional* hardship, (e.g., preventing you earning a living).

Discharge means you are free to obtain credit and run a new business. Prior to discharge, however, your legal rights are severely affected. In particular, control over your income and property is exercised by the trustee, and you cannot interfere with the trustee's decision. The trustee can sell whichever of your assets he or she chooses and can sue third parties for money that you are owed and keep the proceeds. Undischarged bankrupts cannot be local councillors, stand for Parliament, or hold any office which involves handling public money. Many professional bodies (solicitors and accountants, for instance) do not allow bankrupt members to practice.

Rights of a spouse

Nowadays, a solvent spouse or dependent relative has the legal right to occupy the family home. Thus, if you are declared bankrupt but your husband or wife is not, he or she cannot be evicted in order to sell off the family residential property. However, your 'half' of the family home ceases to belong to you and may be disposed of appropriately. How this will operate in practice has yet to be established. Further complications arise if you are separated or newly divorced, or if unequal contributions to the purchase of the home can be proven. Specialist legal advice is necessary in these circumstances.

Services and bank accounts

The gas, electricity and telephone authorities can cut you off as soon as you are declared bankrupt, unless you have transferred these services into someone else's name. Your bank account is frozen, though you may open another account without declaring your bankruptcy to your new bank provided the account is not overdrawn (which is equivalent to your 'obtaining credit', and is thus illegal). Note that the official receiver is entitled to confiscate any money you deposit in a new account. Life assurance policies with surrender values will be seized, but pension fund entitlements cannot be taken.

A bankrupt who conceals the existence of personal assets or who falsifies records commits a criminal offence for which he or she may be imprisoned. Failure to account for assets and/or to keep proper records are not criminal offences but may result in the court refusing to grant a discharge.

Company liquidation

A company is a separate legal entity and thus must be liquidated in its own right, quite independent of its owners (shareholders). All unpaid share capital is called up on liquidation. Thereafter, the principle of limited liability protects shareholders from personal liability for the company's debts. As with a sole trader, liquidation proceedings can be initiated by the company itself. In this case an extraordinary resolution (requiring the support of 75 per cent of shareholders' votes, or 51 per cent if the company is insolvent) of an official meeting of the company's shareholders is necessary, and the courts need not be involved.

On liquidation, the company may be solvent or insolvent. If it is solvent (e.g., if it was formed for a particular project which has been successfully completed), its members pay off the creditors and simply wind the company up. If it is insolvent then either (a) its creditors form a committee to supervise the voluntary winding up, or (b) one or more creditors present a petition to the court for compulsory liquidation, though in this case the amount owed must exceed £750. Note also that a shareholder may ask the court for a compulsory winding up order.

Compulsory winding up

Other circumstances in which a company may be compulsorily wound up are:

(a) if it fails to register its final accounts with the Registrar of Companies;

(b) if it does not trade for more than a year;

(c) when the number of its members falls below the statutory minimum of two;

(d) if a court decides that it is 'just and equitable' that the company be wound up.

Following a compulsory winding up order the court may appoint its own liquidator, or supervise a liquidator appointed by the company or its creditors. Company liquidation and bankruptcy are essentially similar, although it is obvious from the above that personal bankruptcy is infinitely more painful to the owner(s) of the firm. In the case of a company it is the company and not you personally that is responsible for the business's debts – your direct liability is restricted to your personal shareholding (normally £100 for a small private company). Clearly, it is wise to become a company if your business is such that its failure might leave you with a large accumulation of debt (although limited companies themselves have serious problems – see Chapter 10). If you do not operate as a limited liability organisation you should regularly examine trends in your cash flow to assess their implications for your personal financial liability if the business suddenly fails.

The liquidator of a company is equivalent to the trustee of a bankrupt. Instead of the appointment of an interim receiver in bankruptcy, a company has a 'winding up order' issued against it, the effect of which is to place the company's assets in the liquidator's hands. Then the company has to prepare a statement of affairs, and a meeting of creditors is arranged. Legal actions against the company (e.g., warrants of execution) are cancelled as soon as the liquidation begins in order to protect all creditors equally.

Administration orders

Administration orders analogous to those used to avoid personal bankruptcy have been possible for companies since 1987, as are compositions (i.e., 'so much in the pound' settlements) involving the minimum legal interference and fuss. The issue of an administration order by the court enables the company to continue trading, albeit under the supervision of an administrator appointed by the court, and the company is not wound up. The administrator acts as the company's agent. He or she is empowered to:

- borrow money on the company's behalf
- appoint and dismiss directors
- sue in the company's name
- meet with creditors and shareholders and determine changes in the company's organisational structure.

During the period an administration order is in effect the fact must be stated on all company documents, together with the administrator's name and reason for appointment.

13

Receivership

If the creditor initiating court action is a debenture holder whose debenture is secured under a fixed or floating charge (see Chapter 11 and Note 2 below) the court may appoint a 'receiver' rather than an administrator and the company is said to be 'in receivership'. The role of a receiver is essentially similar to that of an administrator. Note that it is unusual these days for a company's bankers *not* to have a fixed or floating charge debenture in respect of substantial loans made to the company, so that banks typically enjoy the right to appoint receivers for insolvent companies.

There can be no public examination of the 'company' as such, although its individual directors may now (since 1987) be so examined. Whereas a bankrupt is 'discharged', a company is given an 'order for dissolution'.

Charges

Company debts secured against floating charges receive priority over unsecured creditors, but are paid only after (i) fixed charges, (ii) the costs of liquidation, and (iii) other preferential claims (taxes, wages and National Insurance) have been settled. Note that for both company liquidation and for personal bankruptcy, a secured creditor who petitions for the business's liquidation or for individual bankruptcy automatically relinquishes his or her right to possession of the particular secured asset, which is now sold off with the proceeds going into a general pool for distribution to creditors in the order previously outlined. And other creditors may have equally ranking secured claims on the firm and will thus share in the money available for secured creditors.

The way ahead

Bankruptcy and company liquidation can be emotionally and psychologically harrowing. But remember that some of the most successful business people around are individuals who at some time or another have had to wind up an enterprise. If your firm is a failure, learn from the experience and use it to your best advantage – having failed once you are not likely to make the same mistakes in the future.

Summary

Bankruptcy is bad news - really bad news; and you must avoid it at all costs. Cease trading immediately you suspect bankruptcy might be possible: liquidate your assets and clear off your debts. It is simply not worth running the risk of bankruptcy just to try and earn a few extra pounds.

Small businesses with substantial cash flows should become limited companies *before* they begin to accumulate large amounts of debt. Disadvantages such as the costs and inconveniences of company formation, the need to employ an accountant to audit the company's books, and the requirement that final accounts be available for public inspection are easily outweighed by the benefits of incorporation in these circumstances.

As a bankrupt you are not allowed to start another new firm without declaring to customers and suppliers that you are a bankrupt, and are personally liable for the failed business's debts. Your spouse and other family will suffer, and you could be subjected to the humiliating experience of a public examination in open court.

Yet, if it happens, it happens! Do not be too despondent, learn from your past mistakes and never be afraid to try again.

Notes

13

1. Such evidence used to be called an 'act of bankruptcy'. At the time of writing the law is being changed and abolition of 'acts of bankruptcy' is proposed. How courts will assess whether a person's actions imply insolvency has yet to be established.
2. Non-incorporated businesses must secure loans against specific, named items in the firm's asset structure. Limited companies in contrast may secure loans against a floating charge covering any or all of the company's assets, including stock and work in progress, and outstanding debts owed to the business. A floating charge is said to 'hover' over the property until liquidation, at which time it attaches to any assets currently available.

Index

Accidents, 114
Accounts packages, 127
Acid test ratio, 38
Acquisition of other businesses, 211
Administration of Justice Act 1970,
    82
Administration orders, 244, 251
Administrative routines, 129–30
Advertising, 138, 165
    outdoor, 167
Advertisements, copy for, 165
After-sales service, 61, 138
Agencies, recruitment, 107
Agency, debt collection, 82, 228
Agent, company registration, 208
Arbitration, 85
Arbitration, Conciliation and
    Advisory Service (ACAS), 98
Articles of association, 207–8
Assets, valuing, 234
Attachment:
    debts, of, 87
    earnings, of, 76, 87
Auditing, management, 3
Automatically unfair dismissal, 102

Banded packaging, 169
Bankruptcy, 89, 229, 241, 243, 245
    notice, 245
Banks, loans from, 229
Body copy, 166, 182
Bonuses, 111
BRAD press guide, 180
Brand:
    images, 148
    names, separate, 148
Branding, 146–7
Break even point, 22
Break-up value of a business, 235
Budgets, 48
Building Society Loans, 220

Bulk:
    purchases, discounts on, 34, 40
    puchasing, 58, 142
Business:
    environment, 19
    expansion, 42
    image, 10, 149
    logos, 147
    name, 144, 150–1, 166
    premises, 55
    risk, 65

Capital employed, 31
Cash flow problems, 20
Certificate of Incorporation, 209
Charging orders, 88
Close companies, 207
Codes of Practice, 106
Commission for Racial Equality,
    106
Commission systems, 61
Companies Act 1985, 209
Companies (Tables A to F)
    Regulations 1985, 209
Company:
    documents, 208
    formation, 208
    liquidation, 250
    off-the-peg, 206
    secretary, 208
Competition, 18, 168
Competitions, for sales promotions,
    172
Competitors, 35
Composition settlement, 246
Compulsory liquidation, 250
Computer:
    hardware, 129
    systems, 121
Computerised accounts, 128
Consequential loss, 64

Constructive unfair dismissal, 102
Consumer Credit Act 1974, 193
Consumer:
  groups, 140
  protection, 187
Consumer Protection Act 1987, 59,
      148, 173, 175, 187
Contract of employment, 101
Control problems, 27
Co-operatives, 204
Corporate image, 50
Corporation tax, 207
Cost:
  centres, 47
  cutting, 47
  sales, of, 39
Costs:
  administrative, 54
  indirect, 48
  photocopying, 49
County court, 83
Coupons, 168, 171
Covenant, 223
Credit, 75–6
  agencies, 226
  control, 78
  factor, 83
  reference agency, 196
  worthiness, 76
Crisis policies, 219
Cross-couponing, 169–70
Current:
  assets, 37
    valuation of, 234
  liabilities, 37
  ratio, 37–8
Customer support services, 57

Data bases, 124–5, 129
Data Protection Act 1984, 133
Data Protection Registrar, 134
Debentures, 231
Debt:
  collecting, 80, 83
  collection period, 79
Deed:
  arrangement, of, 244

partnership, 202
Defective products, 59, 187
Depreciation, 24, 37
Direct:
  expenditures, 48
  mail, 179, 182–3
  manufacturing costs, 41
Directors, 211
Directors' report, 210
Dirty tricks from competitors, 18
Disabled Persons Employment Act
      1944, 117
Discharge from bankruptcy, 248
Discount for prompt payment, 80
Discounts, 175
Discrimination in employment,
      105–6
Dismissal, 99–100, 103
Display, 177–8
Distribution costs, 35
Diversification across markets, 7
Dump displays, 178

Electricity accounts, 226
Employers' Liability (Compulsory
      Insurance) Act 1969, 117
Employers' Liability (Defective
      Equipment) Act 1969, 116
Employers' liability insurance, 64
Employment agency, 109
Employment Protection (Consoli-
      dation) Act 1978, 100
Enforcement:
  County court judgements, of, 86
  orders, 242, 245
Environmental conditions, 25
Equal Opportunities Commission,
      106
Equitable:
  execution, 88
  mortgage, 231
Eviction from premises, 223–4
Excessive stockholding, 39
Exit interviews, 113
Expansion problems, 31–5

Face-to-face selling, 156

Factories Act 1961, 116
Family brand, 148
Filing systems, 53
Fire certificates, 116
Fire Precautions Act 1971, 116
Fixed:
  assets, tangible, 37
  charge, 232, 247
Flashpacks, 170
Floating charge, 231, 252
Flowcharts, 52
Forward buying discounts, 175
Fraud, 68
Fraudulent trading, 205
Free:
  gifts, 168, 173, 176
  samples, 143

Gaming Act 1968, 172
Garnishee orders, 87
Going concern, 233, 235
Goodwill, 236
Gross misconduct, 101
Growth, unplanned, 31
Guarantee payments, 100
Guarantees, 232

Hardware and software, 130
Health and Safety at Work Act 1974,
  113
Hire purchase, 229
Hypothecation, 232

IBM compatible computers, 131
Illustrations for advertisements, 166
Images of firms, 150–1
Inadequate performance, 101
Incentive schemes, 111
Incorporation of a limited company,
  199
Indemnity, principle of, 66
Industrial Tribunals, 102, 107
Inland Revenue, 24
Insolvency Act 1986, 205, 247
Inspections, 114
Insurance:
  contract, 67
  cost of, 63
    house contents, 55
Interim receiver, 245
Interviewing, 107–8
Introduction of new products, 9
Inventory turnover, speed of, 39
Invoices, 127

Job:
  descriptions, 93
  design, 110
  enrichment, 94

Labour efficiency, 42
Landlord and Tenant Act 1987, 238
Lanz, Karen, 93
Late payers, 79
Lazy staff, 23
Leases, 222
Legal:
  mortgage, 231
  structures for businesses, 199
Liabilities, current, 37
Licences, property, 222
Life assurance policies, 231
Limited:
  liability companies, 199–200, 203,
    205, 250
  partnership, 201
Linked-product offers, 169
Liquidation proceedings, 250
Liquidity:
  business, of a, 37
  ratio, 38
Loan sharks, 229
Loans to directors, 211
Logos , 146–7, 151, 166
Lotteries and Amusements Act
  1976, 177

Machine:
  capacity ratios, 40
  efficiency, 41
Mail:
  drop literature, 182
  -ins, 173
  merge, 123

order, 180–1
  costs, 61
  selling, 179
Mailing list brokers, 179
Maintenance:
  bills, 24
  contracts for computers, 131
Make or buy decisions, 60
Malingering by workers, 95
Management information systems, 8
Managing risk, 65
Marketing, 165
  costs, 60
  methods, 137
  strategy, 139
Market:
  segmentation, 139–40, 145
  surveys, 160
Maternity rights, 104
Medicines Act 1968, 177
Memorandum of Association, 206, 208
Merchandising, 177
Mergers, 233
Misleading price indications, 190
Misrepresentation Act 1967, 191
Money-off:
  coupons, 180
  offers, 168
Mortgage arrears, 225
Mortgages, 220, 231
  charges, and, 77
Motivating workers, 110

Net current assets, 40
New products, 9
Newspaper Publishers Association, 181
Notice:
  default, of, 196
  period of, 104
Novation, contract of, 203

Objects clause, 206
Occupiers' Liability Act 1984, 117
Office of Fair Trading, 181

Offices, Shops and Railway Premises Act 1963, 116
Official receiver, 243–4, 249
Off-the-peg companies, 208
One piece mailer, 182
Operating ratios, 40
Oral examination, 86
Organisation:
  methods, and; do-it-yourself, 51
  charts, 96
Organisational difficulties, 31
Overdrafts, 220
Overheads, 48
Own brand products, 148
Own label versions of products, 35

Packaging, 35, 138, 141
  banded, 168
  materials, 62
Parkinson's law, 33
Particulars of Claim, 84
Partnership, 200, 242, 247
Partnership Act 1890, 201
Part-time workers, 93
Payments moratoria, 228
Payroll:
  packages, 127, 132
  system, 129
Penetration pricing, 142
Personal selling, 154
Petition, bankruptcy, 242–3, 245
Piece rate systems, 111
Plaint Note, 84
Planning permission, 71
Possession order, 225
Posters, 167
Pregnant employees, 105
Premises, 220, 223
  choice of, 54
  insurance on your, 66
  low cost, 55
Press releases, 152
Pricing, 141–2
  policies, 21
Private limited companies, 205, 208
Product:
  diversification, 7

liability, 64
positioning, 139
withdrawal, 10
Products, 7, 144–6
Professional liability, 64
Profitability, 31
Profit sharing, 112
Promotion, types of, 169
Promotional:
    methods, 143
    strategy, 168
Promotions, 143
Proofs of purchase, 170, 174, 176
Property:
    conversion, 221
    repair of, 223
Public:
    companies, 208
    liability insurance, 64
    relations, 152
Purchasing, 58

Quantity discounts, 175
Questionnaires, 161
Quick ratio, 38–9
Quinn, P., 186

Race Relations Act 1976, 106
Rate:
    arrears, 225
    return on capital employed, of, 37
Rates, 223
Receivership, 252
Recruitment, 107
Redemption rates on sales
        promotions, 170–1
Redundancy, 99
    payments, 212
Registrar of Companies, 201, 208
Rehabilitation of Offenders Act
        1974, 108
Rent, 222
    arrears, 222, 224–5
    reviews, 223
Request for Entry in Default, 84
Request form, 84
Research, marketing, 158

Reservation of title, 77
Revival plan, 213, 230
Risk, 65
    management, 65

Safety:
    legislation, 115
    policy, 114
    representatives, 114
Sale and leaseback, 56, 220
Sale of Goods Act 1979, 191
Sales:
    literature, 165
    promotions, 165, 168, 174
        law, 176
    revenues, 21
Secured:
    creditors, 247
    loan, 77
Security, 230
    bank loans, for, 24
Segmentation of markets, 140
Self-liquidating offers, 174
Selling, 154
    business, a, 233
    proposition, major, 166
Service contracts, 192
Sex Discrimination Act 1975, 105
Shareholders, 205, 208
Shoplifting, 69
Single-person business, 199
Single product policy, 6
Small:
    claims procedure, 83
    value mail orders, 62
Software maintenance, 132
Sole trader, 199–200
Spare capacity, 26
Spreadsheets, 125
Staff:
    turnover, 112
    utilisation, 58
Statement of affairs, 251
Stock:
    control, 126, 129
    money tied up in, 34
    turnover, 39

Stockholding, 59, 62
Stores procedures, 59
Strategy, marketing, 138
Strengths and weaknesses of a firm, 5
Sub-letting, 56, 221, 224
Summary dismissal, 100
Summons, 84, 225
Suppliers, 8
Supply of Goods and Services Act 1982, 192
Surveys, telephone, 161
Systems analysis, 129

Tag-lines, 166
Targeted maildrop, 180
Technical change, 146
Telephone sales, 158
Theft, 68–9
Time:
　management, 69
　rates, 111
Trade:
　deals, 175–6
　descriptions, 190
　names, 146
　unions, 114
Trading cycle, 39
Transport, 63
Trustees, 242–3, 246–9
Turnaround measures, 11

Two bin stock control system, 60

Unfair Contract Terms Act 1977, 192
Unfair dismissal, 98
Unique selling points, 142, 144
Unit profitability, 31
Unprofitable expansion, 31, 42
Unsolicited Goods and Services Act 1971, 193

Valuation of stock, 37
Valuing a business, 234
Venture financing, 218
Vicarious liability, 117
Victimisation, 106

Warehousing, 62
Warrant of execution, 87, 246, 251
Weights and Measures Act 1985, 193
Wholesalers, 34–5, 62
Winding up order, 250–1
Word-processing, 51, 123
Working capital, 37
Work space, premises, 56
Wrongful:
　dismissal, 103
　trading, 205

Zero-base budgeting, 48

Fill the gaps in your NatWest Small Business Bookshelf!

The books in the NatWest Small Business Bookshelf contain all you need to know about managing your small business. Written in a concise, readable style, each book is a handy and authoritative reference on important aspects of small business management.

Titles in the NatWest Small Business Bookshelf are:

A Business Plan
Alan West
A guide for strategic planning for profit. Evaluates key areas and includes case studies and spreadsheets

Starting Up
Gary Jones
How to find ideas for new enterprises and build up to a successful start-up

Selling
Peter Allen
How to understand customers and cashflow, choose your market position and sell correctly

Hiring and Firing
Karen Lanz
How to recruit, manage, pay and part with staff effectively and within the law

Small Business Survival
Roger Bennett
How to manage operational matters more effectively and turn your business into a profitable venture

Retailing
Gary Jones
How to open and run a shop of any sort effectively and profitably

Managing Growth
Maureen Bennett
A guide for the business on the brink of major expansion, focusing on resources management, finance and leadership

Book-keeping and Accounting
Geoffrey Whitehead
A guide for the small trader which looks at simple bookkeeping systems, and explains business accounts, ratios and other performance indicators

Exporting
James Dudley
How to plan for export marketing, new markets and sell profitably overseas

Franchising
Peter Hall and Rob Dixon
A guide for both the business owner seeking to franchise a business and the would-be franchiser

Titles in the NatWest Small Business Bookshelf are available from all good bookshops. In case of difficulty, contact the publisher.

Sales Department, Pitman Publishing, 128 Long Acre, London WC2E 9AN
Tel: 01 379 7383